THE ROAD FROM DAMASCUS

McMaster New Testament Studies

The McMaster New Testament Studies series, edited by Richard N. Longe-necker, is designed to address particular themes in the New Testament that are of concern to Christians today. Written in a style easily accessible to ministers, students, and laypeople by contributors who are proven experts in their fields of study, the volumes in this series reflect the best of current biblical scholarship while also speaking directly to the pastoral needs of people in the church today.

The Road from Damascus

The Impact of Paul's Conversion on His Life, Thought, and Ministry

Edited by

Richard N. Longenecker

WILLIAM B. EERDMANS PUBLISHING COMPANY
GRAND RAPIDS, MICHIGAN / CAMBRIDGE, U.K.

© 1997 Wm. B. Eerdmans Publishing Co.
255 Jefferson Ave. S.E., Grand Rapids, Michigan 49503 /
P.O. Box 163, Cambridge CB3 9PU U.K.

Printed in the United States of America

02 01 00 99 98 97   7 6 5 4 3 2 1

Library of Congress Cataloging-in-Publication Data

The road from Damascus : the impact of Paul's conversion on his life,
  thought, and ministry / edited by Richard N. Longenecker.
     p.   cm. — (McMaster New Testament studies)
  Papers presented at the H.H. Bingham Colloquium in New Testament,
McMaster Divinity College, second session, June 17-18, 1996.
  Includes bibliographical references.
  ISBN 0-8028-4191-0 (alk. paper)
  1. Paul, the Apostle, Saint — Conversion — Congresses.
I. Longenecker, Richard N. II. H.H. Bingham Colloqium in New
Testament (2nd : 1996 : McMaster Divinity College) III. Series.
BS2506.R59   1997
225.9'2 — dc21   97-7870
                                             CIP

Contents

CONTENTS

Contributors

BRUCE CORLEY   Professor of New Testament, Southwestern Baptist Theological Seminary, Fort Worth, Texas, USA

TERENCE L. DONALDSON   Professor of New Testament and Biblical Languages, College of Emmanuel & St. Chad, Saskatoon, Saskatchewan, Canada

JAMES D. G. DUNN   Lightfoot Professor of Divinity, Department of Theology, University of Durham, Durham, England, UK

GORDON D. FEE   Professor of New Testament and Dean of Faculty, Regent College, Vancouver, British Columbia, Canada

JUDITH M. GUNDRY-VOLF   Associate Professor of New Testament, Fuller Theological Seminary, Pasadena, California, USA

G. WALTER HANSEN   Associate Professor of New Testament and Director of Global Research Institute, Fuller Theological Seminary, Pasadena, California, USA

SEYOON KIM   Professor of New Testament and Director of the Korean Doctor of Ministry Program, Fuller Theological Seminary, Pasadena, California, USA

BRUCE W. LONGENECKER   Post-Doctoral Fellow in New Testament Studies, Tyndale House, and Affiliated Lecturer, Faculty of Divinity, University of Cambridge, Cambridge, England, UK

CONTRIBUTORS

RICHARD N. LONGENECKER   Distinguished Professor of New Testament, McMaster Divinity College, McMaster University, Hamilton, Ontario, Canada

I. HOWARD MARSHALL   Professor of New Testament Exegesis, Department of Divinity with Religious Studies, King's College, University of Aberdeen, Aberdeen, Scotland, UK

STEPHEN WESTERHOLM   Associate Professor and Chair, Department of Religious Studies, McMaster University, Hamilton, Ontario, Canada

Preface

THIS IS the second volume in the McMaster New Testament Studies series (MNTS), sponsored by McMaster Divinity College, Hamilton, Ontario, Canada. The series is designed to address particular themes in the New Testament that are (or should be) of crucial concern to Christians today. The plan is to prepare and publish annual symposium volumes, with the contributors being selected because of their proven expertise in the area assigned and their known ability to write intelligibly for readers who are not necessarily academics. Each article included in the symposium volumes, therefore, will evidence first-class biblical scholarship, but will also be written in a manner capable of capturing the interest of intelligent laypeople, theological students, and ministers. In purpose, the articles will be both scholarly and pastoral. In format, they will be styled to reflect the best of contemporary, constructive scholarship, but in a way that is able to be understood by and speaks to the needs of alert and intelligent people in the church today.

This second symposium volume deals with a subject that is intrinsic to the Christian religion. It has often been treated in an exegetical and theological manner, as well as from a comparative-religions perspective and a social-psychology approach. We believe, however, that it needs firmer rootage in the biblical materials and better personal application than it usually receives in either the popular press or scholarly writings. In particular, we believe that what is needed is a clearer grasp of the nature of Paul's conversion, a more informed understanding of the impact that experience had on his life, thought, and ministry, and a better appreciation of how

Paul's experience functions as a paradigm for Christian conversion, life, thought, and ministry today. Our prayer, therefore, is that this second MNTS volume will prove to be of significant help to many earnest Christians who seek to think and live in a more Christian fashion, and so have a positive impact on the church at large.

Our heartfelt thanks are expressed to Dr. William H. Brackney, Principal and Dean of McMaster Divinity College, and to the faculty, administration, and boards of the college, for their encouragement and support of the entire project. We also express our deep appreciation to the family of Herbert Henry Bingham, B.A., B.Th., D.D., a noted Canadian Baptist minister and administrator of the previous generation, which has generously funded the "H. H. Bingham Colloquium in New Testament" at McMaster Divinity College, the second session of which was held during June 17-18, 1996. It was at that colloquium that the authors of the present volume presented their papers and received criticism from one another, from a large number of scholars, graduate students, and clergy in attendance, and from the editor, before then reworking and polishing their papers, as necessary, prior to final editing and the normal publication process. Most heartily, however, we thank those who have written articles for this volume, for they have taken time out of very busy academic schedules to write in a more popular fashion — in many cases, distilling from their earlier academic publications material of pertinence for the Christian church generally. We also thank Dr. Allan W. Martens, my able assistant, and Dr. Daniel C. Harlow, Editor of Biblical Studies at Eerdmans, for their expert editorial work on the volume. And we thank Bill Eerdmans and the Wm. B. Eerdmans Publishing Company for their continued support of the series.

THE EDITOR

Introduction

CONVERSION is intrinsic to the Christian religion. Jesus began his ministry with the proclamation: "The time has come; the kingdom of God is near. Repent and believe the good news!" (Mark 1:15). Peter closed his Pentecost sermon by exhorting his hearers: "Repent and be baptized, every one of you, in the name of Jesus Christ so that your sins may be forgiven, and you will receive the gift of the Holy Spirit" (Acts 2:38). And Paul commended his Thessalonian converts for having "turned to God from idols to serve the living and true God, and to wait for his Son from heaven, whom he raised from the dead — Jesus, who rescues us from the coming wrath" (1 Thess 1:9-10; cf. 2 Cor 3:15-16 for another instance of conversion language with unbelievers "turning to the Lord," and Gal 4:8-9 for its converse of believers "turning back again" into bondage).

Understanding Christian conversion, however, has often been difficult. Frequently it is discussed anecdotally in terms of one's own experience, whether by way of testifying to its validity and salutary effects or in disparagement of the same. It has, of course, been treated exegetically and theologically. And it has been analyzed from a comparative-religions perspective and a social-psychology approach. Yet what is needed for most of our theories about Christian conversion, we believe, is a firmer rootage in the biblical materials. In particular, what is needed for our thought and practice as Christians are (1) a clearer grasp of the nature of Paul's conversion, (2) a more informed understanding of the impact that experience had on his life, thought, and ministry, and (3) a better appreciation of how Paul's experience functions as a paradigm for Christian conversion, life, thought, and ministry today.

INTRODUCTION

1. An Overview of Paul's Conversion and the Questions to Be Asked

The most remarkable conversion recorded in the New Testament is that of Saul of Tarsus, who later became known as Paul and was the preeminent Christian apostle to the Gentile world. Most Christians consider Christ's encounter of Paul on his way to the city of Damascus to be a prototype of Christian conversion generally — though no one, it seems, takes that experience to be normative in all of its details. The prototypical nature of Paul's conversion, in fact, has become so accepted that references to a "Damascus Road experience" or a "Damascene conversion" have become quite common when speaking about a radical change of mind or stance about almost anything. This is true not only in religious parlance for atheists or agnostics who become theists or Christians, or adherents of some "revealed" religion. It is also true in secular jargon for politicians, for example, who suddenly espouse a position diametrically opposed to what they held before, or for economists who renounce some supposedly outmoded understanding of money, commerce, or business and "convert" to what they consider a more workable model.

But a number of vexing questions come to the fore when one looks carefully at Paul's conversion, as alluded to in some of his letters (principally 1 Cor 9:1; 15:8-10; Gal 1:13-17, and Phil 3:4-11) and as reported in the Acts of the Apostles (i.e., 9:1-28; 22:1-21; 26:4-23). Of immediate concern are questions regarding a proper historical methodology. Should one work primarily — or, perhaps, exclusively — from Paul's own letters, since they most surely bring us closer to the actual consciousness of the apostle himself than do the accounts of Luke, his biographer? Or should one begin with the reports of Paul's conversion in Acts, since they are longer, more structured, and more detailed, and then seek to integrate Paul's more passing references into Luke's more deliberate portrayals? The question involves the difference between primary historical writings (i.e., Paul's own letters, which express his consciousness in a direct manner) and secondary historical writings (i.e., Luke's Acts, which speaks about Paul's thoughts and actions only "at arm's length," however accurate the portrayals might be).

Furthermore, how does one evaluate the data given in the Pauline letters and Acts regarding that conversion experience — particularly regarding the apostle's initial understandings of the nature and impact of the event? For both Paul's letters and Luke's Acts were written sometime later than the event itself, and so must be seen to reflect something of a later understanding and developed appreciation of what occurred and of what it all meant. Likewise, both Paul's allusions to and Luke's reports of that experience are set in contexts that have other purposes, and so must be read in the light of their authors' respective intentions — without forcing them to say more than their authors intended, or accusing their authors of distortion because their purposes prohibited them from saying everything that might be thought to be important for our purposes.

With respect to the nature of Paul's conversion, the most obvious question is: Should the Damascus Road experience be understood primarily in terms of a "conversion," a "transformation," an "alternation," or a "call"? That is, should it be seen as (1) a radical change of thought, outlook, commitments, and practice, which involves either an overt or a subconscious break with one's past identity (i.e., "conversion"), (2) a new perception and a marked change in form or appearance, but not necessarily a break with the past (i.e., "transformation"), (3) a shift in perspective and practice, but without any distancing from one's past (i.e., "alternation"), or simply (4) a summons to a new career or a particular pursuit (i.e., "call")? Or are two or more of these ways of understanding appropriate — in some manner and to some degree — for the data at hand? Furthermore, it must be asked: Did that experience, which he later speaks about as a "revelation" (cf. Gal 1:12, 16; Eph 3:3; also Rom 16:25; 1 Cor 15:8), provide Paul with new revelational content or with a new revelational perspective on the content he already knew? Was what he received on the way to Damascus something that was fully formed in his mind at the time, or is there evidence of development in his understanding? And to what extent is that "revelation of Jesus Christ" to be understood as a given to be simply proclaimed or as a catalyst for further reflection?

Likewise with regard to effects, it needs to be asked quite directly: How did the Damascus Road experience affect Paul's own life, thought, and ministry? Was his experience corporate in nature, or purely personal and private? And to what extent should his conversion be seen as a paradigm for Christian experience today?

2. A Word About Focus and Style

What follows are attempts by a number of first-rate New Testament scholars to deal with (1) the nature of Paul's Damascus Road experience, (2) the impact of that experience on his life, thought, and ministry, and (3) the question of how his experience functions as a paradigm for Christian thought and action today. Reference must be made, of course, to what took place in Paul's experience on "the Road *to* Damascus." The focus of this volume, however, is on what took place in Paul's life, thought, and ministry on "the Road *from* Damascus" — that is, the impact of that experience on his succeeding life, thought, and ministry. Other topics could also have been included, but for various reasons have been excluded from the present volume. What has been included, however, while not "ringing the changes" on all aspects of his Christian understanding, seeks to deal with questions of origin(s) and development(s) — with particular attention to the impact of his conversion on such factors — with respect to many of the most crucial themes in Paul's missionary letters.

Unabashedly, the authors of the articles in this volume have taken varied critical stances and used various interpretive methods in their respective treatments. Likewise, their presentations, while reflecting a certain "sense of center," evidence also a certain degree of diversity in their understandings of Paul and the particular themes being treated. Neither diversity amidst commonality nor unity within diversity, however, is to be deplored. Rather, the union of the two in the presentations that follow is to be applauded, for thereby is set before the reader a fuller presentation of the biblical data — with then, it is hoped, a deeper, broader, and more perceptive understanding able to emerge.

The articles that follow build on the scholarly expertise of their respective authors. But they are presented in a manner that is intended to be understood by intelligent laypeople, theological students, and ministers. They each have a Selected Bibliography of no more than sixteen entries for further study, with many of the works cited being foundational for the articles themselves. They are, however, devoid of all discussion-type footnotes that either interact with competing positions or bring in subsidiary materials. Even documentary-type footnotes are held to a minimum, and then only set in abbreviated form in parentheses in the text when felt to be absolutely necessary. The full publication data for in-text references with only short titles may be found in the Selected Bibliography of the respective chapters.

Likewise, scholarly discussions on a host of critical matters and interpretive methods that have to do with the study of the New Testament generally have been kept to a minimum. This is not because these matters are unimportant. Rather, it is because the purpose of this volume is to explicate the nature, impact, and significance of Paul's conversion for a more general audience, and not to be a collection of learned treatments that deal extensively with the critical issues or methodologies associated with the various themes or topics being considered. Admittedly, no topic of any importance in the New Testament can be dealt with apart from one taking certain critical stances and adopting certain interpretive methods. The authors of the articles in this volume know that well, and so have been quite up-front in their handling of the issues and their proposals regarding proper methods of interpretation. What they have attempted to do is to use traditional designations, common parlance, and standard methods — building on the fruits of contemporary biblical scholarship and giving basic reasons for positions taken. But they have not endeavored to interact extensively with other views or to nuance their own positions in a highly academic fashion.

It is expected that the academic expertise of the authors will be evident in what they write, even though their presentations are directed to a more general audience. More than that, however, it is hoped that through their efforts a deeper, broader, and more perceptive understanding of Paul's conversion — its nature, its impact on the apostle's own life, thought, and ministry, and its significance for Christians today — will emerge. What is prayed for, in fact, is that by such a truer understanding, a better and more effective practice of the Christian religion will come about.

THE EDITOR

Interpreting Paul's Conversion —
Then and Now

BRUCE CORLEY

The scene and its parts are so familiar as to be a part of each of us who refer to a "Damascus Road" experience:

> And it happened that as Saul journeyed, he was nearing Damascus, and suddenly a light from heaven flashed around him; then he fell to the ground and heard a voice speaking to him. . . . (Acts 9:3-4)

On hearing this narrative, deeply resonant images come readily to mind — a long, arduous journey; a flash of lightning; a falling helpless to the ground; a voice heard. These are common pieces of spiritual autobiography in the West. And whether in comparison or contrast, all "varieties of religious experience" have been shaped by, measured by, and explained in terms of this pivotal and stereotyped event: the conversion of the apostle Paul.

1. A Perspective on Psychology and History

Modern psychology considers Paul's experience a primary archetype of religious conversion. In his Gifford Lectures at the beginning of the twentieth century, William James proposed that the psychology of conversion may be described as either "gradual" or "sudden." "The older medicine used to speak of two ways," James said, "*lysis* and *crisis*, one gradual, the other

1

abrupt, in which one might recover from a bodily disease. In the spiritual, there are also two ways, one gradual, the other sudden, in which inner unification may occur" (*Varieties of Religious Experience,* 183). The *lysis* (Greek for "loosing, subsiding"), or gradual type, may be defined as an introspective and voluntary change that "consists in the building up, piece by piece, of a new set of moral and spiritual habits" (ibid., 206). The *crisis* (Greek for "turning point"), or sudden type (also called "lightning" or "dramatic"), is unexpected and involuntary, featuring a self-surrender. Sudden conversion is an abrupt turnabout, according to James, "often amid tremendous emotional excitement or perturbation of the senses, a complete division is established in the twinkling of an eye between the old life and the new" (ibid., 217). Paul is the "most eminent" representative of the sudden type of conversion.

Paul's Damascus experience shows the triumph of God over the human will. Thus Paul's conversion is a striking instance of a necessary and popular tenet of orthodox Christianity: the primacy of God's grace over human despair. Put in popular terms, "man's extremity is God's opportunity." On the other hand, James (and those who follow his lead) found the "sick soul" — that is, a person given over to melancholy, self-contempt, and morbid despair — to be a more likeley candidate for sudden conversion, whereas the "healthy-minded soul" was more likely to have a gradual conversion.

The sudden conversion model of Paul as a "hero of the introspective conscience," as exhibited also in the conversions of Augustine and Luther, was challenged by Krister Stendahl in his essay of 1963 on "The Apostle Paul and the Introspective Conscience of the West" (reprinted in *Paul among Jews and Gentiles,* 78-96). The problem of the "plagued conscience" had been made all the more acute, said Stendahl, because it was exactly at this point that "Western interpreters have found the common denominator between Paul and the experience of man, since Paul's statements about 'justification by faith' have been hailed as the answer to the problem which faces the ruthlessly honest man in his practice of introspection" (ibid., 79). Especially in Protestant Christianty, which in this matter has its roots in Augustine and the piety of the Middle Ages, the Pauline awareness of sin has been interpreted in the light of Luther's struggles with his conscience. But it is exactly at this point that Stendahl discerned "the most drastic difference between Luther and Paul, between the 16th and the 1st century, and, perhaps, between Eastern and Western Christianity."

2

Stendahl's critique has become a programmatic feature of "the new perspective" on Paul (as J. D. G. Dunn has called it; cf. his "The New Perspective on Paul," *Bulletin of the John Rylands Library* 65 (1983) 95-122; idem, *Jesus, Paul and the Law*, 183-214) that emphasizes the apostle's call, rather than his conversion, and his mission to the Gentiles, rather than justification by faith. Advocates of this new perspective share two common assumptions: (1) the Judaism of Paul's day was not a legalistic religion, where acceptance with God was earned through works of the law; and (2) Paul's preaching of justification by faith implied no critique of the law itself, but addressed the entry of Gentiles into the people of God. This approach represents a frontal assault on the Augustinian-Lutheran paradigm, arguing that that earlier understanding was a drastic misreading of both Judaism and Paul.

Leaving aside questions related to Judaism, our concern here is to probe the historical issues that inform so much of the present debate on the interpretation of Paul. What role has Paul's conversion played in the history of Christianity? Has the Western Church, in particular, fallen prey to a mistaken reading of the apostle, interpreting him through the eyes of Augustine and Luther? Was the interpretation of Paul's conversion a primary factor in the rise of the Reformation paradigm?

A traditional history of interpretation, featuring commentaries and theological treatises, falls into seven time periods: Patristic (AD 100-600), Monastic (600-1000), Scholastic (1000-1350), Reformation (1350-1550), Orthodox Protestant (1550-1700), Enlightenment (1700-1850), and Historical-Critical (1850-present). To consult only the written, academic tradition, however, can be very misleading. For an event of momentous proportions like Paul's Damascus conversion, the impact in society and culture beyond the academy is highly informative. Thus in order to get at the wider "history-of-influence," we will also sample relevant materials in (1) legend and popular devotional literature, (2) biblical illuminations and art, and (3) plays and sermons.

2. The Heretical Paul: Marcion and the Ebionites

The earliest Christian sources from the patristic period give little hint of the disputes that were simmering about Paul. The first two centuries after the writing of the New Testament provide information about Paul mainly from two extremes — either from his misguided admirers or his virulent opponents (cf. Dassmann, *Stachel im Fleisch*). Clement of Rome and Polycarp echoed with unruffled voices Paul's admonition that those saved by grace through faith were to adorn their lives with good works (*1 Clement* 32:4; 34:4; Polycarp, *Letter to the Philippians* 1:3). A storm of controversy, however, which had been set on course much earlier, erupted in the mid-second century with Marcion's radical interpretation of Paul. "Marcion's special and principal work," said Tertullian, "is the separation of the law and the gospel" (*Against Marcion* 1.19.4). The "heretic from Pontus" was a hyper-Paulinist who pressed Paul's critique of the Mosaic law beyond limits. He postulated a creator God of the Jews who was wholly distinct from the redeemer God revealed in Jesus Christ, and so severed Christianity from its Old Testament roots. Marcion's logic was perversely simple: There are two gods; the law belongs to one, Christ to the other (*Against Marcion* 5.19).

Pertinent to our interests is how Marcion shifted the focus of debate through a one-sided reading of Galatians, which stood first in his ten-letter Pauline collection. To counter him, Tertullian and Irenaeus both resorted to lengthy expositions of the theological argument in Galatians 3–4, establishing that the God of Abraham is the same God who justifies believers in Jesus Christ (Tertullian, *Against Marcion* 5.2-4; Irenaeus, *Against Heresies* 4.7-8; 4.8.1). The claim to be an apostle by revelation in Galatians 1 was not a matter to be contested. Tertullian found Paul's abrupt turnabout, wherein he was "transformed from persecutor to preacher" (*Prescription of Heretics* 23.6), to be anticipated in two Old Testament figures — Benjamin and Saul, who were seen by Tertullian to be scriptural types of radical change (*Against Marcion* 5.6.5-6).

Many of the reasons that attracted Marcion and the Gnostics to Paul — who was called by some Church fathers the "apostle of the heretics" because of their use of him (cf. Tertullian, *Against Marcion* 3.5.4) — also made him, however, abhorrent to elements within Jewish Christianity. A cycle of stories fostered in Ebionite circles of the late second and early third centuries vilified Paul as an enemy of the law who was without apostolic legitimacy. A tract called *The Ascents of James* alleged that Paul was a Greek, not a Jew, and that after spending some time in Jerusalem he desired to marry the daughter of the high priest. Only then did he present himself as a proselyte for circumcision. But he failed to get the girl. So stricken by rejection, the account goes, "he flew into a rage and wrote against circumcision, the Sabbath, and the law" (Epiphanius, *Against Heresies* 30.16.8-9).

The pseudo-Clementine writings, which set out a bizarre sketch of how Peter overcame his rival Simon Magus (a thinly disguised caricature of Paul), are prefaced by *The Epistle of Peter to James*. In the letter Peter warns the bishop at Jerusalem that Paul was a threat to the church: "For some from among the Gentiles have rejected my lawful preaching and have preferred a lawless and absurd doctrine of the man who is my enemy" (*Epistle of Peter* 2:3). The legends that follow twice allude to the Damascus event — first, in identifying Paul as an agent of Satan, who "fell like lightning from heaven" (*Homilies* 11.35.5); then in warning against a prophet's claims (like Paul's) that are based on a vision, apparition, or dream, which appear and vanish "like an evil flash of lightning" (*Homilies* 17.14.3-5). Such concoctions tell us nothing about Paul. But they are highly informative in what they tell us about a segment within early Christianity that upheld a "Judaizing" position against the legitimacy of Paul's conversion and apostolic vocation.

Even a pagan Neoplatonist, whom some say was Porphyry, entered the fray, likening Paul to an "uneducated bumpkin" whose vacillation on the Law was pathological: "These are not the pronouncements of a healthy soul, nor the precepts of free reason, but thoughts kindled in a fevered mind and based in a sick understanding" (quoted by Macarius Magnes, *Reply to the Greeks* 3.34.9-10; 3.30.21-23). Orthodox defenders of Paul were obliged to show that, while it did not undermine moral reason, his doctrine of grace was based on revelation. John Chrysostom, for example, asked why an insignificant believer like Ananias should attend Paul rather than an apostle. And he answered:

> It was because it was not meet that he should be induced by man, but only by Christ himself — as, in fact, this man taught him nothing, but merely baptized him. . . . Wishing therefore to deepen his dejection, he [God] made the man blind until the coming of Ananias; and, that he might not imagine the blindness to be only fancy, this is the reason for the scales. He needed no other teaching; that which had befallen was made teaching to him. (*Homily* 20 on Acts 9:10-12)

3. The Vanquished Paul: Augustine and Medieval Piety

In the West, the impact of Augustine (AD 354-430) on the discussion of Paul can hardly be overrated. We owe to the bishop of Hippo a recasting of the grace and free will debate in distinctly new terms. For out of a long spiritual struggle, and on the heels of the Pelagian controversy, Augustine formulated the Christian experience of grace in terms of the Pauline model.

A radical change of perspective, which we now call "Augustinian," can be traced, not to the *Confessions* (ca. AD 400) but to Augustine's *Retractations* on Romans 7 and 9, which were written in 396. No one had ever formulated an interpretation of divine grace and human responsibility like the one Augustine offered in 396 — nor until 396, in fact, did Augustine. So, how did it come about? We need look no further than Augustine's account of Paul's conversion, where he develops a retrospective insight to God's power over the human will:

> The only possible conclusion is that it is wills that are elected. But the will itself can have no motive unless something presents itself to delight and stir the mind. That this should happen is not in any man's power. What did Saul will but to attack, seize, bind and slay Christians? What a fierce, savage, blind will was that! Yet he was thrown prostrate by one word from on high, and a vision came to him whereby his mind and will were turned from their fierceness and set on the right way towards faith, so that suddenly out of a marvellous persecutor of the Gospel he was made a still more marvellous preacher of the Gospel. (*To Simplician* 1.2.22; trans. J. H. S. Burleigh, Library of Christian Classics 6 [Philadelphia: Westminster, 1953] 406)

One can make a persuasive case that "no tender conscience had prompted Saul to call on Christ," for he was sinning with a high hand and enjoying himself. God had redeemed Paul from the errors of his past "mysteriously, ineluctably, even violently," without his deserving it or having the option to refuse it (P. Fredriksen, "Beyond the Body/Soul Dichotomy," 240). Augustine saw himself in his new evaluation of Paul. And a few years later he recorded that perception autobiographically in his *Confessions* (8.7-12).

The famous story of the garden conversion in the company of his friend Alypius in Milan, which happened in the summer of 386, was preceded by a long period of self-doubt and frustration compelled by a troubled conscience. But Augustine did not take the step we might have expected, namely, to connect his preparatory searching with a similar disposition often found in Paul (cf. Hawkins, *Archetypes of Conversion*, 45). For the text favored by so many interpreters for such a link — that is,

Romans 7 — was understood by Augustine to be about the struggles of Paul the Christian, not Saul the persecutor. What Augustine found in common with Paul was not a burdened conscience but a vanquished will. Paul's conversion taught him the power of grace and the inability of human striving.

The Augustinian theme of "the violent capture of a rebel will" dominated all subsequent portrayals of Paul's conversion in the medieval period. Two images were particularly prominent: the wolf made a lamb and the toppled horseman. The exegetical tradition from Augustine to the Carolingians (fifth to ninth centuries) resorted to the imagery of a "wolf" transformed into a "lamb." The remaining sketch of a twelfth-century illumination in the Herrad collection (the *Hortus Deliciarum*), for example, portrays Paul midway in the actual transformation, half-wolf and half-lamb (cf. Morrison, *Understanding Conversion,* viii-xi).

The standard biblical illuminations of the period, however, which were based on the earlier images of Prudentius (fifth century), symbolize the conquered will with the rider being unhorsed — that is, with pride or *superbia* riding before the fall, being overthrown by weakness or *humilitas.* In Byzantine mosaic and manuscript illuminations, Paul is depicted as on foot. But Western art and literature, since the twelfth century, represented him as mounted, brandishing his sword and decked with armor (cf. von Dobschütz, "Bekehrung des Paulus," 95). Thus the fierce warrior astride his charger, who was an idealized figure in the age of chivalry, was vanquished by the Christ of weakness.

The Venerable Bede alluded to this pride-humility contest in Christ's identification of himself to Paul:

> "I am Jesus, whom thou persecutest." He did not say: "I am God, or the Son of God," but he said: "Take on the weakness of my humility and shake off the scales of pride." (*Commentary on Acts,* chap. 9)

Bede's interpretation reappears as a primary source in the standard medieval commentary on Acts 9, the *Glossa Ordinaria*. Likewise, in one of the most popular devotional picture books of the period, the work entitled *The Art of Dying Well (Ars Moriendi),* the page illustrating "inspiration against despair" shows the proud Saul prostrate in the foreground, atop the horse but in a pose of comeuppance (cf. Steinberg, *Michelangelo's Last Paintings,* 26). And in what became the standard collection of medieval lore, compiled by Jacobus de Voragine in the thirteenth century (ca. 1265), *The Golden Legend (Legenda Aurea)*, the vanquishing theme from both Augustine (who is quoted four times on Paul's conversion) and Bede is cited to the effect that Christ overcame Paul's pride by his own humility, making the wolf into a lamb: "He was thrown to the ground in order to be straightened up in his perverse intentions."

God's power over the human will also became the dramatic theme for playwrights and preachers like Bernard of Clairvaux, Gregory the Great, and Peter Lombard. And Bernardo Ochino, who before his conversion to the Reformation in 1542 was considered the foremost Catholic orator of his generation, referred to Paul's conversion in such conventional ways as "Christ drew him with great force"; and again, "Paul, illuminated by Christ, was drawn with such violence that he was ravished up even to the third heaven"; also, "in the meanwhile that Paul went with so great anger to Damascus, Christ assaulted him by the way; he used violence with him and by force converted him" (quoted from Steinberg, *Michelangelo's Last Paintings*, 27).

The imagery of a toppled horseman being thrown to the ground dominated, in fact, the artistic tradition during the Renaissance. The motifs of force and assault are best seen in the last work of Michelangelo, which was unveiled in 1550 — that is, the fresco in the Pauline Chapel of the Vatican entitled "The Conversion of St. Paul." The scene is diffused with power: (1) Christ in the air amidst a multitude of angels, focused on (2) Paul below, thrown in fear and amazement to the ground by his horse, not able to look in the direction of the blinding light above; surrounded by (3) a retinue of twenty-three soldiers, some engaged in lifting him, while others, stunned by the voice and glory of Christ, flee in varied postures, all bewildered and terrified, with a bolting horse dragging along one who is trying to restrain it. It is pell-mell disorder with one overwhelming motif — the toppled man in the foreground has been vanquished.

At the end of the Middle Ages, in the Digby play *The Conversion of St. Paul* (ca. 1502), one of two surviving full texts of "saints' plays," we have a sketch of the model we have described, "the bringing of the human will into conformity with the will of God in response to an intervention of God's grace" (cf. Jeffrey and Bossière, "Paul," 590). Medieval piety, not unfairly, can be called Augustinian in its view of conversion — that is, a period of gradual awakening, marked by guilt and conviction of sin, followed by a resolution in God's grace. But not so in its view of Paul's conversion. For in medieval piety the Damascus exemplar served a different, contrastive function. Three reasons are summarized in *The Golden Legend* for hallowing Paul's conversion above all others: (1) an example that no one should despair of pardon, no matter how sinful; (2) a great joy by the turning of one who brought the Church such great sorrow; and (3) the miracle wrought by the Lord when so cruel a persecutor was made so true a preacher. The Damascus exemplar in the Middle Ages recalled the vanquished will of a proud sinner, not the introspective conscience of a troubled persecutor.

4. The Thundering Paul: Luther, Calvin, and the Puritans

If the reformers are to be charged with innovation, it must lie in their vigor for the ancient word. "We shall test everything," Zwingli asserted, "by the touchstone of the Gospel and the fire of Paul." The fire, however, prevailed. "The reformation," as Albert Schweitzer wrote in the first sentence of his history, "fought and conquered in the name of Paul." One hardly exaggerates in naming Paul the *Donnerschlag* or "thunderclap" who rang the truths of grace and faith in the ears of Luther, Calvin, and their followers.

The crises of the young Luther fit the medieval paradigm well. Having been stirred by study of the Latin Bible discovered in the college library at Erfurt, as well as troubled by a sickness that brought him near death, the twenty-one-year-old was traveling with his friend Alexis through the Thuringian Forest when a sudden storm broke. The thunder rolled and lightning blazed. A bolt struck his companion dead by his side, tearing up the ground at his feet. It seemed that the "day of wrath" had arrived. And "compassed with terror and the agony of death," as Luther himself described his fearful state (*Letters* 2.101), he devoted himself to God.

Luther's terrifying experience, however, like that of Augustine, was but a first step. The distance between the lightning strike and the place where Luther found "justification by faith" was much greater than that traveled by Paul to the street called Straight. Luther's immediate cry was, "Save me, Saint Anne, and I will become a monk." The thunderstorm and lightning flash were signs of divine judgment, the last of a series of events that drove Luther into the cloister and utter frustration. But the breakthrough came with the "tower experience" *(Türmerlebnis)* some ten years later, when Luther, the monk, grappled with that "one word" — *dikaiosynē*

9

("justice/righteousness") — in Rom 1:17 and asked what Paul meant by "the justice/righteousness of God is revealed in it [the gospel]." As he reflected on that experience later, he wrote:

> I did not love, nay, rather I hated, this righteous God who punished sinners. . . . I raged in this way with a wildly aroused and disturbed conscience, and yet I knocked importunately at Paul in this passage, thirsting more ardently to know what Paul meant. At last, God being merciful, as I thought about it day and night, I noticed the context of the words, namely, "the justice/righteousness of God is revealed in it; as it is written, the just shall live by faith." Then and there, I began to understand the justice/righteousness of God as that by which the righteous man lives by the gift of God, namely, by faith. . . . This straightway made me feel as though reborn and as though I had entered through open gates into Paradise itself. From then on, the whole face of Scripture appeared different. . . . And now, much as I had hated the word "justice/righteousness" of God before, so much the more sweetly I extolled this word to myself now, so that this passage in Paul was to me a real gate to Paradise (*Lectures on Romans,* trans. W. Pauck, Library of Christian Classics 15 [Philadelphia: Westminster, 1961] xxxvi-xxxvii).

What surprises us about Luther is his relative lack of interest in Paul's conversion as a topic of reflection and preaching. When he did preach on the event, late in his life in 1546 (see his "Predigt von der Bekehrung S. Pauli," in *Luthers Werke* 51 [Weimar: Böhlaus Nachfolger, 1914] 135-48), Luther avoided the word "conversion," although he delivered the sermon for the feast day celebrating Paul's conversion. Rather, as Karl Morrison notes, he "dwelt on external aspects of Paul's mission — call, ordination, and mission — rather than on inward change of heart" (*Understanding Conversion,* xx) — which is, of course, a line of direction that would have pleased the architects of "the new perspective" on Paul. He abstained from drawing any analogy between his own pilgrimage with a "troubled conscience" and Paul's experience. Luther's view of Romans 7 hardly permitted him to do otherwise, for he followed Augustine in reading that chapter as referring to Paul's Christian experience (*Lectures on Romans,* trans. W. Pauck, Library of Christian Classics 15 [Philadelphia: Westminster, 1961] 200-201).

What can be seen in Luther's experience and biblical exegesis is the dilemma that presented itself to the leaders of the Reformation, and which was an emerging issue of faith that would disturb some quarters of Protestantism for the better part of three centuries. Should we expect, they asked, that the manner of our conversions match that of Paul's? Some of the early reformers said "Yes" and frowned on talk of a preparation for grace. In England, for example, William Tyndale (and later Peter Martyr) taught the seizure model of grace as a lighting flash, in accordance with Paul's experience. On the continent, Zwingli was the staunchest defender of sudden grace: "The Word of God is so sure and strong that if God wills, all things are done the moment that he speaks his Word." He denied that there is something we can do of our own nature. Paul "was thrown to the ground and rebuked," Zwingli argued, and his recognition of Jesus "was not due to his own understanding or judgment but to the light of God which surrounded him with visible radiance" (*On the Clarity and Certainty of the Word of God*, Library of Christian Classics 24 [Philadelphia: Westminster, 1953] 66, 68, 82).

Another sentiment, however, was gaining ground, and would finally hold sway. Thomas Aquinas had already foreseen the problem and posited two ways in which God converts the soul — two ways that, remarkably, anticipated the psychological types of William James. The first, "imperfect preparation," happens over a period of time as the soul is gradually brought to Christ. The second, "perfect preparation," is immediate and comes "simultaneous with the infusion of grace." Paul was a recipient of the latter, said Aquinas, for "he received grace suddenly" (*Summa Theologica*, part I–II, quest. 112, art. 2, rep. 1, 2; *Great Books of the Western World*, 2 vols. [Chicago: Encyclopaedia Britannica, 1952] 2.357-58). Luther and Calvin also posited two ways, but spoke more about repentance than conversion and allowed for a preparation preceding grace. Bullinger, at the other extreme from Zwingli, was more radical in his appropriation of the preparation model, arguing that every penitent was to make a preliminary avowal of God's covenant promise — with that avowal opening the secrets of the heart and preparing for grace.

The language of preparation, having created the distinction between external and effectual calling, took center stage among the Elizabethan Puritans. Puritan thought, as Norman Pettit points out (*Heart Prepared*, 45), drew on three options: (1) that grace comes only as an effectual call with no preparatory disposition of the heart (so Peter Martyr); (2) that grace, while entirely a matter of seizure, may nevertheless involve preparation through divine constraint of the heart (so John Calvin); or (3) that grace follows the heart's response to God's offer of the covenant promises in preparatory repentance (so Heinrich Bullinger). The aftermath was that Puritanism, both in England and America, nurtured the concept of "the heart prepared": "Through introspective meditation, within the depths of the self, it was possible and indeed necessary to prepare the heart for salvation" (Pettit, *Heart Prepared*, 2).

In the Puritan "morphology of conversion," Damascus could not be the exemplar of a believer's conversion. Rather, the foremost scriptural example became Lydia, the seller of purple, "whose heart the Lord opened to receive the message spoken by Paul" (Acts 16:14). At the beginning of the seventeenth century, the Cambridge preparationists saw in the description of Lydia's conversion an inward moving of the heart that matched the Puritan experience. Thus Thomas Hooker in 1632 wrote: "Paul was not willing to take up his own heart, for that was mad against the Lord . . . but the Lord must come down from heaven and break open the door by strong hands." By contrast, Lydia looked to God's promises, and God "opened her eyes and melted her heart kindly" (*The Soul's Preparation for Christ* [London: R. Dawlman, 1632] 180-81).

"That turbulent sorrow, that violent disquiet of mind goes not always before," John Preston in 1632 cautioned the more zealous who insisted on such a witness of the heart's preparation to verify a true conversion (cf. his *The Breastplate of Faith and Love* [London: N. Bourne, 1632] 80). His words, however, seem to have had little impact. For by the mid-seventeenth century Puritan orthodoxy had become thoroughly preparationist — as witnessed by an outpouring of spiritual autobiographies, which were considered requisite for membership in the Puritan churches of England and the Massachusetts colony.

The best known of these conversion narratives, John Bunyan's *Grace Abounding to the Chief of Sinners* (1666), details alternating seasons of spiritual comfort and abject despair spread over a period of five years. Early on, Bunyan tells us how he came under conviction of sin while playing a game of tipcat one Sunday in his home village of Elstow, and how — reminiscent of Paul's heavenly vision — he looked up to heaven and "with the eyes of my understanding" saw the Lord Jesus hotly displeased with him (*Grace Abounding*, para. 22). This episode does not end, but begins a long night of the soul that finds no resolution until a hundred pages later.

The momentum of the evangelical awakenings consolidated the Puritan conversion experience in wider circles. Preachers, notably Wesley and Whitefield, trumpeted the conviction of sin through the Law before they opened the bright door of the gospel. Commentators looked for "that turbulent sorrow, that violent disquiet of mind" in the pre-Christian career of the apostle Paul. Not a few of them found it in Romans 7. A law-gospel paradigm has clear precedence in Pauline theology. But its central importance for the Protestant heritage was fueled as much by religious experience as by biblical witness. As for the place of Paul's conversion in this development, it was, by and large, a troublesome afterthought.

5. The Ecstatic Paul: Enlightenment and Modern Criticism

The Enlightenment took matters on a different course. A rising tide of skepticism in the eighteenth century threatened to sweep away the supernatural in Paul's conversion, along with other cherished truths, and called forth a variety of apologetic approaches. Those who doubted the miraculous sought other ways to explain what happened to Paul. One of these doubter's inquiries seems to have had an unexpected result. Early in the century at the end of an academic term, two Oxford scholars, George Lyttelton and Gilbert West, set a task for themselves during long vacation to undermine two salient truths of Christianity. Each intended to demonstrate, respectively, that the conversion of Paul (Lyttelton) and the resurrection of Jesus (West) were falsehoods that did not happen as reported in the New Testament. When they met again in the autumn, they shared an astounding reversal. For Lyttelton had become convinced of Paul's conversion and West of Jesus' resurrection. Both published their findings as apologetic tracts for the faithful.

Lyttelton's eighty-page pamphlet, *Observations on the Conversion and Apostleship of St. Paul* (London: R. Dodsley, 1747), was widely circulated and is still reprinted today. His argument proceeded on the assumption that the facts surrounding Paul's conversion, by necessity, could be explained in only one of four ways: (1) Paul was an imposter who reported what he knew to be false; or (2) he was an enthusiast who was driven by an overheated imagination and thereby deceived; or (3) he was deceived by the fraud of others, whether human or demonic powers; or (4) what he declared about the cause and consequences of his conversion was true and, therefore, the Christian religion is a divine revelation. In the course of

13

offering proofs for the last alternative, Lyttelton posted warning flags of objections that would not go away, especially those related to Paul's mental state — in particular, the often proposed "overheated imagination" that Lyttelton associated with temper, melancholy, ignorance, credulity, vanity, and self-conceit.

Negative readings of Paul's Damascus experience flourished under the sway of rationalism and the emergence of the historical-critical method. Paul was an ecstatic, a crank driven by some physiological or psychological weakness. On the one side stood the opponents of Christianity, who joined with Nietzsche in declaring Paul to be the law-breaker — "violent, sensual, melancholy, and malicious in his hatred" — who single-handedly invented Christianity and deceived the world. On the other side, however, so-called proponents of Christianity did little better for the apostle. Nineteenth-century explanations, in fact, commonly delved into mythic projections of guilt, hallucinations and apparitions, epileptic seizures, or the power of a thunderstorm (cf. Pfaff, *Bekehrung*, 3-97).

What may be called "the ecstatic hypothesis" — that is, that Paul was in a state beyond reason — was constructed in various ways. But it rested on three assumptions, as summarized in 1845 by F. C. Baur: (1) the narratives of Acts are contradictory and not reliable; (2) a miracle on the Damascus road is no longer tenable; and (3) Paul's vision of the risen Christ was a mythic objectification of a subjective impression (*Paul, the Apostle of Jesus Christ*, 2 vols., trans. E. Zeller [London: Williams & Norgate, 1876, from 1846 German edition] 1.63-75). Others supplied explanations for the various details, often more absurd than they had imagined Paul to be. For example, while fighting off a pernicious fever in the region of Damascus, Paul encountered a thunderstorm of great violence on the slopes of Mt. Hermon; he mistook a flash of lightning for an apparition of the "sweet master" (E. Renan). Or again, Paul's epilepsy was the culprit, transforming "an immanent, psychological act of his own spirit" into a vision of Christ (C. Holsten). Yet more popular, a "painful condition of inner division" born of failure to fulfill the Law was terminated on the Damascus road, where the tension under which Paul had groaned was relaxed by the light of Christ (H. J. Holtzmann).

The psychological underpinning of the ecstatic hypothesis was the primary target of W. G. Kümmel's influential monograph, *Römer 7 und die Bekehrung des Paulus* (Leipzig: Hinrichs, 1929), which attempted to demolish the autobiographical reading of the passage as a description of Paul's pre-Christian struggles with the Law. Kümmel argued that the "I" of Rom 7:7-25 is a rhetorical device used by Paul to identify himself as a spokesman for humanity in general. Furthermore, he pointed out that the "wretched man" of the chapter hardly fits the description that Paul gives in Phil 3:4-6 of his life in Judaism as being blameless. Thus, Kümmel concluded, Romans 7 does not record the cry of Paul's troubled conscience as a Pharisee, but that of any person under the law. Whether Kümmel has been altogether persuasive does not diminish the fact that his work marks the end of a notable chapter in Pauline interpretation and introduces us to the current scene.

6. A Retrospective on Theology and Mission

We have now come full circle in our survey of past interpretations of Paul's conversion, and so need here to review the ground that has been covered. Three major points must be highlighted, with various subpoints under each noted.

First, the term invariably used in the history of interpretation for Paul's experience at Damascus was "conversion," although the word itself is not found in the biblical accounts. The church apparently saw little to gain in another concept because the significance of the event lay in Paul's "turning" from persecutor to preacher. Contemporary definitions, based on sociological and psychological criteria, suggest at least three shades of meaning associated with conversion: (1) a gradual change of life that grows out of the past is an "alternation"; (2) a sudden change of life that rejects the past and takes a new direction is a "conversion"; and (3) a cognitive change of life that reconceives the past is a "transformation" (cf. Gaventa, *Darkness to Light*, 10-13). No one would contest that what Paul experienced was a transformation. With regard to conversion, he certainly rejected some aspects of his Jewish past — in fact, he rejected enough of Jewish theology and praxis to render him apostate in the eyes of his fellow Jews (cf. Segal, *Paul the Convert*, who subtitles his book *The Apostolate and Apostasy of Saul the Pharisee*). To speak of Paul's experience as only a calling, however, is not adequate to describe the "turning from" the past that his conversion connotes.

Second, the role of Paul's conversion in the history of the Western Church is more complicated than Stendahl's analysis suggests. One cannot draw a straight line from Luther back to Augustine — and then back to Paul — associating them all with an "introspective conscience." Both Augustine and Luther give us narrative descriptions of such spiritual introspection. But neither of them suggests Paul as the archetype of their anguish. On the contrary, they find in him the promise of sudden grace. The law-gospel paradigm that stands prominently in Paul's thinking contributed to two movements that more nearly provide evidence for Stendahl's case — that is, the Puritan preparationists, who established a theological necessity for a plagued conscience to precede a true conversion, and the Enlightenment rationalists, who established a psychological necessity for a plagued conscience to induce a questionable conversion. Having seen these alternatives, we must dissent from the judgment of "the new perspective." Augustine and Luther are still better guides to Paul's thought than either of these two movements.

Third, the models for understanding Paul's conversion in the history of interpretation have their counterparts today, much in the way that Thomas Aquinas anticipated William James. Many of the approaches to Paul's conversion today are multifaceted, and so tend to resist a neat definition. Yet it is useful to propose the following four models as an index to current thinking about the impact of Paul's conversion on his theology.

1. *Soteriological:* Damascus revealed Christ as the end of the law (Rom 10:4); the crucified Messiah overcame the curse of the law by his resurrection and offered salvation apart from the law (so, e.g., J. Dupont, U. Wilckens, and P. Stuhlmacher).

2. *Christological:* Damascus revealed Jesus as the Messiah of Israel (Gal 1:12), whose death and resurrection inaugurated the "Age to Come" and fulfilled the covenant promises of the Old Testament Scriptures (so, e.g., P. H. Menoud, R. B. Hays, and N. T. Wright).

3. *Missiological:* Damascus revealed the divine intention (Rom 1:5) to incorporate the Gentiles into the people of God by faith and to claim Paul for a world mission (so, e.g., J. Munck, E. P. Sanders, and J. D. G. Dunn).

4. *Doxological:* Damascus revealed Jesus as the Lord of glory (2 Cor 4:6), whose radiance intimated the very presence of God and the eschatological glory to come (so, e.g., S. Kim, A. Segal, and C. C. Newman).

Selected Bibliography

Dassmann, E. *Der Stachel im Fleisch: Paulus in der frühchristlichen Literatur bis Irenaüs*. Münster: Aschendorff, 1979.

Dobschütz, E. von. "Die Bekehrung des Paulus." *Repertorium für Kunstwissenschaft* 50 (1929) 87-111.

Dunn, J. D. G. *Jesus, Paul, and the Law: Studies in Mark and Galatians*. Louisville: Westminster/John Knox, 1990.

Fredriksen, P. "Beyond the Body/Soul Dichotomy: Augustine's Answer to Mani, Plotinus, and Julian." In *Paul and the Legacies of Paul*, ed. W. S. Babcock. Dallas: Southern Methodist University Press, 1990, 227-51.

Gaventa, B. R. *From Darkness to Light: Aspects of Conversion in the New Testament*. Philadelphia: Fortress, 1986.

Hawkins, A. H. *Archetypes of Conversion: The Autobiographies of Augustine, Bunyan, and Merton*. Lewisburg, PA: Bucknell University Press, 1985.

James, W. *The Varieties of Religious Experience: A Study in Human Nature*. London: Longmans and Green, 1902.

Jeffrey, D. L., and La Bossière, C. R. "Paul." In *A Dictionary of the Biblical Tradition in English Literature*, ed. D. L. Jeffrey. Grand Rapids: Eerdmans, 1992, 588-93.

Kim, S. *The Origin of Paul's Gospel*. 2d ed. Tübingen: Mohr-Siebeck, 1984.

Morrison, K. F. *Understanding Conversion*. Charlottesville: University Press of Virginia, 1992.

Newman, C. C. *Paul's Glory-Christology: Tradition and Rhetoric*. Leiden: Brill, 1992.

Pettit, N. *The Heart Prepared: Grace and Conversion in Puritan Spiritual Life*. New Haven: Yale University Press, 1966.

Pfaff, E. *Die Bekehrung des h. Paulus in der Exegese des 20. Jahrhunderts*. Rome: Officium Libri Catholici, 1942.

Segal, A. F. *Paul the Convert: The Apostolate and Apostasy of Saul the Pharisee*. New Haven: Yale University Press, 1990.

Steinberg, L. *Michelangelo's Last Paintings: The Conversion of St. Paul and the Crucifixion of St. Peter in the Cappella Paolina, Vatican Palace*. New York: Oxford University Press, 1975.

Stendahl, K. *Paul among Jews and Gentiles and Other Essays*. Philadelphia: Fortress, 1976.

A Realized Hope, a New Commitment, and a Developed Proclamation: Paul and Jesus

RICHARD N. LONGENECKER

BASED ON an analysis of 1 and 2 Thessalonians, I have argued, in concert with others, "that Paul's basic Christian conviction and the starting point for all his Christian theology was not apocalypticism but functional christology — that is, that his commitment was not first of all to a programme or some timetable of events but to a person: Jesus the Messiah" (Longenecker, "The Nature of Paul's Early Eschatology," 93). If that thesis be true, then we need to deal first with how Paul's conversion affected his view of Jesus before we go on to consider how it affected his life, thought, and ministry in all sorts of other ways as well. For if his commitment was first of all to Jesus as Israel's Messiah, then all other matters on his agenda as a Christian, while of importance individually, must be seen as being dependent on that central conviction.

With respect to method, our procedure will be to work primarily from Paul's own letters. We consider the Acts of the Apostles to be also an important source for understanding Paul's conversion, convictions, preaching, and ministry (cf. my "Acts," in *The Expositor's Bible Commentary,* ed. F. E. Gaebelein [Grand Rapids: Zondervan, 1981] 9.207-573). But because it is an account "about" Paul and not "from" Paul — and so, compared to Paul's letters, a secondary historical source and not a primary source — it will be used only in a supplementary manner. Furthermore, due recognition

18

will be given to the facts (1) that Paul's letters were written approximately twenty to thirty years after his conversion, and (2) that what he says in his letters about his conversion is set within the respective purpose of each of those letters. So we must constantly be aware that we are not reading immediate responses to the event itself, but later perceptions that have been nuanced by their author in line with the respective purposes he had in writing each of the letters under consideration. And what is true of Paul's letters as to their dates and purposes must also be taken into account when dealing with Acts — indeed, since it is a secondary historical source, even more so.

1. Saul of Tarsus and Jesus of Nazareth

Before dealing directly with Paul's conversion and its impact on his view of Jesus, some consideration must be given to the relationship of Saul of Tarsus to Jesus of Nazareth and his followers. In particular, three rather well-worn questions that have a bearing on Paul's later christology arise: (1) Had he personally known the historical Jesus? (2) What factors impelled him to persecute believers in Jesus? and (3) How significant for him was what he later called "the scandal of the cross"?

Saul and the Historical Jesus

Extensive debate has taken place over the past century and a half as to whether or not Paul had any interest in the historical Jesus — even, in fact, whether before his conversion he had actually met or known Jesus. And usually 2 Cor 5:16, which reads "though we once knew [or, "regarded"] Christ according to the flesh *(ei kai egnōkamen kata sarka Christon)*, now we know/regard [him in that manner] no longer *(alla nyn ouketi ginōskomen)*," has been viewed as the crucial passage in that debate.

On one side of the argument, Ferdinand Christian Baur (1845), Karl von Weizsäcker (1886), Hans Hinrich Wendt (1894), Wilhelm Wrede (1905), Wilhelm Heitmüller (1912), Rudolf Bultmann (1948), and Gunther Bornkamm (1969), to cite only a few prominent scholars, have claimed that Paul's kerygmatic Christ actually displaced all interest in his mind in the historical Jesus and that 2 Cor 5:16 clearly evidences such a disinterest. On the other side of the argument, however, Heinrich Paret (1858), George Matheson (1881), Adolf Hilgenfeld (1894), Adolf Harnack (1901), Paul Feine (1902), James Moffatt (1908), W. D. Davies (1948), and C. F. D. Moule (1969), again to name only a few representative scholars, have argued (1) that Paul's kerygmatic Christ actually presupposes a knowledge of the events and teaching of Jesus, (2) that various allusions in his letters to Jesus' life and teaching suggest that Paul was indeed interested in the historical Jesus, (3) that where Paul is silent regarding the historical Jesus it is because his letters are pastoral in nature (that is, addressed to specific problems in his churches), and so do not reflect all that he proclaimed in his evangelistic preaching, and (4) that 2 Cor 5:16 has no direct bearing on the question, for the expression "according to the flesh" *(kata sarka)* refers not to a disavowal of interest in the historical Jesus but to a disavowal of a former human view or worldly perspective regarding Jesus — just as it does in the first part of the same verse where Paul affirms: "now we regard no one from a human [or, "worldly"] point of view" *(hēmeis apo tou nyn oudena oidamen kata sarka).*

In defense of Paul's interest in the historical Jesus, Johannes Weiss went so far as to assert that "the express statement of the apostle himself in 2 Corinthians v.16" clearly reveals that "Paul had actually 'known' Jesus and had been impressed by His human personality and His teaching, though Paul afterwards regarded this impression as external, superficial, and 'carnal'" *(Paul and Jesus,* trans. H. J. Chaytor [London/New York: Harper, 1909] 41 and 54). Furthermore, Weiss proposed that "the simplest and most natural assumption is that he had seen Jesus during His last visit to Jerusalem and perhaps had heard Him speak; he may have been a witness of Jesus' Passion and Crucifixion, a supposition likely enough in the case of a passionately enthusiastic pupil of the Pharisees" (ibid., 54; see pp. 39-56 for his entire discussion).

Weiss's thesis had some currency among scholars during the first half of the twentieth century. But it has few, if any, advocates today. Most today are prepared to see Paul's pre-conversion knowledge about Jesus as having been obtained entirely from Pharisaic sources, which he trusted. Certainly Saul of Tarsus thought that he knew all that needed to be known about Jesus of Nazareth, for he would hardly have persecuted those early believers in Jesus had he not felt that he was in possession of the essential facts and their correct interpretation. But his knowledge then, as he later confesses in 2 Cor 5:16b, was from a purely human or worldly perspective. And though as a result of his conversion he saw those facts in a new light — and though, as we will point out later, the emphasis in his Gentile mission was on the kerygmatic Christ and the title "Lord," rather than on the historical Jesus and the title "Christ" — Paul never denigrated the historical Jesus. Rather, the story of Jesus' life and teaching, which Paul learned in a proper fashion from some of Jesus' closest followers (cf. Gal 1:18-19) and from the church's early confessions (portions of which he quotes in his writings), underlies much of what he wrote in his letters (cf., e.g., R. B. Hays, *The Faith of Jesus Christ,* esp. 139-91).

Factors Impelling Saul to Persecute

Various factors have been proposed to explain Saul's persecution of the early believers in Jesus. One common explanation, which had its heyday during the latter part of the nineteenth century and the first half of the twentieth, focused on Paul's supposed Hellenistic religious orientation: (1) that he had been heavily influenced by Diaspora Judaism during his youth in Tarsus; (2) that his Hellenized Judaism was a poorer religion than existed in Jerusalem; and so (3) that his persecution of Christians reflects more his own moral frustrations and misguided sense of logical consistency under such an inferior form of religion, and not at all the tolerance and joy of mainline Judaism (cf. my *Paul, Apostle of Liberty,* 21-64 for a detailing of such positions and my evaluations). But Paul expressly refers to himself as "a Hebrew of Hebrews" (Phil 3:5; cf. 2 Cor 11:22). And since W. D. Davies' *Paul and Rabbinic Judaism* of 1948, which E. P. Sanders rightly calls "a watershed in the history of scholarship on Paul and Judaism" (*Paul and Palestinian Judaism,* 7), it has been almost universally accepted that Paul's pre-conversion religious experience — including his persecution of the early followers of Jesus — cannot be credited to such a Hellenistic orientation.

Another explanation, which had currency for approximately the same period of time as the first, viewed Saul the Pharisee as generally in line with mainline Pharisaic teaching, as later codified by the rabbis, but interpreted the Talmud and its cognate writings as comprising a thoroughly legalistic system of religion that emphasized external actions over inward piety and elevated the human ego over a theocentric orientation. Coupled with such a view of the rabbinic literature and Saul's Pharisaism, Rom 7:7-25 was taken to be an autobiographical account of Paul's pre-conversion struggles under the tyranny of the Mosaic law. Thus various psychological analyses attempted to show how the passage's depiction of an inner spiritual struggle "fit like a glove" Paul's earlier experience, where "the shoe pinched" for him, and in what way his persecution of Christians served "to purge the demons in his own soul," which obedience to the law was unable to conquer.

In 1928, however, Werner G. Kümmel argued persuasively that the pronoun "I" in Rom 7:7-25 is a stylistic device meaning "one" or "anyone" — as it often is elsewhere in Paul's letters and other Greek writings — and so is not to be read autobiographically but refers to anyone apart from Christ (*Römer 7 und die Bekehrung des Paulus* [Leipzig: Hinrichs, 1928]). And in 1977 E. P. Sanders captured the day in arguing that the religion of the earlier rabbis quoted in the Talmud (i.e., the "Tannaim") was not a legalistic system, but rather should be characterized by the expression "covenantal nomism" (*Paul and Palestinian Judaism;* cf. also my treatment of "The Piety of Hebraic Judaism," in *Paul, Apostle of Liberty,* 65-85, where already in 1964 the term "nomism" is coined to describe the religion of the better representatives of Early Judaism). In light of such studies, as Beverly Gaventa points out, "contemporary New Testament scholars almost universally reject the notion that Paul describes his own conversion here [in Rom 7:7-25]"; in fact, "there is near consensus at this one point: Romans 7 does not provide information about the conversion of Paul" (*Darkness to Light,* 34). So we are properly warned "to be extremely wary of interpretations of Paul that contend that while still a persecutor, he experienced some prolonged period of personal questioning, of either a theological or a moral nature" (ibid., 36).

Paul's own recollections of his pre-conversion experience speak of his impeccable Hebraic ancestry, his "extreme zeal" for his ancestral traditions, and his being "blameless" in his worship of God and lifestyle (cf. Gal 1:14; Phil 3:5-6) — with the additional word found in 1 Tim 1:13 (whether by Paul himself, a companion who served as an amanuensis or as a co-author, or a later Paulinist) that his persecution was done "in ignorance and unbelief." But he does not give even a hint of any theological uncertainty or moral frustration. Rather, it seems that what motivated Saul of Tarsus to persecute early believers in Jesus was his firm commitment to the Jewish religion and his wholehearted acceptance of the Pharisaic interpretation of that religion (cf. my *Paul, Apostle of Liberty,* 86-105).

To a great extent, Saul's persecution of Christians was probably impelled by his Jewish understanding of the Messiah — or, what might be called his "pre-conversion christology." For in addition to being theocentric in orientation (that is, focusing on God, who had secured redemption for his people preeminently in the Exodus) and nomistic in lifestyle (that is, observing the law in response to what God had done in establishing his covenant with Israel and redeeming his people from Egyptian bondage, and not in keeping God's commandments in order to gain merit), Saul awaited with eager anticipation "the Coming One" who would be God's "Anointed One" — that is, "the Messiah." Therefore, he was undoubtedly deeply disturbed by the fragmentation of loyalties that was taking place within the nation with the rise of a new messianic movement that looked to Jesus of Nazareth as the Messiah.

From his perspective, those who believed in Jesus as God's Messiah were terribly mistaken. They were, in fact, sinful, and in their sin were leading many Jews astray. And while such variant thinking might be allowed for individuals, it could not be tolerated as a movement within the nation — particularly at a time when messianic expectations were high. For, as Joseph Klausner has pointed out, the common view among Pharisees of that day was that "sins cannot completely frustrate the [coming eschatological] redemption; but they can delay it" (*The Messianic Idea in Israel*, trans. W. F. Stinespring [London: Allen & Unwin, 1956] 404). So in days of "messianic travail," when the time for the appearance of the Messiah seemed to be drawing close, every effort must be expended to thwart apostasy and unite the people in a common response to God. Probably even violent action was justified in Saul's mind by such precedents as Moses' order to kill all the idolatrous and immoral Israelites at Shittim (cf. Num 25:1-5), Phinehas' killing an immoral Israelite man and Midianite woman in the plains of Moab (cf. Num 25:6-15), and Mattathias and the Hasidim rooting out apostasy among the people (cf. 1 Maccabees 2:23-28, 42-48) — perhaps also by the exhortation of 2 Maccabees 6:13: "It is a mark of great kindness when the impious are not let alone for a long time, but punished at once."

The Scandal of the Cross

More particularly, it seems that what most repelled Saul with respect to Jesus — and what ultimately compelled him to act against followers of

Jesus — was what he later speaks about in Gal 5:11 as "the scandal of the cross" (cf. 1 Cor 1:23): that an acclaimed Jewish Messiah should have been put to death by crucifixion on a Roman cross. For Deut 21:23 plainly declares that God's curse resides on "anyone who is hung on a tree." The verse originally had reference to the exposure of a criminal executed for a capital offense, whose dead body was hung on a tree for public ridicule. But it came to be viewed by Jews as also referring to the impalement or crucifixion of a living person on a pole or a cross (both a pole and a cross being parts of a tree).

The early Christians and Paul later resolved this problem by viewing God's curse of Christ as an "exchange curse" — that is, a curse that Christ bore on behalf of humanity in exchange for which humanity is offered the righteousness of God by being united with Christ (cf. 2 Cor 5:21; Gal 3:13; Morna Hooker has dealt extensively with this concept, most recently and popularly in her *Not Ashamed of the Gospel* [Grand Rapids: Eerdmans, 1994] 32-36). But in his pre-conversion experience, Paul undoubtedly shared his Jewish compariots' repugnance at the idea of a crucified Messiah, as suggested by the way in which he nuances his references to that "scandal." And so, again it may be said, his opposition to any messianic claims for Jesus of Nazareth and his persecution of those who would make such a claim were essentially based on his "pre-conversion christology."

2. The Nature of Paul's Conversion

Much of the hesitancy of scholars to speak about Paul's conversion stems from (1) the brevity and diverse contexts of Paul's own references to his conversion, (2) suspicions about the accuracy of the portrayals of his conversion in Acts 9, 22, and 26, particularly when compared to the apostle's own statements but also when comparisons are made among the three accounts themselves, and (3) the difficulty of developing a general definition of conversion and then applying that definition to Paul's experience, for he speaks of that event in ways that are not always compatible with our standard definitions and reflects a consciousness of having never left his ancestral faith. Nonetheless, as Alan Segal rightly maintains, "Conversion is an appropriate term for discussing Paul's religious experience, although Paul did not himself use it" (*Paul the Convert,* 72).

Paul's Own References

As Beverly Gaventa points out regarding Paul's own references to his conversion: "Paul tells us very little about himself. Paul is not self-preoccupied, self-reflective, introspective, or narcissistic" (*Darkness to Light*, 20). In fact, he refers to his own experience only in contexts where he deals with other issues — that is, in defending the gospel that he proclaimed to his Gentile converts in Gal 1:13-17; in countering certain "supra-spiritual" believers who were evidently attempting to denigrate him in 1 Cor 9:1 and 15:8-10; and in rebutting certain Jewish Christians who were trying to "Judaize" his converts in Phil 3:4-11.

Yet in those brief, allusive references, Paul sets out the essential features of his conversion experience: (1) He had personally "seen Jesus our Lord" (1 Cor 9:1). (2) What he saw was on a par with all of Jesus' other post-resurrection appearances, whether to Peter and "the Twelve," as referred to in the early confessional statement quoted in 1 Cor 15:3b-5, or to five hundred other believers at one time, to James, and to all the other apostles, as he enumerates in 1 Cor 15:6-7 — even though that appearance was highly unusual because of his own spiritual condition (i.e., even though he was a spiritual "abortion," 1 Cor 15:8). (3) What he experienced was of the nature of a revelation (Gal 1:11-12, 16a). (4) Jesus Christ was the agent of that revelation (Gal 1:12, understanding *Iēsou Christou* as a subjective genitive). (5) The content of that revelation was "his [God's] Son," who was also the agent of the revelation (Gal 1:16b). (6) The ultimate purpose of that revelation was "so that I might preach him [God's Son] among the Gentiles" (Gal 1:16c). And (7) Christ's appearance to him had a revolutionary effect on his life, so that he came to consider "everything [particularly his past Jewish credentials and accomplishments] a loss compared to the surpassing greatness of knowing Christ Jesus my Lord" and to focus only on "knowing Christ," with all that such a consuming passion involved (Phil 3:7-11).

Paul's few references to his own experience make no use of such terms as "repentance" *(metanoia)* or "turning/conversion" *(epistrophē)*, as one might expect in a conversion account — though he uses the verbs "to turn" *(epistrephein)* and "to believe" *(pisteuein)* with respect to the reception of the gospel by others (cf. 2 Cor 3:15-16; 1 Thess 1:9-10; conversely Gal 4:8-9) and the verb "to be transformed" *(metamorphousthai)* in admonition of believers (Rom 12:1-2). Rather, in Gal 1:15, by saying that God "set me

25

apart from my mother's womb" *(aphorisas me ek koilias mētros)* and "called me by his grace" *(kalesas dia tēs charitos autou),* he lays emphasis on that experience as being a call to a particular service — that is, his Gentile ministry — which he seemingly compares to the call of the Old Testament prophets (cf. Jer 1:5) and the Servant of Yahweh (cf. Isa 49:1-6). But Paul's language regarding conversion, it needs to be recognized, was neither as precise nor as restrictive as our modern definitions seem to require, as witness his reference to the conversion of believers at Corinth as being a "call": "For consider your call *(tēn klēsin hymōn),* brothers and sisters, for not many of you were wise by human standards; not many were influential; not many were of noble birth" (1 Cor 1:26).

Likewise, in Paul's own references to his conversion there is no mention of a trip to Damascus (though Damascus is associated with his conversion at two later times in 2 Cor 11:32 and Gal 1:17) and no narrative detailing what took place, as in Acts. No light, no voice, no companions, no blindness, and no Ananias to interpret the significance of it all. But there is certainly an impression given in the dramatic shift depicted in both Gal 1:13-17 and Phil 3:4-11 — that is, from a description of his earlier life to an immediate portrayal of his present stance — that what Paul experienced in that event was a change of commitment, values, and identity that was sudden and unexpected.

The Portrayals in Acts

There are three accounts of Paul's conversion in Acts, in chapters 9, 22, and 26. That may seem a trivial matter to note, but it is actually highly significant. For, as Ernst Haenchen rightly observes: "Luke employs such repetitions only when he considers something to be extraordinarily important and wishes to impress it unforgettably on the reader. That is the case here" (*The Acts of the Apostles,* trans. R. McL. Wilson [Philadelphia: Westminster, 1971] 327).

Source criticism has had a field day with these accounts, often attributing the repetitions to a plurality of sources and the differences to divergent perspectives among those sources. The differences among the three accounts, of course, are notorious, with such questions as the following being repeatedly asked: Who heard the voice? Who saw the light? What did the heavenly voice say? Was Saul's conversion an objective or a subjective experience? How did he learn of his future ministry to Gentiles, and to what extent was that ministry revealed to him? Likewise, there are differences between Paul's allusive references and Luke's explicit accounts, as we have noted above. The materials are impossible to harmonize completely. Yet taking into consideration the redactional purposes of Paul in his letters and Luke in his portrayals, it is possible to understand why certain matters were included and other matters omitted in their respective presentations (cf. my Acts commentary).

Most important to note, however, is the fact that in all three of his accounts, Luke makes one dominant point: that Christ was the one who brought about the change in the strategy of divine redemption that occurred in Paul's Gentile ministry — that is, that it was not a plan that Paul thought up or a program given him by another; rather, it was instigated by a commission that came directly from Christ himself (just as Christ had commissioned the Eleven for their ministries in Acts 1:4-8). So Luke emphasizes the miraculous circumstances of Saul's conversion and the supernatural nature of his call. And with that point, though with variations in spelling out the details, Paul was in full agreement.

Definitions and Applications

What, then, should we call what Paul experienced? Certainly it involved a "paradigm shift" in his life and thought — that is, a different way of looking at what he had previously known, a different set of questions than he had previously asked, and a different way of evaluating all that he had previously accepted. It could, therefore, be called an "alternation" (i.e., a shift in perspective and practice, without distancing oneself from one's past) or a "transformation" (i.e., a new perception and a marked change in outward form or appearance, but not necessarily a break with the past). For now he viewed everything from the perspective of fulfilled messianism, with Jesus of Nazareth being identified as Israel's Messiah and the realization of the nation's ancestral hope. Now having received a revelation from God, he could no longer live or think simply in the old ways. The revelation of "his Son in me" had taken precedence over all that he had ever experienced or contemplated.

Yet the grammatical counterpoint between *formerly* a persecutor of "the church of God" but *now* a persecuted teacher of "the faith he once tried to destroy" (1 Cor 15:9-11; Gal 1:13-17, 23, and Phil 3:6-7) indicates quite clearly, as Alan Segal rightly asserts (*Paul the Convert,* 117), that Paul's own self-consciousness was that of having undergone a conversion. Admittedly, at a time when Christianity was not yet defined as being different from Judaism, Paul had no desire to disassociate himself from his ancestral faith. And with an outlook that viewed commitment to Jesus as the fulfillment of his people's expectations, he understood his stance as being in direct accord with the ancient promises of God (cf. Gal 3:6-18; 4:21-31; Rom 9:6–10:33) and his relationship with his nation as that of being part of the "remnant" or "elect" of Israel (cf. Rom 9:6; 11:1-10). Still, in that his self-consciousness and sense of identity were radically altered, Paul can be seen as having experienced a conversion.

It was, in reality, a new commitment that Paul made when he responded affirmatively to Christ's encounter. It was a new identity that he took on as a follower of Christ. It may have been difficult for him to relinquish his ties with Pharisaism and to think of himself as anything other than a fulfilled Jew. The Jewish world, however, seems to have been even more perceptive than Paul on this matter, and to have recognized his break with the past. For in 2 Cor 11:24 there is the statement: "From the Jews five times I received forty lashes less one." Just where and when Paul received these lashings is uncertain. But there is no doubt that they were "synagogue whippings" or "stripes" that were administered by synagogue officials as a severe form of punishment for some type of serious deviation from Jewish thought or practice. And there is no doubt that Paul viewed them as afflictions that he suffered as a "servant of Christ" and because of his witness for Christ (cf. vv. 23-29).

2 Corinthians 11:24, in fact, speaks quite dramatically of how reticent Paul was to separate himself from his Jewish past and of how far he would go in being "to those under the law as one under the law" (1 Cor 9:20). But it also suggests how the Jewish world, even at such an early time, viewed his commitment to Jesus, and how for them that commitment was anathema to the Jewish religion (cf. 1 Thess 2:14). Likewise, Acts depicts how Paul repeatedly attempted to minister in various Diaspora synagogues, but how he constantly was opposed by Jews and forced to leave those synagogues (often even forced to leave the respective cities and areas as well) if he wanted to continue to express his new identity as a missionary of Jesus Christ (cf. Acts 9:20-25, 28-30; 13:14-51; 14:1-7, 19-20).

The principal factor when one deals with conversion is that of identity.

Paul never forgot his Jewish past or his Jewish training, and emotionally he still identified with his Jewish compatriots (cf. Rom 9:1-5; 10:1-2). A great deal of his past, in fact, he brought into his new experience. But while Paul carried over into Christianity much of what he learned in Judaism, "he inverts the values of his past in a way that is consonant with his new commitments" (Segal, *Paul the Convert*, 125). And chief among those new commitments was his commitment to Jesus as Israel's Messiah — from which, then, sprang his new identity as being no longer simply a Jewish Pharisee or even a fulfilled Jew, but a "Christ follower" or "Christian" (cf. the parallel consciousness reflected in the use of "Christian" in Acts 11:26; 26:28; 1 Pet 4:16).

3. Immediate Christological Implications

Paul considered all that he learned and experienced in Judaism, in one way or another, to have been important, for he seems to have viewed it all as a pre-stage for his Christian life, thought, and ministry. But his conversion, which he characterized as God's revelation of "his Son in me" (Gal 1:16), was, as James S. Stewart rightly identified it, "far and away the most vital and formative influence of Paul's life" (*A Man in Christ: The Vital Elements of St. Paul's Religion* [London: Hodder & Stoughton, 1935] 82). Like the first disciples, who began from their Easter experience and viewed everything from the standpoint of that historical and existential occasion, Paul looked back on his former hopes, life, and thought in the light of Christ's encounter, and from that perspective (1) affirmed everything that the earliest believers held to be true about Jesus, (2) transposed some of their statements into language that would be more meaningful for Gentiles, and (3) developed his own distinctive christological proclamation. The straining of his ancestral faith had suddenly given way to realization and fulfillment, as is most readily seen in his affirmation, transposition, and development of the early church's christology.

Reaffirmed Theocentricity

As a Jew, Paul well knew that it is the God of holy Scripture, the One who is both Creator and Redeemer, who alone is to be credited as the initiator, sustainer, and final agent of human redemption. What took place in Paul's conversion, therefore, was not a setting aside of God in favor of Jesus, as though espousing a "Unitarianism of the Second Person" or a "Jesus Only" theology. Rather, what occurred was an overwhelming realization that God's salvific purposes for both creation in general and humanity in particular are now to be understood as focused in the work and person of Jesus of Nazareth. Thus in words probably drawn from some of the church's early confessions, Paul affirms the basic theocentricity of the Christian gospel: (1) that Christ's redemptive work was "according to the will of our God and Father" (Gal 1:4); (2) that "God sent his Son" (Gal 4:4-5); (3) that "God was in Christ reconciling the world to himself" (2 Cor 5:19); (4) that believers are "being justified freely by his [God's] grace" (Rom 3:24); (5) that "God presented him [Christ] as a sacrifice of atonement" (Rom 3:25); (6) that it is God who shows "justice," is himself "just," and who "justifies sinners" (Rom 3:26); (7) that "God exalted him [Jesus Christ] . . . and gave him the name that is above every name" (Phil 2:9); (8) that the worship of Jesus and the confession "Jesus Christ is Lord" are "to the glory of God the Father" (Phil 2:10-11); and (9) that "God was pleased to have all his fullness dwell in him [Christ], and through him to reconcile all things to himself" (Col 1:19-20).

Messiah/Son of God/Lord

Understanding, therefore, that God's redemptive purposes are now to be seen as focused in Jesus, the most immediate implication of Paul's conversion was the conviction that "Jesus is Israel's Messiah [the Christ]," who acted as God's agent in inaugurating the Messianic Age and in bringing about divine redemption. Most often, of course, Paul used the Greek term *Christos* as a proper name and not a title (which is a phenomenon we will speak about more fully later). Yet there are a number of places in his letters where his reference to Christ reflects a Jewish understanding of messiahship. Such a titular usage comes to the fore most clearly in Rom 9:5, where, at the conclusion of a list of Israel's advantages, he says: "From them [the people of Israel] comes the Christ [the Messiah], according to the flesh."

Connected with the theme of Jesus as the Messiah is the theme of Jesus as the Son of God. Many earlier comparative religionists have claimed that "Son of God" was an alien import into the New Testament, being derived from polytheistic notions that were circulating in the Hellenistic world. But with its appearance in some of the writings of Second Temple Judaism that express their authors' messianic expectations — in particular, in *1 Enoch* 105:2; 4QFlorilegium frags. 1-3, 1:10-12 (on 2 Sam 7:14); and 4 Ezra 7:28-29; 13:32, 37, 52; 14:9 (roughly dated between 200 BC and AD 100) — the title "Son of God" when used of Jesus in the New Testament is today being viewed in a more Jewish and functional manner to denote Jesus' unique relationship with God and his obedience to the Father's will. For just as Israel was understood to be uniquely God's own "son" (or, "child") among all the peoples of the earth and Israel's anointed king to be in a special manner God's "son" — with both the nation and its king pledged to a relationship with God of loving obedience — so Jesus, who exemplified obedience to God in an unparalleled manner, was seen to be the Son of God *par excellence.*

Sixteen times in his letters Paul speaks of Christ as God's Son: three times as "Son of God" (Rom 1:4; 2 Cor 1:19; Gal 2:20); twice as "the Son" (1 Cor 15:28; Col 1:13); and eleven times as "his Son" (Rom 1:3, 9; 5:10; 8:3, 29, 32; 1 Cor 1:9; Gal 1:16; 4:4-6 [twice]; 1 Thess 1:10). Four times his reference to Christ as God's Son appears in a quoted confessional fragment (i.e., Rom 1:3-4 [twice]; Gal 4:4-6 [twice]); once in a traditional eschatological climax (i.e., 1 Thess 1:10); and at other times in polemical contexts (e.g., Gal 1:16; 2:20) — all of which seems to suggest that not only did Paul use "Son" with regard to Christ relatively infrequently (compared to its use elsewhere in the New Testament), but also that his use of that title was fairly traditional and often quite circumstantial.

An additional immediate result of Paul's conversion was that he came to affirm the lordship of Jesus. The preaching of Jesus' earliest disciples had made this connection between "Christ" and "Lord," as Luke's report of Peter's exhortation on the Day of Pentecost evidences: "Therefore let all the house of Israel know assuredly that God has made him both Lord and Christ, this Jesus whom you crucified" (Acts 2:36). And Paul's quotation of various early Christian confessional statements that speak of the lordship of Christ (e.g., Rom 10:9; 1 Cor 12:3; 2 Cor 4:5; Phil 2:11; cf. Col 2:6) testifies to his own acceptance of what the church was confessing about Jesus.

Thus in Luke's first account of Paul's conversion in Acts 9, the newly converted apostle is portrayed as almost immediately proclaiming in Damascus that "Jesus is the Christ" (v. 22) and "Jesus is the Son of God"

(v. 20), and that soon afterwards in Jerusalem he was "speaking boldly in the name of the Lord" (v. 28). Undoubtedly Paul's immediate perceptions and first attempts at preaching his new convictions were primarily functional in nature — that is, with an emphasis on the supremacy of Jesus in the divine strategy of redemption and on what God had done redemptively through Jesus, as Peter is portrayed as doing in his Pentecost sermon of Acts 2:14-36. And undoubtedly he called for a response of repentance and faith, as Peter did at the conclusion of his sermon in Acts 2:38-39. For both as a former Pharisee and a new believer in Jesus, Paul knew that being justified before God was not a matter of human endeavor, but that it had to do with a person's response of faith in God, who has acted redemptively for his people (cf. Gal 2:15-16).

4. Transposed Christological Features

As time went on after his conversion, certain ways of expressing those immediate christological convictions became, it seems, transposed — that is, became altered as to sequence or changed as to order, if we understand "transposed" in a literary fashion; though probably it is better to think along musical lines of a composition that is arranged or performed in a key other than originally written. Most obvious of these transpositions is the move in Paul's letters from the single name "Jesus" and the title "Christ" (or, "Messiah") to the use of "Christ" (or, "Jesus Christ"/"Christ Jesus") as a name and an emphasis on "Lord" as the associated title. But there are other identifiable transpositions as well.

From "Jesus is the Christ/Messiah" to "Christ is the Lord"

In the four canonical Gospels, the use of the single name "Jesus" is, by far, most common, usually with the article (ho Iēsous). Likewise, in Hebrews the common designation is "Jesus" (ten times: 2:9; 3:1; 4:14; 6:20; 7:22; 10:19; 12:2, 24; 13:12; 13:20) as opposed to "Jesus Christ" (three times: 10:10; 13:8, 21). And in the confessional portions quoted by Paul, the usual designation is also simply "Jesus" — as, for example, in Phil 2:10 ("that at the name of Jesus every knee should bow, in heaven and on earth and under the earth"); 1 Thess 4:14a ("that 'Jesus died and rose again'"); Rom 10:9

("that if you confess with your mouth 'Jesus is Lord' "); and 1 Cor 12:3 ("no one can say by the Spirit of God 'Jesus is cursed,' and no one can say 'Jesus is Lord' except by the Holy Spirit"; cf. also Rom 3:26b; 1 Cor 11:23; 2 Cor 4:8-11, 14; 11:4; 1 Thess 1:10).

In Paul's letters, however, apart from the confessional material he quotes, "Jesus" is usually transposed into "Christ," "Christ Jesus," or "Jesus Christ." There are, of course, exceptions to this pattern. But frequently the exceptions are to be found in a traditional grace benediction at the close of his letters (cf. Rom 16:20; 1 Cor 16:23), a traditionally conditioned doxological statement (cf. 1 Thess 3:11, 13), a comment on confessional material previously quoted (cf. 1 Thess 4:14b), a reference to something historical, such as Jesus' afflictions, death, and resurrection or Paul's own conversion (cf. Rom 4:24; 1 Cor 9:1; 2 Cor 4:10, 14; Gal 6:17; 1 Thess 2:15), or in roughly parallel statements, with "Jesus" and "Christ" (or "Jesus Christ") appearing in the parallelism as equivalent names (cf. Rom 8:11; Eph 4:20-21; also 2 Thess 1:12). Only a handful of other exceptions can be cited — Rom 14:14; 1 Cor 5:4 (twice); 2 Cor 1:14; 11:31; Eph 1:15; Phil 2:19; Col 3:17; 1 Thess 4:1, 2; 2 Thess 1:7, 8; 2:8; Phlm 5. The use of the single name "Jesus" in Paul's letters, therefore, while not scorned by the apostle, must be seen as being exceptional in comparison to his much more abundant use of the name "Christ," "Christ Jesus," or "Jesus Christ."

Likewise, Paul's frequent reference to Christ as "Lord" should be seen as something of a transposition on his part. For while the early church certainly confessed that "Jesus is Lord" (e.g., Acts 2:36; Rom 10:9; 1 Cor 12:3), it is in Paul's letters that the title "Lord" receives particular prominence and that the lordship of Christ resounds in a higher key and with greater explication. The situation is somewhat comparable to Luke's use of "Lord" for Jesus in his Gospel (forty-two times) vis-à-vis the christological use of that title in Mark (four times) and Matthew (nineteen times); also to Luke's use of the synonym *epistata*, "Master," on the lips of the disciples in his Gospel (seven times) and of "Lord" in Acts (fifty-three times, though since "Lord" is used in Acts for both God and Jesus it is sometimes difficult to determine when it specifically refers to Jesus).

Why this transposition of name and title in Paul's letters? Probably it had much to do with the ways in which "Jesus," "Christ," and "Lord" were perceived by Gentiles, whom Paul was attempting to evangelize. For the name Jesus, which carried a distinctly Jewish flavor, Paul probably thought best to tone down when addressing Gentiles by using Christ as a name or

Christ Jesus/Jesus Christ as the double name. Furthermore, the title Christ would likely have been understood by Gentiles to signify someone who had been medicinally anointed or rubbed with oil in preparation for an athletic contest, and so would not have suggested to them the significant notion of "God's Anointed One" or the idea of supremacy. The title Lord, by contrast, would have conveyed to Gentiles the note of supremacy, needing then only clarification regarding the nature of that supremacy.

A rationale for such a transposition of name and title, however, should also likely be attributed to Paul's own consciousness. For his relationship with Jesus had not been historical in nature, as was true of the earliest believers portrayed in the Gospels, but was supra-historical. It came about by means of a heavenly encounter at his conversion, by various mystical experiences (cf. 2 Cor 12:1-6; also Acts 22:17-21; 23:11), and by continued personal communion. In addition, his Christian understanding of all of the Jesus traditions that he quotes (e.g., 1 Cor 15:3b-5; 1 Thess 4:1-9; Phil 2:6-11) and of all of the Jesus narrative substructure that he builds on in his letters (e.g., 2 Cor 1:5; 4:10; 5:14; 8:9; 10:1; Gal 1:4; 3:1, 13; 4:4-5) was probably mediated to him through the church's leading figures (e.g., Peter and James, as referred to in Gal 1:18-20) and the church's confessions. Thus the title "Lord" would have been more approrpiate in his own conscious-ness, with "Christ" retained but used by Paul mostly as a name.

Other Identifiable Transpositions

Other christological images and titles used by Jewish Christians could also be cited as having been transposed by Paul in his Gentile mission (cf. the discussion of "Distinctive Imagery and Motifs," in my *The Christology of Early Jewish Christianity* [London: SCM, 1970] 25-62; also some of the titles spelled out under the caption "Messiahship and Its Implications," 63-119). Representative of such christological ascriptions is the title "God's Salva-tion," "Israel's Salvation," or simply "The Salvation," which was used in messianic fashion by Jews during the Second Temple period (cf. *Jubilees* 31:19; 1QIsa[a] 51:4-5; 1QH 7:18-19; CD 20:20 [9:43]; 20:34 [9:54]; also note the rabbinic tractate *b. Berakoth* 56b-57a) and is reflected in some of the materials of the New Testament (cf. Luke 1:69, 71, 77; 2:30; 3:6; John 4:22; Acts 4:12). Paul, however, seems to have transposed that ancient title by speaking of "the Lord Jesus Christ" as "Savior" (Phil 3:20; cf. Eph 5:23;

2 Tim 1:10; Titus 1:4; 2:13; 3:6; Acts 13:23). It may also be argued that he transposed the christological image "Son of Man," which appears extensively in the Gospels (cf. also Acts 7:56; Rev. 1:13; 14:14), into a "Second Adam" typology or a "Son of God" ascription. But I doubt the validity of both those latter views.

More to the point is the transposition that seems to take place in Paul's shift from the theme of Jesus' obedience, which appears prominently elsewhere in the New Testament (especially in the confessional materials that he quotes, in Matthew's Gospel, and in Hebrews), to his use of the expression *pistis Christou,* which seems to be the dominant way in which he highlights that obedience. The expression is admittedly difficult, as the current, extensive discussion of it indicates. But when *Christou* is read as a subjective genitive and *pistis* understood in terms of the Hebrew word *'ĕmûnah,* which means both "faith" and "faithfulness," then it is not too difficult to view Paul as talking about "the faith/faithfulness of Christ" in Rom 3:22; Gal 2:16 (twice); 3:22; Eph 3:22, and Phil 3:9 (cf. also Gal 3:26 in P^{46}) in much the same way as he speaks about "the faithfulness of God" in Rom 3:3 and "the faith of Abraham" in Rom 4:16.

That Paul found this expression already rooted in the vocabulary of early Jewish Christianity can be argued from the appearance of the phrase *ek pisteōs Iēsou* at the conclusion of the quoted material in Rom 3:24-26. And that Paul also, at least once, spoke directly of Christ's "obedience" *(hypakoē)* can be seen by reference to Rom 5:19. But his more usual way of speaking of Christ's obedience was, it seems, by the use of the expression "the faith/faithfulness of Christ" *(pistis Christou),* thereby transposing that theme into another key. And so by transposing the theme in this manner, he was, it appears, able to set up a parallel between (1) the objective basis of the Christian gospel, that is, Christ's "faith" or "faithfulness," understood as the perfect response of obedience that Christ rendered to God the Father both actively in his life and passively in his death, and (2) the subjective response of "faith" that is required of all human beings whom God reconciles to himself through the work of Christ.

5. Distinctive Christological Proclamation

In addition to his affirmation of the early church's acclaim of Jesus and his transposition of some of the ways in which that acclaim took form, Paul also may be said to have developed certain distinctive christological emphases. Some of the nuancing of these emphases may be credited to the catalyst of his Gentile mission, for he needed to make his preaching not only understandable but also relevant to his Gentile audiences. In the main, however, it seems that many of the distinctive christological features in Paul's proclamation were rooted primarily in his conversion experience and developed by means of his own reflection on that experience.

Paul's letter to Christians at Rome provides us with an excellent source for identifying some of the particularly significant and distinctive features of Paul's proclamation. For not only is it the longest, most systematic, and least overtly polemical writing among the apostle's extant letters, it also — and more importantly for our present purposes — (1) addresses Gentile believers whom Paul had not evangelized and never met, (2) tells them in the opening thanksgiving section that he wants to include them among his converts and to give them a "spiritual gift" *(charisma pneumatikon)* to make them strong, implying that in so doing he is giving them the essence of what he proclaims to all Gentiles in his missionary activities (1:11-15), and (3) speaks in the concluding doxology of what he has presented to them as being "my gospel," thereby suggesting that it has been something fairly distinctive that he has given them (16:25). But while Romans may be declared to be an excellent source of material for our purposes, it must also be admitted that the letter is extremely difficult to analyze, with numerous proposals being offered today for most of the major issues of provenance and interpretation.

My own understanding of the major issues involved — which, of course, informs my interpretation here, but must await a forthcoming commentary to explicate — includes two important points. First, that the addressees, while ethnically both Jews and Gentiles, were predominantly Gentile believers in Jesus who (1) had been evangelized by Jewish believers from Jerusalem, (2) continued to look to the Jerusalem church for inspiration and guidance, and (3) "kept up some Jewish observances and remained faithful to part of the heritage of the Jewish Law and cult, without insisting on circumcision" (to quote R. E. Brown, *Antioch and Rome: New Testament Cradles of Catholic Christianity* [New York/Toronto: Paulist, 1983] 104, whose thesis J. Fitzmyer has agreed with in his *Romans* [Anchor Bible; New York: Doubleday, 1993] 33-34, though without drawing out the hermeneutical implications of such a position). Second, that Paul's major purposes in writing were (1) to give Gentile believers whom he had not evangelized and did not know, but who as Gentiles were within the orbit of his mission, teaching that he considered to be uniquely his, which he characterizes as his "spiritual gift" to them (cf. 1:12-15; 15:15-18), and (2) to seek their assistance for his proposed ministry to the western regions of the Roman empire (cf. 1:10b, 13; 15:23-32) — with the setting out of "my gospel," as he calls it in 16:25, meant not only to prepare them for his coming, but also so that they might understand and appreciate what he is preaching in his ministry to Gentiles.

An additional problem that confronts interpreters of Romans, and one that is of pertinence for our discussion here, is the rather decided difference that exists between the first major section of the letter, that is, 1:16–4:25 (or wherever the body of the letter begins, whether at 1:13, 1:16, or 1:18), and the second major section, that is, 5:1–8:39 (or possibly 5:12–8:39, with 5:1-11 being a hinge section between the two). For whereas 1:16–4:25 contains some fifteen to eighteen biblical quotations located at eight or nine places, biblical quotations in 5:1–8:39 are notoriously lacking (only at 7:7, used illustratively, and at 8:36, within a quoted confessional fragment). Furthermore, these two sections seem fairly different in their overall presentations, with 1:16–4:25 being quite Jewish in its vocabulary, rhetoric, and argumentation — with those same Jewish features being carried on in the third section of 9:1–11:36 — but 5:1–8:39 seemingly devoid of such Jewish features and given over more to the universal themes of "death," "life," "peace," and "reconciliation," and to such distinctive emphases as being "in Christ" and being "in the Spirit."

Perhaps the differences between 1:16–4:25 and 5:1–8:39 should be seen as supporting the thesis that chapters 1–11 of Romans contain two Pauline sermons: one to a Jewish audience that was originally made up of material now in chapters 1–4 and 9–11, but whose parts have somehow become separated; the other to a Gentile audience as represented in chapters 5–8 (cf. R. Scroggs, "Paul as Rhetorician: Two Homilies in Romans 1–11," in *Jews, Greeks, and Christians: Religious Cultures in Late Antiquity. Essays in Honor of William David Davies,* ed. R. Hamerton-Kelly and R. Scroggs [Leiden: Brill, 1976] 271-98). More likely, however, is the view that in 5:1–8:39 Paul is presenting what he spoke of in the thanksgiving section of the letter as his "spiritual gift" to his Roman addressees that is given for their strengthening (1:11) — that is, the form of the gospel that he customarily proclaimed within his Gentile mission, which in the concluding doxology he calls "my gospel" (16:25).

Approaching the relationship of chapters 1–4 and 5–8 from the perspective of this latter thesis, 1:16–4:25 can be seen as the type of proclamation that Paul knew was held in common by all Jewish believers in Jesus — including Gentile believers who traced their origins back to the Jerusalem church and who looked to Jerusalem Christianity for their inspiration and support. That form of Christian proclamation, it may be posited from 1:16-17 and 3:21-26, laid great stress on such Jewish concepts as "the righteousness of God," "the witness of the law and the prophets," "justification," "redemption," and "expiation/propitiation," seeking only to focus attention on Jesus as Israel's Messiah and on faith as one's proper response to God — features that both Jewish Christians and Paul believed were inherent in Israel's religion (cf. Gal 2:15-16). It proclaimed the fulfillment of God's promise to Abraham in Jesus' ministry and the church's message, honored the Mosaic law as the God-ordained "pedagogue" for the nation Israel, cherished the traditions of the Jerusalem church, and supported its proclamation by a christocentric reading of holy Scripture.

With this form of Christian proclamation Paul was thoroughly in agreement, and so he begins Romans with a section that presents his agreements with his addressees (i.e., 1:16–4:25) and then goes on to set out his distinctive message (i.e., 5:1–8:39). By way of comparison, it may be pointed out that Paul did something similar in his letter to the Galatians, presenting in his proposition statement of Gal 2:15-21 (the "Propositio") first the points on which he and his addressees agreed (i.e., vv. 15-16, which are spelled out in 3:1-18) and then the points on which they differed (i.e., vv. 17-20, which are spelled out in 3:19–4:11), with a summary of the issues at hand appended (i.e., v. 21). And probably he often presented the gospel in this manner himself when occasion demanded, particularly before a Jewish audience.

In 5:1–8:39, however, it may be claimed, Paul sets out the distinctive features of the gospel that he proclaimed in his Gentile mission, to those who had no Jewish heritage and no biblical instruction. The material in 5:1-11 may be seen either as a thesis statement for what follows in 5:12–8:39 or as a hinge between chapters 1–4 and 5–11 — or, in fact, as both. But what seems evident is that in 5:12-21 Paul presents his readers with what could be called a "new, constitutive redemption story" that has universal dimensions, as opposed to the more limited story of redemption from bondage in Egypt that Jews held as being central. Paul's redemption story speaks of (1) sin coming into the world through "one man," (2) death and its effects reigning over all people, but (3) grace and life being available to everyone "through Jesus Christ our Lord." And throughout 5:1–8:39 Paul highlights, in explication of this universal redemption story, such matters as "peace with God," "reconciliation" with God and others, deliverance from sin and death, being "in Christ," the gift of the Holy Spirit, and being unable to be separated from "Christ's love," and so from God's love and protection.

Chapters 5–8 have frequently been viewed as the apex of Paul's argument in Romans. They deal with the central factors of human existence — namely, with sin, death, life, and relationship with God and others. These are matters that can be based, by analogy, on God's past dealings with Israel as recorded in Scripture. But they are also matters, evidently, that were not directly demonstrable to Gentiles by specific biblical texts. Nor, it seems, would such an approach have been meaningful to or appreciated by Gentiles. Rather, Paul's emphases on "peace with God," "reconciliation," life "in Christ," life "in the Spirit," etc. (as in chapters 5–8) appear to have stemmed primarily from his conversion experience and his own reflection on its significance — with his practice in his Gentile mission being to present such matters without any necessary reference to the Jewish Scriptures.

Christ's confrontation of Paul, with all that went into the apostle's subsequent understanding of it, confirmed for him what the early Jewish believers in Jesus were proclaiming — which, of course, he also proclaimed (so Rom 1:16–4:25). In addition, however, it gave him a new understanding of (1) relationship with God, (2) relationships with others, and (3) the logistics for a Gentile mission (so Galatians 1–2). Therefore, in writing to Gentile Christians at Rome, who were largely dependent on the theology and traditions of the Jerusalem church, he speaks at the beginning of wanting to give them a "spiritual gift" (1:11) and refers in closing to "my gospel" (16:25). And in 5:1–8:39 he presents that spiritual gift and his gospel, which turns out to be his own distinctive and developed christological proclamation that has to do with "death," "life," "peace," "reconciliation," being "in Christ," being "in the Spirit," and being unable to be separated from "the love of God that is in Christ Jesus our Lord."

6. A Christological Paradigm in Paul's Conversion Experience?

At least one further question, however, needs to be asked when we consider the impact of Paul's conversion on his view of Jesus: Did Paul understand his conversion experience to be a paradigm for the experience of every Christian? And if so, in what way and to what extent?

In 1 Cor 4:16 and Phil 3:17 Paul exhorts his converts: "Be imitators of me!" *(mimētai/symmimētai mou ginesthe)*. The Corinthian exhortation refers to his readers' attitudes toward their present life "in Christ Jesus" vis-à-vis their former lives, for now they are not to boast about past attainments but to boast "in the Lord" (cf. 1 Cor 1:26-31). The Philippian exhortation has also to do with a radical change of perspective, for now "having been taken hold of by Christ Jesus," his addressees are asked to follow Paul's example in counting everything from their past as garbage in comparison to "the surpassing greatness of knowing Christ Jesus [their] Lord" (cf. Phil 3:4-16). And in 1 Cor 11:1 and 2 Thess 3:7, 9 he asks his converts to imitate him in other matters as well (also in Gal 4:12 and Phil 4:9, though without the use of the term "imitate").

Furthermore, in Gal 3:26-29 Paul says that those who have expressed "faith in Christ Jesus" and have been "united with Christ in baptism," and so in their conversion have been "clothed with Christ," have come into an entirely new relationship with God and with others. It is, as he spells it out in that passage, a relationship where one's identity is changed (i.e., now "children of God," those who "belong to Christ," and those who are truly "Abraham's seed" and "heirs according to the promise") and where social relationships are altered, with judgments no longer to be made on the basis of traditional human categories but on the basis of new redemptive categories (i.e., now "no longer Jew or Greek, slave or free, male and female, for you are all one in Christ Jesus").

As a result of his conversion, Paul's self-identity and thinking were dramatically changed. Christologically, he saw Jesus in an entirely new way, affirming as true all that the early church had claimed him to be: Israel's Messiah, the Son of God, and humanity's redemptive Lord. Also on the basis of his conversion — coupled with his own reflections on that experience and the needs of his Gentile mission — Paul came to transpose some of the language of those early affirmations and to develop his own distinctive christological proclamation.

Paul's conversion is never portrayed as being paradigmatic in the specific details of that event, as those details are narrated in Luke's Acts. But it is presented in Paul's letters as a paradigm for all Christians in terms of a radical reorientation of thought about Jesus and of life now lived "in Christ." Furthermore, there is the suggestion of the need to follow his example in (1) transposing the gospel proclamation into forms more readily understandable and relevant for today, and (2) developing a distinctive proclamation that better explicates the truths of the gospel in various situations and to various audiences addressed. For, as seen in Paul's practice, contextualization of the gospel must always take place — both by way of transposing certain traditional features and by way of developing certain new significances, with those transpositions and developments being always in line with the testimony of Scripture and Christ's transforming and illuminating encounter.

Selected Bibliography

Boyarin, D. *A Radical Jew: Paul and the Politics of Identity.* Berkeley: University of California Press, 1994.

Davies, W. D. *Paul and Rabbinic Judaism: Some Rabbinic Elements in Pauline Theology.* 4th ed. Philadelphia: Fortress, 1980.

Dietzfelbinger, C. *Die Berufung des Paulus als Ursprung seiner Theologie.* Neukirchen-Vluyn: Neukirchener Verlag, 1985.

Donaldson, T. L. "Zealot and Convert: The Origin of Paul's Christ-Torah Antithesis." *Catholic Biblical Quarterly* 51 (1989) 655-82.

Gaventa, B. R. *From Darkness to Light: Aspects of Conversion in the New Testament.* Philadelphia: Fortress, 1986.

Dunn, J. D. G. "'A Light to the Gentiles': The Significance of the Damascus Road Christophany for Paul." In *The Glory of Christ in the New Testament,* ed. L. D. Hurst and N. T. Wright. Oxford: Clarendon, 1987, 251-66.

———. "The New Perspective on Paul." *Bulletin of the John Rylands Library* 65 (1983) 95-122. Reprinted in *Jesus, Paul and the Law: Studies in Mark and Galatians.* London: SPCK; Louisville: Westminster, 1990, 183-214.

Hays, R. B. *The Faith of Jesus Christ: An Investigation of the Narrative Substructure of Galatians 3:1–4:11.* Chico, CA: Scholars Press, 1983.

Hurtado, L. "Convert, Apostate or Apostle to the Nations: The 'Conversion' of Paul in Recent Scholarship." *Studies in Religion/Sciences Religieuses* 22 (1993) 273-84.

Kim, S. *The Origin of Paul's Gospel.* Tübingen: Mohr-Siebeck, 1981; Grand Rapids: Eerdmans, 1982.

Longenecker, R. N. *Paul, Apostle of Liberty.* New York: Harper & Row, 1964; Grand Rapids: Baker, 1976; Vancouver: Regent College Bookstore, 1993.

————. "The Nature of Paul's Early Eschatology." *New Testament Studies* 31 (1985) 85-95.

Sanders, E. P. *Paul and Palestinian Judaism.* Philadelphia: Fortress, 1977.

Segal, A. F. *Paul the Convert: The Apostolate and Apostasy of Saul the Pharisee.* New Haven: Yale University Press, 1990.

Stendahl, K. *Paul Among Jews and Gentiles and Other Essays.* Philadelphia: Fortress, 1976.

Wenham, David. *Paul: Follower of Jesus or Founder of Christianity?* Grand Rapids: Eerdmans, 1995.

A New Understanding of the Present and the Future: Paul and Eschatology

I. HOWARD MARSHALL

1. Development in Early Christian Theology

There is a suspicion in the world of scholarship that New Testament students of a conservative tendency dislike the idea of development in Christian doctrine. They want to argue, it is held, that Christians everywhere throughout the New Testament period believed much the same things, and that what was happening in Christian writings was simply that the various authors drew on a common, static store of teaching — the only changes made being to adapt and apply that common body of teaching to different audiences. The idea that Jesus could have developed in his understanding of God the Father and God's kingdom is thought to be anathema. For surely he was omniscient, or at least knew all that he needed to know as a man through revelation from the Father. Jesus' disciples, of course, did not fully understand him during his earthly life. But the special seminars they had with their risen Master during the forty days from the resurrection to the ascension sufficed to give them a full and mature understanding of Christian doctrine right from the earliest days of the Church. As for Paul, conservative students of the New Testament are often viewed as believing that he learned a great deal from Christians at Damascus and that he imbibed even more during the next three years, whether through visions or his own thinking, so that when his writing career began he was already mature in his understanding of his new faith. The alleged attraction of this view —

43

whether presented as a characterization or a caricature of a certain group — is that it is then possible to claim that all the New Testament documents are in essential agreement with one another and that each presents different but harmonious facets of a common Christian faith.

No doubt this characterization is largely a caricature. Nonetheless, there is sufficient truth in it to make some of us who might be regarded as members of this group feel a little hot under the collar. For discussions by conservative scholars of development and growth in the thinking and teaching of Jesus are few and far between. And when C. H. Dodd argued for significant developments in Paul's theology — with the implication that Paul's later views on such a topic as "eschatology" were more correct and acceptable than his earlier ones, and that his earlier views can be quietly ditched — this was hardly congenial to conservative students.

But development can hardly be denied in a proper understanding of the New Testament. It is not until Acts 10 and 11, for example, that Peter realizes that Gentiles are acceptable to God without first being circumcised and that Jewish food laws no longer hold for Christians. Likewise, the victory for freedom depicted in Acts 15 was not gained without a struggle. As for Paul himself, it is possible to show that controversies with Judaizers and other opponents led to fresh expositions of his theology in which previously unknown thoughts came to expression. His developing use of the metaphor of the body is a good example.

Yet the basic instinct of conservative students of the New Testament is correct. For it is the case that the central lines of Christian doctrine were laid down remarkably swiftly, and that we can recognize a core of belief and practice that can be traced back to the earliest days. In concert with Martin Hengel, I believe that the first twenty years of the church were decisive for the development of its theology. In fact, some of the key elements in Paul's thinking are already present in his earliest writings. I share the view of the editor of this volume that Galatians is probably the earliest surviving letter of Paul. If this view is incorrect, then the palm must be awarded to 1 Thessalonians. On either assumption, however, not only is there a maturity of understanding in Paul's earliest letter, but also we gain the firm impression that much of what he is saying was not thought up freshly for the occasion but represents his settled views. Likewise, the fact that he can assume so much common understanding on the part of his recipients confirms that he was not suddenly producing new ideas that nobody had ever heard of previously.

In this essay we will concentrate our attention on the question of how far Paul's views on eschatology were determined and settled by his conversion. Needless to say, we subsume under the term "conversion" not just the momentary experience outside Damascus but also the associated complex of events and intense personal reorientation that filled the immediately ensuing period.

2. Eschatology

It would perhaps have been better for theologians if the term "eschatology" had never been created. But now that we have it, we find it difficult to do without it. Properly speaking, eschatology refers to doctrine or teaching concerning the "last things" — that is, concerning what is going to happen in the future, or rather at the end of time or of this world.

The various religions and philosophies of the Greco-Roman world had differing views regarding eschatology. The Stoics, for example, believed that the world would come to an end with a conflagration in which everything would be destroyed. Probably most ordinary people, however, had little concern about the world coming to an end and were more preoccupied with their own deaths and what would happen to them individually in the hereafter. So the mystery religions offered immortality to pious individuals who accepted initiation into their rites.

Many Jewish writings looked forward to some kind of divine intervention in the history of the world at some time in the indefinite future. That intervention would bring the present state of affairs to an end and lead to the establishment of God's kingdom. To use Jewish phraseology that was taken over by Christians, "This Age" would be succeeded by the "Age to Come" (Matt 12:32; cf. Gal 1:4; Eph 1:21). The new age would see the establishment of God's kingdom, in which people would be governed justly and enjoy peace. This new state of affairs was expected to go on forever, particularly since all opponents would be destroyed and all who were counted worthy of entry into it would be transformed. Thus "the last things" would not signal the end of God's being or activity. Rather, they would constitute the eternal last phase that would be introduced by the end of the present world-order. It was not uncommon for people to believe that this transitional crisis was not far distant in time. There were, therefore, numerous cases of disappointed hopes and numerous fresh formulations of the people's expectations.

Jewish thought of the kind we have been describing is often labeled "apocalyptic." This term refers loosely to the kind of documents that depict the transmission of heavenly secrets to a human being — whether through a vision, or some kind of inspiration, or as a result of a heavenly journey. They unfold mysteries otherwise unknown. In their content they reflect a type of thinking in which God and evil stand opposed to one another: the present world is under the grip of evil, which may well get worse; but the writers have the certainty, born of revelation, that God will triumph in the end by some kind of powerful intervention in world history. The language used to refer to this event is characterized by bizarre imagery and symbolism, and includes descriptions of various cataclysmic events.

The term "eschatological" is sometimes used to denote a type of outlook that is dominated by what people believe (and hope) God is going to do in the future. In many situations in life, of course, what has already happened determines what one does now. After the birth of a child, especially a first child, a mother's (and father's) life is dominated by what has just happened (and its continuing effects). After a catastrophe, people concentrate their attention on repairing the damage that has been caused. But what is about to happen can also be decisive for one's planning and action. Before a wedding, for example, a bride's thinking and planning are largely determined by what is about to happen. In fact, in the now-familiar situation of a "countdown" of whatever nature, everything is determined by what is intended to happen at a specific future time. Similarly, any group of people whose life was (or, is) dominated by their hope of God's future intervention in the world will have an eschatological outlook, especially if they expected (or, expect) God to act in the near future.

3. The Eschatological Outlook of the Earliest Christians

It is a common interpretation of earliest Christianity that it had such an apocalyptic, future-dominated outlook. On this view, Jesus was concerned with the imminent intervention of God to establish his rule in the world, and he spoke about the coming of a "Son of Man" who would play a leading role in this event. When Jesus died, his followers were dominated by the hoped-for fulfillment of this prophecy more than anything else. They thought of themselves primarily as "the community of the end-time," who had been gathered together by Jesus in preparation for this cataclysmic event and who were assured of a place in the coming kingdom. Then, as time went on, their hopes were not fulfilled, and so they became conscious of what has been called "the delay of the parousia." The continuing non-fulfillment of their original hopes compelled them to reformulate their theology — in particular, (1) to value the present time more positively as a time for continuing mission and service, and (2) to attach increasing importance to what had happened in the past. Their faith became increasingly centered on the past events of the death and resurrection of Jesus and on their present experience of spiritual power in the church, with the "parousia" ("coming" or "presence") of the Son of Man moved to a much less central place in their thought. So they settled down to an indefinite period of life in this world. And while they never wholly abandoned their hope, eschatology did not actively affect their thinking in the same way as at first.

The temporal point at which the church became conscious of this alleged "delay" and began to alter its theological outlook is debated. A popular theory a few years ago was that Luke was largely responsible for such a reformulation of Christian theology, doing so in order to face the "long haul" of the church in the world. This hypothesis would place the change fairly late in the first century. This is, however, a misinterpretation of the evidence of Luke and Acts. The church's development of a theology in which the structural principle is the working out of God's plan in history (sometimes referred to as "Salvation History" or *Heilsgeschichte*) can be traced back to a much earlier period than the composition of the Gospels. Nevertheless, this still leaves open the question of the relationship between past, present, and future in the thinking of the earliest Christians. This matter is of particular concern to us here because some interpreters hold that such a shift from an originally future-oriented theology to a past/present-oriented theology was part of the legacy bequeathed to the church by Paul.

4. Paul's Thinking about the Future

Before attempting to assess what effect Paul's conversion had on his thinking about the future, we need to discover what his orientation actually was and whether it shifted in any way in the course of his life. For it is not very wise to ask how Paul's conversion affected his eschatology if we do not know what that eschatology was!

We consider, then, the common modern view that Paul held first to an apocalyptic eschatology that only gradually gave way to a recognition of the importance of other aspects of Christian faith. Richard Longenecker identifies Albert Schweitzer as the first scholar to argue that Jewish apocalypticism was the matrix for Paul's thought (cf. his "The Nature of Paul's Early Eschatology," 85, citing Schweitzer's earlier works on Jesus and his *The Mysticism of Paul the Apostle,* trans. W. Montgomery [London: Black, 1931], particularly 52ff.). Ernst Käsemann, among others, also considered apocalyptic to be the "mother" of early Christian theology (cf., e.g., his *New Testament Questions of Today,* trans. W. J. Montague [London: SCM, 1969] 236-37). This means that in essence Paul's earliest thought as a Christian was future-oriented and future-dominated.

In his article "The Nature of Paul's Early Eschatology," Longenecker sets himself to dispute this view. He investigates 1 and 2 Thessalonians and makes three points. First, the theme of the letters is not eschatology. The passages dealing thematically with this topic are limited. 1 Thessalonians is largely about encouraging the church in Paul's absence during some kind of hostile situation. In fact, the ethical and eschatological materials of 1 Thessalonians are introduced in 4:1 by a "finally" *(loipon),* which suggests to Longenecker that 4:1–5:22 does not contain the main theme or themes of that letter. It is not, then, that eschatology was unimportant for Paul in these letters, but rather that it is not the dominant theme. Second, right from the beginning the basis for hope for the future is firmly based on what has happened in the past — specifically on the death and resurrection of Jesus (1 Thess 4:14) and on the teaching of Jesus (1 Thess 4:15). And, third, the purpose of the discussions of the future in 1 and 2 Thessalonians is pastoral and supportive rather than being to present what is central in the faith. For Paul, then, teaching about Christ is what is central rather than apocalyptic hopes for the future. Longenecker picks up the phrase "fulfilled messianism" from W. D. Davies to sum up his understanding of Paul's outlook. And he concludes that "Paul's basic Christian conviction and the starting point for all his Christian theology was not apocalypticism but functional christology — that is, that his commitment was not first of all to a programme or some timetable of events but to a person: Jesus the Messiah" (ibid., 93).

This conclusion is basically sound, although I would demur from some of the details of the argument. First, it seems to me that the context of all that is said in 1 and 2 Thessalonians is the future advent of Jesus, which occupies a much greater role in these letters than elsewhere in Paul's writings. This may reflect a greater awareness of the future advent of Jesus in this particular community at this early date (though it is not so conspicuous in Galatians, which was written around the same time). Second, the letters were written to deal with problems regarding the future hope of believers, and one cannot say that the materials of 1 Thess 4:1–5:22 comprise virtually an addendum to an already complete letter.

Nevertheless, the essential point is correct. The center of gravity in Paul's theology lies in the past and not in the future, although the future hope is one pole of the context for Christian living now. This is demonstrated beyond doubt by reference to 1 Cor 15:3-5, a passage in which Paul summarizes the gospel he has received and now preaches. It is a gospel that is concerned with the death, burial, resurrection, and appearances of Jesus. Other passages in 1 Corinthians also indicate that this was the content of Paul's preaching: "we preach Christ crucified" (1:23; cf. 1:17-18; 2:2), not "Christ who is to come." Paul works within the horizon of the future coming of Christ and the establishment of the kingdom of God, and for him this is a living hope. But the central content of his message is not the future coming of Christ but his incarnation, death, and resurrection. And the heart of his Christian experience is union with the risen Lord, which is expressed in a whole variety of ways — with the centrality of the phrase "in Christ" to describe that experience and a focus on the presence of the Spirit being particularly important in this connection.

We can also see in Paul's writings, as elsewhere in the New Testament, that the parousia or future coming of Jesus occupies a secondary place compared with other aspects of his person and work. For example, it is insignificant in Galatians. The big exception is provided by the two letters to the Thessalonians, and it is not special pleading to point out that its prominence in 2 Thessalonians is due to the need to deal with misunderstandings of Paul's doctrine. In both 1 and 2 Thessalonians, however, it is certainly prominent, and indications are that it must have figured largely in Paul's oral teaching and evangelism (cf. 2 Thess 2:5). Nevertheless, it is only a part of the message and not the center.

5. The Nature of Paul's Eschatology

How, then, are we to characterize Paul's thought about the future? The fact that the first coming of Jesus is central in his message leads us to observe that for him (as also for other early Christians) there was a sense in which the final intervention of God in history had already taken place. Jesus was the Messiah who had already come, and he was the first to be raised from the dead! Therefore, the end time had already commenced.

In the opinion of most interpreters, Paul and other early Christians believed that they were already living in the end time. They were those on whom the end of the ages had come (1 Cor 10:11). This was a belief that could be understood and misunderstood in various ways. There were certainly some people who believed that the end of the world had fully come and that they were now living and reigning in the new world (1 Cor. 4:8). Thus there was nothing more to look forward to. The resurrection had already taken place (2 Tim 2:18), and there would be no future resurrection of the dead (1 Cor 15:12). This must have been a view that required looking at the world through rose-colored spectacles and ignoring the suffering and evil still around. It is hard to see how people reconciled the evidence of their senses with a belief that the end had fully come.

There were also people, however, who believed that they were living in the very last time before the return of the Messiah. The last days had begun. But these "last days" were simply a brief prelude to "the last day" itself, with nothing standing between them and the coming of the final end. This appears to have been the belief that Paul had to correct in 2 Thessalonians (cf. 2:1-12).

Over against such beliefs, Paul's own view was that people were living in the overlap of the ages — that is, that the new age had indeed already dawned with the coming of Jesus and the pouring out of the Spirit, and that believers were therefore experiencing the power of the Spirit and communion with Christ, but that the old world was also still very much in existence. Paul writes that our salvation is nearer than when we first believed (Rom 13:11), but he did not attempt to work out a timetable of eschatological events and appears to have left the course of those events quite open. He stressed the reality of the new life and the new creation, but equally he recognized the continuing existence of the old life and the old world — believing that God had still to bring about the consummation of his new creation. He held, in fact, that the last days had dawned, but he does not appear to have expected an immediate end of the world.

Such, at least, are his settled views in his major writings. The questions that arise here, however, are basically two: Were these views fixed throughout his period of activity as a Christian missionary, or did his thought develop in some manner from one view to another? And, What effect did his conversion have on these eschatological views?

6. Hypotheses of Development

There have been one or two different theories about a change or development in Paul's thinking. There is the case argued by C. H. Dodd, which sees some kind of crisis between the writing of 1 Corinthians and the writing of 2 Corinthians that resulted in Paul giving up his earlier belief in the imminence of the end of the world and coming to a more positive evaluation of the present world (cf. his "Mind of Paul: II"). This interpretation has been effectively refuted in the past (cf. esp. Lowe, "Examination of Attempts to Detect Developments"), and therefore does not here need further attention. Nevertheless, Dodd was right to the extent that there is a change in emphasis as we move chronologically through the letters of Paul. That is to say, the prominence given to the parousia in 1 Thessalonians is not found in later letters. There is, therefore, development but not transformation.

Perhaps the best exposition of this change of emphasis is provided by William Baird, who reaches two conclusions. First, that there is a reduction in the amount of apocalyptic language used by Paul, and this reflects an increasing concern with the past and the present. Second, that Paul's thought becomes more concerned with personal issues, especially as he faces the prospect of his own death and the likelihood that he will not be alive to experience the parousia (Baird, "Pauline Eschatology in Hermeneutical Perspective").

A very different hypothesis regarding development, however, has been set forth by C. L. Mearns, who holds that Paul's teaching developed and changed very early in his career *before* the writing of 1 and 2 Thessalonians (Mearns, "Early Eschatological Development"). Basically, as Mearns proposes, Paul originally shared the belief that the exaltation of Jesus in his resurrection was the fulfillment of the predictions about the future. Christians, therefore, were already living the new life of the world to come in the power of the Spirit. But problems arose when some of them died: How was this possible for those who were already risen with Christ? Moreover, those who held to such an understanding of fulfillment had an overly glorious view of their present existence with its charismatic endowments.

To counter these attitudes Paul introduced new teaching about the future coming of Jesus, which can be seen in the letters to Thessalonica. One stimulus to his new ideas about Jesus' coming was the excitement caused by the Emperor Caligula's attempt to have a statue of himself set up in the Jewish temple in Jerusalem, and the subsequent defeat of that venture. This was seen, Mearns contends, as evidence of the prevailing power of wickedness that could be defeated only by the imminent Day of the Lord.

Mearns ascribes to the early Paul what is sometimes called "realized eschatology," that is, that the expected future events *have already taken place*. This is obviously very different from the theory that Paul held that the future events *were about to take place in the near future* — although both views ascribe a sense of great excitement to the Christians who held them. Mearns's hypothesis is discussed by L. J. Kreitzer, who is attracted by various features of the position but in the end rejects it (Kreitzer, *Jesus and God in Paul's Eschatology*). The fatal flaw of the theory is that it presupposes that Paul (and other believers in Jesus) had not dealt with questions regarding the death of Christians and their resurrection in the earliest years of the church, which is highly unlikely (ibid., 177-79).

Nonetheless, we can see how such a hypothesis as that of Mearns is possible. It is possible because there are, indeed, elements of "realized eschatology" in Paul's thinking, and these were held alongside his belief that there are divine events still to come. The erratic feature in Mearns's position, however, is the ascription to Paul of the view that Jesus' resurrection was his parousia. It seems more probable that Paul as a Christian always held together the two beliefs that the last days had dawned and that history had still to run its course to its consummation.

7. Paul's Conversion and His Recognition of Jesus as the Messiah

The case for associating the birth of some aspects of Paul's theology with his conversion depends on (1) analyzing the content of the conversion experience to see what happened to Paul's beliefs as a direct result of it, and (2) showing that there is no reason to suppose that a particular conviction developed late, was preceded by some other conviction, or required some other catalyst.

Whether we regard this crisis in the life of Paul as a conversion experience or a call to ministry — or, as is surely the correct view, a combination of the two — it undoubtedly caused a significant change in his beliefs. In the case of his eschatology, we can confidently assume that his pre-Christian views were not significantly different from those of Second Temple Judaism generally, as we have already outlined them. He would, therefore, have held to a Jewish understanding of the successive nature of "This Age" and the "Age to Come."

From the very beginning, Christians certainly believed that Jesus was the Messiah. The evidence for this is strong: (1) Luke says so in Acts (e.g., 2:36; 3:18, 20). (2) The early confessional formulae preserved in Paul's letters refer to the death and resurrection of the Messiah (cf. Rom 5:6, 8; 1 Cor 8:11; 15:3; Gal 2:21); presumably a person who had died could be regarded as Messiah only if raised from the dead. (3) The earliest Christians were conscious of the power of the Holy Spirit in a new way, both as conveying an inward conviction of the reality of their salvation and as the worker of "signs and wonders" in their communities. The interpretation given in Acts 2:33 that this was the gift of the exalted Jesus is confirmed by the description of the Spirit as "the Spirit of Christ" in Rom 8:9 (cf. Gal 4:6), for the Messiah is the bearer of the Spirit.

Paul's own conversion is comprehensible only if it consisted in a reevaluation of Jesus in some way. The crucial elements in his experience are concerned with (1) the revelation to him of Jesus as God's Son and (2) the commission to preach him to the Gentiles (Gal 1:16). When Paul describes his experience in 1 Cor 9:1, he says that he has seen "Jesus our Lord"; in 1 Cor 15:1-11 the subject revealed to him is "Christ" (not "the Christ"); in Phil 3:4-11 the prevailing term is again "Christ," but he is also spoken of as "the Christ" and "Christ Jesus my Lord." The use or non-use of the definite article with names and designations in Greek is decidedly haphazard. The use of the article could signify that the following noun is a title ("the Christ," i.e., "the Messiah"), but it need not do so. Likewise, the absence of the definite article need not imply that "Christ" by itself is a name rather than a title. Although Paul tends, in my opinion, to use "Christ" more as a name, the sense that it is a meaningful name derived from a title is strong. And that is probably how it should be understood in the cases cited above.

We have, then, three designations that are all associated with this initial conversion experience by Paul in his later writings: "Christ," "Lord," and "Son of God." This observation is corroborated by the evidence in Acts. For in Acts 9, Saul (as he was then called) addresses the heavenly figure as "Lord" (v. 5), which may have been simply an expression of respect, and thereafter proclaims "that Jesus is the Son of God" (v. 20) and sets out to prove "that Jesus is the Christ" (v. 22). And according to Acts 26:23 he preached "that the Christ would suffer and, as the first to rise from the dead, would proclaim light to his own people and to the Gentiles." The evidence of Acts, therefore, agrees with that of Paul's own letters. But it must be remembered that in all of these cases, including those found in Paul's writings, the influence of later reflection may be present.

Paul's experience of Jesus was that of a heavenly being who had been raised from the dead. The titles "Christ," "Lord," and "Son of God" are therefore used by him as designations of a heavenly being. The associations of the designations "Son of God" and "Lord" with the image of God motif have been carefully worked out by Seyoon Kim in his *The Origin of Paul's Gospel,* which is the first major study of the implications of Paul's conversion. Kim's case rests partly on the assumption that Paul knew before his conversion that these designations were being applied to Jesus by the early Christians (ibid., 105). Certainly according to Acts 2:36, Peter spoke of Jesus as having been made "Lord" and "Christ" by God. But there is no explicit mention in Acts of "Son of God" being used before Paul's own use recorded in 9:20.

Part of the evidence for the earliest Christians using "Son of God" (or, "his [God's] Son") as a christological title is in Rom 1:3-4, which Kim regards as a "pre-Pauline confession" (ibid., 111). The phrase in question, however, is ambiguous. The most that can be deduced is that the wording used by Paul in these verses is not his own formulation but represents a form of words used by other Christians and then taken over by him — and used with whatever adaptation he deemed appropriate. To take the further step of claiming that the phrase predates Paul's conversion is to run beyond the evidence, especially if Paul's conversion is dated, as it must be, within some three years at most of the death of Jesus. To assign all "pre-Pauline" material to that narrow period of time is thus unwarranted.

Despite this caveat, there is still a strong case to be made for the earliest Christians, from the very beginning, regarding Jesus as the Messiah/Christ. Without some such recognition the Christian movement would not — and, in fact, could not — have begun. We can, therefore, take it as certain (1) that for Paul his conversion experience established that Jesus was the Messiah, and (2) that this term, or its Greek equivalent "Christ," was explicitly used with reference to Jesus by Christians before Paul.

The important question is, then, whether the attestation that the Messiah has come and has been raised from the dead constitutes evidence for the beginning of the new world or for the start of some other new eschatological conception. We may take it as certain that the converted Paul came to believe that the resurrection was the corroboration of the *existing status* of Jesus, and not that he had *become* the Christ only at his resurrection. There is no evidence from his letters that would suggest anything other than the former understanding. The traditional language that he took over spoke of Christ as dying and being raised from the dead — which does not suggest that the person in question became Christ as a consequence of dying and being raised. Moreover, the persecutor was attacking those who were followers of Jesus, and it was because of the claims that they proclaimed about Jesus that he attacked them. It is highly unlikely that for the converted Paul the term Christ did not apply to the status of Jesus during his earthly life.

If so, this means that the coming of the Messiah is to be dated not from Easter but from the birth of Jesus, as Paul certainly believed by the time he wrote Gal 4:4 — that is, that the beginning of the messianic age predates Easter. Our interpretation would be reinforced if it were possible to show that for Paul the kingdom of God began with the coming of Jesus, but the evidence for this is lacking. The most that can be said is that for Paul the kingdom — whether of God or of Christ — is not only future but also present. This is established by Rom 14:17, where the kingdom is spoken about as being already present and associated with the experience of the Holy Spirit. The new age, in fact, has already begun. Furthermore, since Paul regarded Jesus as being the Messiah, and not as a sort of Messiah-designate who would take up office later — and since a Messiah cannot exist without a kingdom — the coming of Jesus and his present status as Lord mean that the kingdom is present here-and-now and that it has been in existence since whatever point it was established.

In any case, for Paul both the coming of Jesus and his resurrection were past events at the time of his conversion. It follows, therefore, that he viewed the kingdom of Christ as being already present and not as something that was still to come in the future.

Did Paul reach this conclusion because he saw that the Messiah had come in the advent of Jesus? Or, was it because he (and other early Christians) interpreted the resurrection of Jesus as the end-time parousia that inaugurated the kingdom of God? We lack any evidence to show that the resurrection was seen as the fulfillment of the promise of the parousia, and not rather as the ratification of the earthly ministry of Jesus. It is certainly arguable that for the disciples, who had heard prophecies of the coming of the Son of Man, the immediate impact of the resurrection of Jesus could have been to convince them that the parousia had taken place. But supposing that this had happened, how long would this belief have survived? By all accounts, the resurrection appearances of Jesus were limited in time. And once they ceased, could belief that the parousia had taken place have survived for any length of time — other than as a fringe belief that certain groups may have held? It does not seem likely. There is no evidence that Paul himself ever thought of the resurrection as the parousia.

It follows, therefore, that the tension between the "already" and the "not yet," which is so frequently found in the New Testament, goes back to the earliest stage of the church's existence. The conviction that the kingdom of God and salvation are "already" here but "not yet" present in their fullness goes back to this earliest period. In addition, it is vital to bear in mind that for all Jewish expectations the reign of the Messiah takes place on earth, whereas for the early Christians Jesus was no longer on earth. There has to be, therefore, a future parousia to establish the kingdom on earth. This insight must have been developed at a very early stage, and our documents suggest that it was (Acts 3:21).

8. Other Signs of the New Age

This point regarding the tension that exists in Paul's eschatological thought between the "already" and the "not yet" can be corroborated by four subsidiary arguments. The first has to do with the resurrection of Jesus as an anticipation of the general resurrection. For while *the resurrection of Jesus* is the basis of Paul's experience, *the resurrection of the dead* is the event that inaugurates the new age, as is clear in 1 Thessalonians. In 1 Corinthians 15 the resurrection of Jesus is the event that anticipates the final, general resurrection, and consequently in some sense there has been an anticipation of the end. So new life from the dead is built into Paul's thought from the start.

It is significant that Mearns has to agree with this point, and so he assumes that Paul taught a (merely) *spiritual* resurrection of believers at the very beginning. It is impossible, however, to see how Paul could have accepted that Jesus rose from physical death with a spiritual body without also having to hold that the resurrection of believers was bodily and not purely spiritual. What is significant is that for Paul the resurrection of Jesus was the "first fruits" of the resurrection from the dead of believers (1 Cor 15:20, 23) — that is, the anticipation of their final resurrection.

Here again, then, we have that combination of the "already" and the "not yet." Believers are not yet risen from physical death, but the powers of the age to come are already at work and they are united spiritually with Christ. Whether the whole of this developed conception was present in Paul's mind just after his conversion, however, is uncertain. At the very least he saw the resurrection of Jesus as the inauguration of the new age that would be consummated with the general resurrection of God's people.

Second, the experience of Christians — including that of Paul — from the very start was tied to *their reception of the Spirit.* At least by the time he wrote Romans, Paul could not conceive of a Christian believer who did not possess the Spirit (Rom 8:9). Earlier still he writes in Galatians on the basis of that same conviction: that the experience of becoming a believer is associated with the reception of the Spirit, and that his readers are people who "began" with the Spirit (Gal 3:3). Acts links the Spirit with Paul's conversion (Acts 9:17), and 1 Thessalonians links it to the earliest experience of his readers (1 Thess 1:5-6; cf. 4:8). These points must be interpreted in light of the fact that the universal outpouring of the Spirit on the people of God was viewed as a sign of the end (cf. Joel 3:1-2 [Hebrew text], cited in Acts 2:17-18).

It is most improbable that this perception developed only at a later stage in the church's experience. In fact, the view that only gradually did Christians come to see the Spirit as a kind of substitute for the second coming of Jesus is quite unsound. On the contrary, from the beginning they appear to have regarded the Spirit as the mark of the new age. The evidence that Judaism regarded the Spirit in this way and that Paul would have taken over this belief has been convincingly argued by W. D. Davies in his *Paul and Rabbinic Judaism* (see esp. 208-26). By the time that Paul wrote 2 Corinthians he could think of the gift of the Spirit as an anticipatory gift, a first installment of the new life in the world to come (2 Cor 1:22; cf. Eph 1:14). But whether he had reached this insight at the time of his conversion is not certain.

For a third piece of evidence we need to refer to the thesis set out by Christian Dietzfelbinger in his *Die Berufung des Paulus als Ursprung seiner Theologie,* which, after Kim's monograph, is the second major study of the influence of Paul's conversion on his subsequent theology. In his discussion of what he calls the turning point for the world, Dietzfelbinger states that for Paul the period between Moses and Christ was *the period of the Torah:*

> World history is the history of the Torah. Through the Torah the world was called to life and preserved in life, history was put in motion, and this already before the Sinai event. If the Torah comes to an end with Christ, then history in its previous sense must also come to an end. From this perspective Romans 10:4 is to be understood: the believer knows that through Jesus the Christ the history borne by the Torah — and Paul knows no other — has found its end. (*Berufung,* 117; my translation)

The Spirit, therefore, is understood by Paul as the counterpart to the Torah. He sees two ages: one of the Torah and one of the Spirit.

This basic insight that Christ supersedes the Torah had already been anticipated by Kim (*Origin of Paul's Gospel,* 331), but the significance of such an insight for an understanding of Paul's eschatology was not developed (so also in Wilckens's earlier article, "Bekehrung des Paulus"). Dietzfelbinger, however, develops the point in some detail and claims that this insight derives from Paul's conversion. In the advent, death, and resurrection of Christ, the age of the Torah has come to an end and the new age has begun. But whereas, in Dietzfelbinger's view, other early Christians believed that they were living in the end time and expected the return of the Son of Man almost immediately, Paul proclaimed that the new age had already begun and that it overlaps with the old age until the final judgment — which is, says Dietzfelbinger, why Jews cannot believe that Jesus is the Messiah, since in their view the coming of the Messiah will bring the end of world history as we know it.

The decisive point in this argument is that the coming of the Messiah brings to an end the old age, which was dominated by the Torah, since Christ is the replacement of the Torah. Whether, however, Paul realized immediately at his conversion that the Torah had been superseded by Christ is dubious in my opinion. The replacement of a *thing* by a *person* is a rather subtle kind of shift. I suspect that it may not have presented itself in quite that way at the outset, but was a more gradual development — particularly in light of controversies with Jewish Christians about the admission of Gentiles to the church.

A fourth argument, it seems, carries somewhat more weight. For Paul's conversion included within itself a calling, akin to that of the prophets, to be a witness to the risen Lord and specifically *to proclaim him among the Gentiles* (Gal 1:16). There has been some debate whether this consciousness of a calling to witness specifically to Gentiles belongs to the original experience of Paul or was later realized by him to be inseparably bound up with an experience whose implications he did not at first fully recognize. Be that as it may, Paul firmly links his calling with his mission to the Gentiles. And that call to a Gentile mission marks a new and decisive stage in the fulfillment of God's plan of salvation. For Paul it is the essential preliminary to the final saving of "all Israel," and so it takes its place as an eschatological event. Consequently, the inauguration of the Gentile mission is a further sign of the dawn of the new age.

9. Conclusion

We have now examined five main lines of evidence: (1) the messiahship of Jesus, (2) his risen status, (3) the gift of the Spirit, (4) the age of the Torah as superseded by the age of the Messiah, and (5) the mission to the Gentiles. Every avenue we have followed has led us to the same destination. Paul's conversion was a revelation to him of a Messiah whose kingdom was inaugurated, whose resurrection was an anticipation of the general resurrection, whose gift was the Holy Spirit experienced both in the individual believer's inward consciousness and in the communal life of the Church, whose presence superseded that of the Torah (although this realization may well not have dawned until later), and whose command was to proclaim the good news not only to Jews but also to Gentiles in fulfillment of God's plan for the last days. These implications of his conversion experience were seen from as early a stage as we can trace. They combined to lead to a new kind of eschatology (which, we believe, was already present in Jesus' teaching) in which the advent and resurrection of Jesus are the proof of the presence of the new age, but in a way that overlaps with the old age. There is no need for any factor other than the conversion of Paul — which includes both his individual experience of Jesus and his incorporation into the community of other believers — to account for the development of this belief. It follows, therefore, that Paul's conversion was the origin of his eschatology, or rather the event that decisively shaped it. We do not have to look for other influences.

It is thoroughly understandable that in the beginning a longing for the promised coming of the Son of Man and an expectation of the appearance of that event would have been close to the center of Paul's religion. But what he awaited was the fuller revelation of what he was already experiencing, rather than something new which he had not yet tasted. By the time he wrote Philippians, however, he understood clearly that the greatest thing in life was to know Christ and that the goal for the future was to know him even more fully (Phil 3:7-11). And that means that we can now finally drop that slippery term "eschatology" and speak instead of God's personal saving intervention in the world that was accomplished through his Son and by his Spirit, which marks the end of the old world and the beginning of the new age.

Selected Bibliography

Baird, W. "Pauline Eschatology in Hermeneutical Perspective." *New Testament Studies* 17 (1971) 314-27.

Davies, W. D. *Paul and Rabbinic Judaism: Some Rabbinic Elements in Pauline Theology.* 2d. ed. London: SPCK, 1955.

Dietzfelbinger, C. *Die Berufung des Paulus als Ursprung seiner Theologie.* Neukirchen-Vluyn: Neukirchener Verlag, 1985.

Dodd, C. H. "The Mind of Paul: I" and "The Mind of Paul: II." In *New Testament Studies.* Manchester: Manchester University Press, 1953, 67-82 and 83-128. Originally published as "The Mind of St Paul: A Psychological Approach." *Bulletin of the John Rylands Library* 17 (1933) 91-105 and "The Mind of Paul: Change and Development." *Bulletin of the John Rylands Library* 18 (1934) 69-110.

Kim, S. *The Origin of Paul's Gospel.* Tübingen: Mohr-Siebeck, 1981; Grand Rapids: Eerdmans, 1982.

Kreitzer, L. J. *Jesus and God in Paul's Eschatology.* Sheffield: Sheffield Academic Press, 1987.

———. "Eschatology." In *Dictionary of Paul and His Letters,* ed. G. F. Hawthorne and R. P. Martin. Downers Grove, IL/Leicester, UK: InterVarsity Press, 1993, 253-69.

Longenecker, R. N. "The Nature of Paul's Early Eschatology." *New Testament Studies* 31 (1985) 85-95.

Lowe, J. "An Examination of Attempts to Detect Developments in St Paul's Theology." *Journal of Theological Studies* 42 (1941) 129-42.

Marshall, I. H. "Slippery Words: 'Eschatology.'" *The Expository Times* 89 (1977-78) 264-69.

―――. "Is Apocalyptic the Mother of Christian Theology?" In *Tradition and Interpretation in the New Testament,* ed. G. F. Hawthorne with O. Betz. Grand Rapids: Eerdmans; Tübingen: Mohr-Siebeck, 1987, 33-42.

―――. "The Parousia in the New Testament and Today." In *Worship, Theology and Ministry in the Early Church,* ed. M. J. Wilkins and T. Paige. Sheffield: Sheffield Academic Press, 1992, 194-211.

Mearns, C. L. "Early Eschatological Development in Paul: The Evidence of I and II Thessalonians." *New Testament Studies* 27 (1981) 137-57.

Segal, A. *Paul the Convert: The Apostolate and Apostasy of Saul the Pharisee.* New Haven/London: Yale University Press, 1990.

Stuhlmacher, P. "Gegenwart und Zukunft in der paulinischen Eschatologie." *Zeitschrift für Theologie und Kirche* 64 (1967) 423-50.

Wilckens, U. "Die Bekehrung des Paulus als religionsgeschichtliches Problem." *Zeitschrift für Theologie und Kirche* 56 (1959) 279-93.

Israelite, Convert, Apostle to the Gentiles: The Origin of Paul's Gentile Mission

TERENCE L. DONALDSON

1. Introduction

People who know anything at all about the New Testament tend to know at least three things about Paul: (1) that he was a persecutor of Christians; (2) that he experienced a conversion on the road to Damascus; and (3) that he became an apostle to the Gentiles. Furthermore, they have an intuitive sense that these three features are to be somehow linked — that is, that Paul's role as early Christianity's most visible missionary in the wider non-Jewish world somehow resulted from the combination of his personal formation and pattern of life within Judaism *and* his conversion experience near Damascus, where, as he perceived and expressed it, Christ "appeared also to me" (1 Cor 15:8). This intuition is not without foundation, for Paul himself seems to link these three elements in Gal 1:13-16.

But how might such a linkage be understood? What is the connective thread? If Galatians 1 provides us with an accurate portrayal of Paul's conversion experience, why was it that he viewed a mission to the Gentiles as a necessary component of his new set of convictions about Christ? The question, while an important one, has only recently been receiving the attention it deserves.

To bring the question into focus, it is instructive to compare Paul's career with that of James. Both of their stories begin with an initial period of antipathy toward Christ — Paul, of course, a zealous persecutor of the

62

church (Gal 1:13; 1 Cor 15:9; Phil 3:6); James, according to the traditions in the Gospels, apparently cool to Jesus and his mission (John 7:5; Mark 3:21, 31-35). Both had an experience in which the risen Christ "appeared" to them (for James' experience, see 1 Cor 15:7). And in both cases, evidently, it was this experience that radically transformed their earlier estimation of things and propelled them into apostolic leadership within the new movement. But from that point on their careers unfolded quite differently. For Paul understood his experience as a "call" to "proclaim [God's Son] among the Gentiles" (Gal 1:15-16), and he was prepared to live as a Gentile in order to carry out that calling (Gal 2:14; 1 Cor 9:21). James, by contrast, while ultimately not opposed to the inclusion of Gentiles, nevertheless remained in Jerusalem — within, it seems, the traditional boundaries of Judaism.

The story of James raises more questions than can be pursued here. For our present purposes, the comparison serves simply to illustrate the point that a mission among the Gentiles was by no means a necessary outcome of the kind of conversion experienced by Paul. Other options were available; other outcomes conceivable.

Some interpreters, of course, appealing to the vivid accounts of Paul's conversion in Acts, explain the difference between Paul and James simply on the basis of an explicit verbal commission given by the risen Jesus himself, such as is narrated in Acts 22:21: "Go, for I will send you far away to the Gentiles." But the question should not be so quickly short-circuited.

As most readers of this essay will probably acknowledge, the Christian "testimony" genre — both ancient and modern — often includes, as statements directly attributed to God, perceptions and insights arrived at through more indirect and mediated spiritual processes. Statements such as "God said to me, 'Quit your job and go to seminary'" usually function as a form of theological shorthand for more complex — and verbally less explicit — processes. But even if one were prepared to give full weight to a literal reading of the Acts narratives, the fact remains that for such a divine statement to make any sense at all to its recipient, it would need to be met on the human side by an appropriate framework of understanding.

The attempt to rediscover such a subjective framework for Paul is fully justified. At the same time, however, it is neither easy nor simple. The connective thread being sought has to pass through three complex and controverted aspects of Paul's life and thought: (1) his "former life in

Judaism" (Gal 1:13); (2) his "revelation of Jesus Christ" (Gal 1:12); and (3) his subsequent way of presenting and defending "the gospel that [he] proclaim[ed] among the Gentiles" (Gal 2:2).

For items (1) and (2) we are dependent on retrospective accounts written long after the events. Also for (1) we have to reckon with a range of possibilities for Paul's placement within Judaism, his attitudes toward the various aspects of Jewish religious experience, his degree of Hellenization, his initial perceptions of the Christian movement and reasons for persecution, and so on. For (2), while his experience certainly convinced him that God had raised Jesus from the dead and that Jesus was therefore Messiah and Savior, it is not immediately clear what implications these new realizations had for other matters that he had previously been convinced about — that is, for his previous convictions regarding Israel, the law, sin, and forgiveness, and (especially) the Gentiles.

Furthermore, we do not know whether a concern for Gentiles was present from the outset as part of his conversion experience itself, or whether it emerged only gradually, perhaps in response to subsequent experiences. And finally, though Paul's letters provide us with more or less direct access to item (3), because those letters are occasional writings rather than systematic treatises they present us with quite a variety of arguments in support of the Gentile mission. This makes it difficult to differentiate between statements that reflect Paul's fundamental convictions about the Gentiles and their place in salvation and statements that merely function as situationally conditioned arguments in support of a position arrived at on other grounds.

As should be clear from the above, the question regarding the origin of Paul's Gentile mission is not one that can be treated in isolation. The connective thread that we are concerned to trace out runs right through the central pattern of the Pauline fabric. Not surprisingly, then, answers to the question tend to be correlated with larger scholarly reconstructions of Paul's life and thought. This means both that his Gentile mission has been accounted for in a wide variety of ways and that developmental shifts in Pauline scholarship have had concomitant effects on the approach to this particular question.

We currently, for example, find ourselves in the midst of a significant shift of scholarly opinion regarding Paul and first-century Judaism. Precipitated by the work of E. P. Sanders (though not due to him alone), this "new perspective on Paul" (to use J. D. G. Dunn's phrase) has both

(1) raised the question of Paul's Gentile mission in a new and acute form, and (2) provided the framework within which a more satisfactory answer can be found. We will look further at this new perspective and its implications in due course. To move the discussion forward, however, it will be useful first to survey the range of scholarly approaches that have been taken to the question of the origin of Paul's Gentile mission.

2. A Survey of Approaches

There are at least two ways in which the various approaches to the question of the origin of Paul's Gentile mission can be organized and classified. One way, which corresponds to a certain extent with the distinction between the old and the new perspectives on Paul, is to differentiate between those approaches that view Paul's concern for Gentiles as stemming from an abandonment of Jewish particularism and those that account for it in terms of an adaptation of (some form of) Jewish universalism. Another way of categorizing the various approaches is to focus on the biographical point at which a concern for Gentiles first entered the horizon of Paul's vision — whether prior to the Damascus experience, as part of that experience itself, or as a subsequent development. For pedagogical reasons, we will follow the latter option in this section of our essay, presenting the various reconstructions — though in reverse order — according to a chronological schema. The other set of categories, however, will also come into play in the sections to follow (for a much more thorough survey of the discussion, with full bibliography, see my *Paul and the Gentiles*, chap. 1).

Paul's Gentile Concern as a Later Development

Some scholars have viewed Paul's interest in Gentiles as a later development in his thinking — in particular, as the result of an initial, failed mission to Jews. Important in this reconstruction is the argument of Romans 11, where Paul identifies the "rejection" of Israel as that which made Gentile salvation possible (v. 15; also vv. 11-12, 28). Francis Watson is typical of those who understand this argument as being reflective of Paul's own experience, and he therefore constructs the following scenario: Paul began his missionary activity by preaching to Jews; only when this was a failure was he forced to reconsider things, resulting in a turn to the Gentiles (Watson, *Paul, Judaism and the Gentiles,* 32). But most scholars have tended to see Paul's interest in Gentiles as either arising from his conversion or as having been present in his pre-conversion experience.

Paul's Gentile Concern as Part of His Conversion Experience

Other scholars see Paul's Gentile mission as an integral part of the Damascus experience itself. This does not necessarily mean that it was instantaneous. Many who take such a position would be prepared to consider a period of time during which Paul worked out for himself the implications of his experience. But this category differs from the one discussed previously in that it attempts to account for Paul's Gentile mission solely in terms of the dynamics set in motion by his conversion, without drawing in any subsequent factor.

Most of those who take this view perceive Paul's concern for Gentiles as being derivative — that is, as a kind of corollary of some more fundamental new conviction. Most commonly, the dethronement of the Torah is seen to have been the driving force. In fact, this is one of the two most common explanations — an eschatological-pilgrimage approach (which will be treated later) being the other. In his conversion experience, so this line of interpretation runs, Paul abandoned the belief that the Torah is the way to salvation, or at least that it is necessary for salvation. Since one of the roles of Torah was to differentiate Jews from Gentiles, the abandonment of Torah brought with it the eradication of the distinction between Jews and Gentiles — and so, in turn, the rise of the Gentile mission.

But why did Paul's conversion experience require an abandonment of Torah? For some interpreters, even before his conversion Paul had experienced the Torah as being inadequate. Such an approach, however, belongs more properly in the next section, and will be discussed there. For many others, the displacement of the Torah was the result of Paul's new conviction about Christ — that is, that salvation is provided through Christ, and so does not come through the Torah. While the logic leading from "Christ" to "not Torah" is understood in a variety of ways (several of which will be touched on below), the logic of the next step is common: "not Torah" means the eradication of the traditional distinction between

Jews and Gentiles; therefore, a Gentile mission is necessary (see, e.g., Davies, *Paul and Rabbinic Judaism*, 67).

But the dethronement of Torah is not the only route by which Paul's new conviction about Christ might have led to a concern for Gentiles. Less frequently, but still quite plausibly, the connective link is found in christology itself — in particular, Paul's perception of Christ as having been raised to an elevated, cosmic status. As Phil 2:9-11 demonstrates, the early confession "Jesus is Lord" can easily be taken to imply "Jesus is Lord of all" — which leads, quite naturally, to the inclusion of the Gentiles. In Seyoon Kim's reconstruction, for example, Paul's Damascus christophany led him to equate Christ with the exalted figure found in Jewish visions of the heavenly throne room, such as in Ezekiel 1 and Daniel 7. Consequently, Paul perceived Christ to be invested with universal significance, which led — via the intermediate, but not fully necessary, step of Adam christology — to the Gentile mission (Kim, *Origin of Paul's Gospel*, chap. 6; see esp. the summarizing diagram on p. 268).

In contrast to these approaches, however, we need to take note of an additional position — that is, one where concern for the Gentiles is understood not as a corollary of a more fundamental aspect of the Damascus experience, but as the essence of that experience itself. Krister Stendahl's insistence that Paul's experience must be seen as a "call" rather than a "conversion" represents the most prominent example of this position (Stendahl, *Paul among Jews and Gentiles*, 7-23). In this way of reading Paul, the call to be an apostle to the Gentiles is what the Damascus experience was all about.

Finally, there is the approach advocated by Heikki Räisänen and others, in which Paul is understood to have converted into a Christian community that was already involved in a mission to the Gentiles, a mission in which Paul himself became engaged (Räisänen, *Paul and the Law*, 251-63). Most of those who view the receiving community in this light also believe that in the process of becoming a member, Paul worked out for himself the theological implications of the community's position. For Räisänen, however, the theological implications began to be worked out only later, when conflict emerged. Thus the Gentile mission was spawned by a spontaneous eschatological enthusiasm within Hellenistic Jewish Christianity. When Paul converted into this community, he simply adopted the community's unreflective liberalism and accepted the validity of a Gentile mission without having worked through the theological implications of his shift of position.

TERENCE L. DONALDSON

Paul's Gentile Concern as a Pre-conversion Disposition

A number of other scholars have posited that the most significant factor leading to Paul's Gentile mission is to be found in various attitudes and convictions already present in his Jewish experience. This does not mean that the significance of his Damascus experience is ignored or undervalued. But in contrast to the previous approaches, where the Gentile mission is accounted for in terms of factors first put into play by the conversion experience itself, here that experience interacts in decisive ways with factors already present.

This group of approaches can be subdivided into two basic stances, one decidedly more positive than the other in its estimation of Paul's formative Jewish experience. On the negative side are those approaches in which Paul's Damascus experience is understood as representing the resolution of an already existing problem, one which concerned the Gentiles either directly or indirectly. One instance of such a stance, which is encountered frequently in older writings on the subject (e.g., Stewart, *Man in Christ*, 83-122), is the view that prior to his conversion Paul had been a frustrated Jew, overwhelmed by his inability to live up to the demands of the Law (as Romans 7 has frequently been interpreted). The substance of his conversion, then, was the process by which he found the solution to his dilemma in Christ — in particular, in the doctrine of justification by faith. His conversion, therefore, was at the same time an abandonment of Torah religion and a corresponding universalizing of his apostolic vision.

Other approaches, equally negative with respect to Paul's "former life in Judaism" (cf. Gal 1:13), center instead on Judaism's exclusiveness. In the older history-of-religions approach there was a tendency to see Paul as having been drawn to Hellenism — or, perhaps, as torn between Judaism and Hellenism — and his conversion as representing a decision in favor of the wider Hellenistic, and therefore Gentile, world (cf. Boyarin's revival, in modified form, of this view in his *Radical Jew*).

More recently there has been a readiness to understand the pre-Damascus Paul as troubled by the exclusion of the Gentiles from salvation, with his conversion serving to resolve, in one way or another, his "uneasy conscience" (Davies, *Paul and Rabbinic Judaism,* 63) or his "secret dissatisfaction" (Sanders, *Paul, the Law, and the Jewish People,* 152) or his own personal "quandary" concerning their fate (Gaston, *Paul and the Torah,* 28).

On the other hand, and more positively, there have been approaches that begin not with Judaism's exclusion of the Gentiles, but with one or the other of the Jewish "patterns of universalism." These approaches take note of various ways in which Judaism, without compromising its own covenantal self-understanding, was able to conceive of the inclusion of Gentiles within the sphere of salvation. It is possible, of course, that the pre-Damascus Paul should be located within one of the gloomier and more pessimistic segments of Judaism (as found, e.g., in *Jubilees* 15:26). Nevertheless, the fact remains that Judaism as a whole contained several strands that were more optimistic about the fate of the Gentiles. Judaism, despite its covenantal particularism, had its own forms of universalism. And it is plausible that as part of his Jewish formation, Paul had adopted one of these approaches to the Gentile world. His conversion, therefore, would only have served to place his native concern for Gentiles within a new convictional framework that centered in Christ, with the result that a Gentile mission emerged from the interplay between the two.

Here we can do little more than give a brief description of the three main patterns in the tapestry of Jewish universalism — with, then, further discussion and critical assessments reserved for section 4 below (for a full discussion, however, see my *Paul and the Gentiles*, chap. 3). One pattern focused on the eschatological pilgrimage of Gentiles to Jerusalem as a by-product of the end-time restoration of Israel, anticipating that Gentiles would abandon their idols, seek God, and so come to share in salvation. Another pattern centered on "righteous Gentiles," arguing that while the Torah is God's special gift to Israel, Gentiles — as Gentiles, and not just as converts to Judaism — can be granted a share in salvation on the basis of a more universal standard of righteousness, as seen in the case of Noah. A third pattern emphasized Gentile proselytes, believing that since the Torah is a universal means of salvation, Gentiles can become part of the covenant people through full conversion. My own position is that Paul's mission to the Gentiles is to be accounted for in terms of his prior commitment to Jewish proselytism, and so could be seen as following out the lines of this third pattern. But this must be developed in more detail later.

It is not possible here to deal in any detail with all of these approaches. Several of them, in my opinion, are improbable, requiring only the following brief comments: (1) In the high-stakes situation of Galatians, the vigor with which Paul argues that he had been proclaiming his law-free version of the gospel from the beginning makes it unlikely that his interest in the Gentiles developed only later, as a result of a failed mission to Jews.

(2) While it is probable that Paul was aware of his "call" from the beginning, simply to describe his experience as a call, without providing any indication of how he came to understand it in these terms, leaves the central question unaddressed. This approach amounts to little more than a tautology: the reason Paul's Damascus experience resulted in his becoming a missionary to the Gentiles is that his experience was a call to become a Gentile missionary. (3) While one might be prepared to grant the possibility that pre-Pauline Christianity was already engaged in a Gentile mission, it is much more difficult to believe that someone who had persecuted the movement on principled grounds — that is, as a "zealot" for the Torah and Jewish tradition (cf. Gal 1:14; Phil 3:6) — would casually abandon those principles by joining such a community without thinking through the theological ramifications, especially since there were other versions of Christianity on offer (cf. James). And, finally, (4) since Judaism itself offered a variety of ways in which Gentiles might be included in the sphere of salvation, there would have been no reason for Paul to look elsewhere for a way to ease a conscience troubled by Gentile "exclusion."

3. An Abandonment of Jewish Particularism?

Many of the reconstructions surveyed in the previous section operate on the assumption that Paul's Gentile mission was grounded in a basic abandonment of Jewish particularism. That is, that while Paul had been nurtured in a world where the distinction between Jews and Gentiles was fundamental, the essence — or, at least, the outcome — of his conversion experience was the realization that in Christ "there is no distinction between Jew and Greek" (Rom 10:12). His conversion, according to many scholars, meant the abandonment of a set of convictions that was rooted in a fundamental Jew-Gentile distinction and the adoption of a new set in which this distinction was of no continuing significance, having been eliminated or transcended in Christ.

The Universalism of Paul's Letters

Given the discourse in Paul's letters — especially in Romans and Galatians — it is easy to understand how such a reading of Paul could emerge, for

Paul consistently hammers away at the theme of universalism in contrast to Torah-based particularism. The most salient aspects of Paul's argument in this regard have to do with the following features:

(1) The presence of such a statement as in Christ "there is no distinction between Jew and Greek" (Rom 10:12, as noted above). This particular statement, however, is no isolated *obiter dictum.* Rather, it is but one of a number of similar statements that punctuate Romans and Galatians and serve to summarize the apostle's argument: God shows no partiality (Rom 2:11); all, both Jews and Gentiles, are under sin (Rom 3:9); there is no distinction in either plight or salvation (Rom 3:22-25; 10:9-13); in Christ there is no Jew and Greek (Gal 3:28).

(2) These explicit statements of universality are embedded in discourses that are characterized by sharp criticism of the law and a law-centered religion. To condense that criticism into a single point: In Rom 10:4 Paul speaks of Christ as the "end" *(telos)* of the law. The word *telos,* of course, can have the sense of goal or completion. But in view of Paul's tendency to draw a sharp temporal contrast between the former situation "under the law" and the new state of affairs made possible by Christ — as, for example, in "now we are discharged from the law" (Rom 7:6; also 6:14-15; 7:1-6; Gal 3:19-26) — the *prima facie* sense of the verse seems to be one of termination. Christ has brought the law — the instrumentality that served, among other things, to differentiate Jews from Gentiles — to an end.

(3) The arguments brought against the Law in Romans and Galatians appear to be founded on universalistic categories: the universality of sin, which is a condition resulting from the sin of Adam, the progenitor of humankind (e.g., Rom 1:18–3:20; 5:12-21); the contrast between faith and works, with "faith" and "works" being mutually opposed human stances vis-à-vis God and capable of being demonstrated by Jews and Gentiles alike (e.g., Gal 2:15-3:14); and the necessity that Jews and Gentiles be seen to stand on equal terms, in both sin and salvation (e.g., Rom 3:29-30).

(4) Elsewhere in Paul's letters, where Jew/Gentile issues are less to the fore, Paul customarily speaks of the gospel in universal terms — as, for example, in speaking of the plight of "all" in sin (1 Cor 15:22) and the role of Christ as Lord and Savior of "all" (2 Cor 5:14; Phil 2:10-11) — with no indication that "all" might be divided into sub-categories of "Jew" and "Gentile."

These four points, admittedly, are highly condensed, functioning merely as markers to more extended aspects of Paul's discourse and subsequent scholarly reconstructions. But they are sufficient to make the point that major strands of Paul's discourse are consistent with the view that his Gentile mission was predicated, in one way or another, on an abandonment of Jewish particularism in favor of an undifferentiated universalism.

The "New Perspective" and Paul's Gentile Mission

While a consistently universalistic reading of Paul is possible, such consistency comes with a price tag — the credibility of Paul's criticism of Judaism. Jewish scholars since the turn of the twentieth century have pointed out that Paul's arguments against the law, taken at face value, represent a significant misunderstanding — or, at least, a misrepresentation — of Judaism. A Jewish interlocutor might respond to Paul's arguments, as they are presented above, in the following ways. First, with respect to *universal sin,* it can be stated that contrary to Paul's apparent assumptions in Romans, the reality of sin does not make a religion that is based on law unworkable. Perfect performance of the law was never expected in Judaism, and the law itself made provision for repentance, atonement, and forgiveness (something that Paul studiously ignores). Second, with regard to Paul's contrast of *faith and works,* law and grace are not fundamentally antithetical. Judaism has always understood law-keeping as a means of responding to God's grace, not as a way of earning God's approval. The Torah is not a system of works. Third, and most significantly for our discussion, as to Paul's background in a *Judaism that excluded Gentiles,* the particularism of the Jewish religion does not necessarily exclude Gentiles from salvation. In fact, Judaism had developed several ways in which the Gentiles could be included in salvation without having to call the law into question.

These criticisms have suggested to some that Paul misunderstood Judaism. Others have been prompted to ask, instead, whether modern interpreters have not misunderstood Paul. Such questioning has resulted in the so-called "new perspective," which is now commonly associated with the work of E. P. Sanders (*Paul and Palestinian Judaism;* also his *Paul, the Law, and the Jewish People*). For Sanders, the various *arguments* that Paul mounts in defense of his law-free Gentile mission do not necessarily reflect the fundamental *reasons* for his commitment to such a mission in the first place. Paul's arguments follow a line moving "from plight to solution" —

that is, from a perceived deficiency with Torah religion to the discovery of a solution in Christ. The difficulty in making sense of these arguments, especially in view of their implications for Paul's perception of Judaism, led Sanders, however, to invert things — that is, to propose instead that we should understand the basic structure of Paul's thought in terms of a movement "from solution to plight." Thus as a result of his conversion experience, Paul became convinced that God had provided Christ as a means of salvation for all — Jews and Gentiles alike — on equal terms.

The immediate corollary of such an understanding is, of course, that if salvation is in Christ and on equal terms for all, it cannot come through the Torah. Everything apart from Christ — Torah-religion included — is to be considered part of the "plight" from which Christ offered deliverance. So Paul's various arguments against the law must be seen not as fundamental reasons for his commitment to a law-free Gentile mission, but as attempts in specific situations to defend his more basic conviction about Christ.

Approaches to Paul carried out within this "new perspective" have had considerable success in making sense of his thought. Justification, the faith-works contrast, the connection between juridical and participatory patterns of thought, and the saving work of Christ — all these characteristic Pauline elements have been construed in fresh and persuasive ways. One of the appeals of this new perspective is that it frees us from having to conclude that Paul misunderstood Judaism. A coherent picture can be constructed of a Paul who began as a covenantal nomist, but who came to believe that Jesus was Messiah and Savior — and who, as a result, found himself looking at his native convictional world from a different angle of perception.

But the question still remains: Why should the Gentiles loom so large in Paul's new field of vision? Though it has yet to be fully recognized, this question emerges as a particularly pressing consequence of the new perspective. We may grant that one can make better sense of Paul by assuming that he began with the conviction that God has provided Christ as a means of salvation for all on equal terms, as Sanders has demonstrated. But what is the origin of his concern "for all"? Sanders himself makes two suggestions — one about Paul's "secret dissatisfaction," as touched on above; the other about Paul's use of the "eschatological pilgrimage" tradition, to be discussed below. But neither of these suggestions has been integrated into his reconstruction. For the most part, the universal sphere of Christ's saving activity is simply taken as axiomatic.

In the old paradigm, which has been dominant at least since the Reformation, a universal framework was also axiomatic. But it was axiomatic precisely because it was implicit in what was understood to be Paul's central concern — namely, How can sinful humanity be accounted righteous before God? If, however, Paul's central concern is to be located with reference to "solution" rather than to "plight" — that is, if he should be seen as a Jew for whom Judaism "worked," but who subsequently came to believe that Jesus was Messiah and Savior — it is no longer possible to take his universalism as axiomatic. Why should such a one necessarily come to believe that the salvation accomplished by Jesus Christ was available to Gentiles as well as Jews, and on equal terms that did not require full Torah observance? To return to the language introduced at the start of this essay: If the first and second of the biographical facts with which we began — that is, his Jewish upbringing and his conversion — are to be understood in these new terms, how are we to position them so that the line between them leads on to the third — that is, his Gentile mission?

As we will see, this new perspective on Paul opens up a promising alternative to the approach that grounds Paul's concern for the Gentiles in an abandonment of Jewish particularism. Before beginning to develop this alternative approach, however, it needs to be observed that the "abandonment of particularism" approach is not restricted to the older paradigm. It continues, in fact, to be found among proponents of the new perspective as well.

In a few cases within "new perspective" scholarship, Paul's rejection of Torah-centered particularism is taken to be axiomatic — not as a consequence of his new Christian convictions, but as something inherent in the logic of Jewish eschatological expectation. The most notable example of such an understanding is to be found in the work of N. T. Wright, who attempts to place Paul's Gentile concerns within the framework of an "eschatological pilgrimage" tradition (Wright, *Climax of the Covenant*). Wright's reconstruction cannot be described here in detail. Suffice it to say that many of its features — in particular, that Paul (and many of his compatriots) saw the exile as a continuing state of affairs; that a plight which called for a solution was therefore very much a part of his starting point; and that his handling of law and sin makes perfect sense in this context — are highly stimulating and worthy of serious consideration.

But while Wright sees eschatological pilgrimage conceptions as providing the general framework for Paul's mission to the Gentiles, when he comes to account for that mission's law-free character he appeals to a fundamental rejection of Jewish particularism, as follows:

> The covenant with Abraham always envisaged a single family, not a plurality of families; therefore the Torah, which creates a plurality by dividing Gentiles from Jews, stands in the way of the fulfilment of the covenant with Abraham; and this cannot be allowed. (*Climax of the Covenant*, 163-64)

Wright, therefore, regards the rejection of any distinction between Jews and Gentiles as a fundamental element of Paul's convictional world. Moreover, he apparently sees it not as having been derived from his new Christ conviction, but as being basic and axiomatic.

The logic of this argument, however, would appear highly curious from a Jewish perspective. For if the covenant had such a single, unified family in view, why is it that the Torah itself could not be the means by which it is to be produced? Furthermore, how is Paul's law-free but Christ-centered gospel any less particularistic (see further my *Paul and the Gentiles*, chap. 5)?

More common within a "new perspective" approach are those scholars who see Paul's abandonment of Jewish particularity as a derived, not a fundamental, conviction. Occasionally, elevated christology is identified as the origin of the assertion that "there is no distinction." Usually, however, it is the consequent dethroning of the law. For since Paul clearly perceived Christ and the Torah to be in some essential way antithetical (though the precise point of the conflict is variously assessed), the vindication of Jesus meant for Paul the end of the Torah as a means to or a mark of righteousness. But since it was Torah that created the distinction between Jews and Gentiles, the end of Torah meant (so the argument goes) the end of that distinction.

J. D. G. Dunn's reconstruction of Paul's thought is fairly typical of a "new perspective" variation on this old theme:

> The vindication of one who had been cursed by the law meant the end of the law in its function of marking the boundary between the righteous and the sinner, the Jew and the Gentile. . . . The *immediate* corollary for Paul would be that God must therefore favour the cursed one, the sinner outside the covenant, the Gentile. ("Light to the Gentiles," 264-65; italics his)

Thus for Paul, the recognition of Christ, the rejection of Jewish particularism, and a new openness to the Gentiles were three inseparable elements of a single experience.

The Significance of "Israel" for Paul's Gentile Mission

But any reconstruction based on the idea of an abandonment of Jewish particularism — whether in the form of the older or the newer paradigms — is difficult to sustain in view of another feature of Paul's letters, namely, the stubborn persistence of "Jew" and (ethnic) "Israel" as categories with ongoing theological significance. For according to Paul, "not Torah" is *not* equivalent to "not Israel" or to "no distinction between Jew and Gentile" — which would need to be the case for the reconstruction to work. To be sure, when the discussion concerns conditions of membership "in Christ," Paul is adamant: "there is no distinction." But where this is not at issue, we find that ethnic Israel — defined in the usual, Torah-determined terms and differentiated from the Gentiles — continues to play an important part in his theology.

The most striking example of Israel's place in Paul's theology is, of course, to be found in Romans 11, where Paul argues for the ultimate salvation of "all Israel" (11:26). While the argument may be considered somewhat unexpected, given the flow of Romans to this point, it nevertheless is highly revealing. For Paul is clearly convinced that to conclude that Israel has no more role in God's plan would be to call into question God's faithfulness to the divine promise, and thus to jeopardize the truth of the gospel itself.

In addition, we can cite the role assigned to the Jewish remnant. Remnant language appears explicitly, of course, only in Rom 9:27 and 11:5. But the concept appears frequently elsewhere throughout Romans (4:11-12, 16; 9:27-29; 11:1-10, 16-17; 15:8-9, 25-27; cf. Gal 3:13-14). And all these passages present us with a distinct Jewish body of believers, which is differentiated from Gentile believers in traditional, Torah-based terms (e.g., circumcision; Rom 4:12) and plays a significant role in the extension of the gospel to the Gentiles (e.g., 15:25-27).

This leads to an additional point concerning the term "Gentile" itself. For though the point is often overlooked, it needs to be noted that the designation "Gentile" depends for its sense on a view of the world where

"Jew" continues to be a significant category. Paul's self-description as an "apostle to the Gentiles" (Rom 11:13; cf. Gal 2:7-9), in fact, betrays a fundamentally Israel-centered view of his missionary activity. He is not to be understood as one who has abandoned his Jewish identity, and now is proclaiming a nonparticularistic message addressed to undifferentiated, generic humanity. No, he is a Jewish apostle (Rom 11:1), who on behalf of Israel and for the sake of Israel's ultimate salvation, is declaring to the other, non-Jewish nations that in Christ they too can be members of the family of Abraham (cf. Romans 4; Galatians 3).

The argument could be fleshed out considerably. It is sufficient here, however, to note that the continuing significance of "Israel" as a category of thought for Paul suggests that his concern for the Gentiles is not to be accounted for in terms of an abandonment of Jewish particularism. Instead, what is needed to understand Paul's Gentile concern is a more Israel-centered framework, to which we now turn our attention.

4. An Adaptation of (Some Form of) Jewish Universalism

Despite its particularism, Judaism was, as noted earlier, in its own way universalistic. And since one of the defining characteristics of "the new perspective" is the search for a Paul who can be understood from the starting point of covenantal nomism, it is not surprising that attempts have been made to account for his Gentile mission in terms of one or other of those patterns of Jewish universalism.

The Eschatological Pilgrimage Tradition

The pattern most frequently appealed to in this connection is that of the "eschatological pilgrimage" tradition. As early as the time of Isaiah, it had been expected that when God finally acted to redeem Zion, the Gentiles would come to their senses, reject idolatry, recognize Israel's God as the one true deity, and come to worship God at the sanctuary in Jerusalem (cf. Isa 2:2-4; see also Tobit 14:5-7; *Sibylline Oracles* 3.716-20). Given the obviously eschatological framework of Paul's thought and mission, it is understandable that scholars would attempt to find the key to his concern for the Gentiles in this eschatological tradition. Thus, according to such a view,

Paul must have thought that since the long-awaited age of salvation had dawned as a result of Jesus' life, death, and resurrection, the time had arrived for the Gentiles to be invited in to share in Israel's blessings. E. P. Sanders's comment is typical: "Paul's entire work . . . had its setting in the expected pilgrimage of the Gentiles to Mount Zion in the last days" (*Paul, the Law, and the Jewish People,* 171).

This reconstruction has a certain *a priori* plausibility. It is often, however, developed in an inadequate way. For the characteristic feature of the eschatological pilgrimage tradition is not simply that the Gentiles will turn to God in the last days. Instead, the salvation of the Gentiles in this tradition is always linked with the restoration of Israel: it is because Gentiles see God's vindication of Israel that they will respond to God and share in Israel's glory. And so it is not enough simply to rest the case on the eschatological framework of Paul's thought in general — as if eschatology per se were sufficient to make the connection.

Nor is it appropriate to speak (as Sanders and many others do) of a simple inversion of the expected eschatological events — that is, where, contrary to expectations, the ingathering of the Gentiles precedes the salvation of all Israel. For the relationship of the eschatological pilgrimage to the redemption of Israel is a matter not simply of sequence, but of consequence: the second event takes place precisely because the first has occurred. Simply to invert the order of the two events so as to explain Paul is to empty the hypothesis of its explanatory power.

What is needed for the eschatological pilgrimage hypothesis to work is the demonstration that Paul somehow sees Israel's restoration as having already been accomplished in Christ. There are two ways in which this might be done. First, it could be argued that Paul saw Christ himself as the personification of Israel, so that Israel's restoration was accomplished in Christ's resurrection. Such an argument is developed, with passion and eloquence, by N. T. Wright (*Climax of the Covenant,* 141, 146, 150-51, 196, 245). The other possibility is to argue that Paul viewed the establishment of the Jewish Christian remnant as the "restoration of Israel," with, then, the ingathering of the Gentiles being predicated on that basis. I attempted to develop such an argument in my article "The 'Curse of the Law' and the Inclusion of the Gentiles."

For reasons that I now find incontrovertible, however, I have been led to change my mind, and to conclude that the eschatological pilgrimage tradition cannot account for Paul's concern for the Gentiles. The decisive factor in my change of mind was Paul's readiness in Romans 11 to predicate the Gentile mission on Israel's stumbling (vv. 11-12), defeat (v. 12), and rejection (v. 15). The question is: How can one use a tradition that was centered on Israel's restoration to explain an element of Paul's thought that he is prepared to account for on the basis of Israel's rejection? He certainly knows the difference between the two, for he is also quite concerned to find a place in his thinking for Israel's restoration (cf. Rom 11:12, 15, 25-26). But for him that event of restoration is clearly in the future. Moreover, it is the event that will bring the Gentile mission to an end (Rom 11:25-26)!

In addition to this consideration — which must be considered decisive in itself — one can also note Paul's failure to quote any of the traditional eschatological pilgrimage texts (e.g., Isa 2:2-4; 25:6-10a; 56:6-8; Zech 8:20-23). In Romans and Galatians he is obviously concerned to provide scriptural justification for his Gentile mission. But it needs to be asked: Why, if his mission was driven by such an eschatological pilgrimage pattern of thought, did he ignore those portions of Scripture on which it could be grounded?

"Righteous Gentiles" Conceptions

The eschatological pilgrimage tradition, however, is not the only pattern for Jewish universalism. Some scholars have pointed to the "godfearing" or "righteous Gentile" phenomenon within Judaism to account for Paul's Gentile mission. Indeed, seen from the outside, Paul's converts look a lot like Rabbi Joshua's "righteous Gentiles" (*Tosephta Sanhedrin* 13:2). For Paul insists that his converts are to be considered righteous even though they have not fully embraced the Torah — particularly in regard to those aspects that differentiated Jews from Gentiles, such as circumcision, food laws, and Sabbath observance. Yet Paul also says that his Gentile converts are subject to a code of behavior that prohibits idolatry (1 Corinthians 8, 10) and sexual immorality (1 Corinthians 5–6), and he enjoins the observance of monotheism (1 Corinthians 8:6) — all elements that are found in the decrees thought to have been given through Noah to the whole of humankind. For Paul, therefore, according to this view, such "righteous Gentiles" exist alongside a body of righteous Jewish believers who are, of course, to be differentiated from Gentiles generally by the usual Torah-based means (cf. Rom 4:12, 16).

This approach to Paul can appear in two forms, one less christocentric than the other. The first of these approaches has been pioneered by Lloyd Gaston, who argues that for Paul the Torah continues to function as a legitimate and sufficient means of righteousness for Jews (Gaston, *Paul and the Torah*). The significance of Christ, however, is that he has made possible a parallel and distinct means of righteousness for Gentiles. Gentiles, therefore, can be righteous while still remaining Gentiles, without having to become Jews. While Gaston does not say so explicitly, this "two paths to righteousness" reading is, in reality, a "righteous Gentile" model for understanding Paul's rationale for his Gentile mission.

In the other form of this approach, Paul is believed to have viewed Christ as the divinely provided means of salvation for both Jews and Gentiles. His thought is, therefore, basically christocentric in its orientation, though "righteous Gentile" patterns have also been brought into his thinking — which accounts for both his interest in the Gentiles and the terms on which he incorporates them into the church. To date there is no fully developed example of this approach, though a beginning in this direction has been made by P. J. Tomson (*Paul and the Jewish Law*).

The major difficulty with a "righteous Gentile" approach in either of its forms is that Paul insists on the full equality of Jews and Gentiles — not only that they share the same status in both plight and salvation, but, more specifically, that "in Christ" they are both full and equal members of Abraham's family (Rom 4:11-16; Gal 3:7, 29). For Judaism, however, righteousness was one thing, whereas membership in Abraham's family was quite another. So while many first-century Jews might have been open to the possibility of "righteous Gentiles," only in the case of full proselytes would they have been prepared to think in terms of membership in Abraham's family.

Paul's arguments in Romans 4 and Galatians 3 are especially instructive with regard to his perspective on the status of converted Gentiles. His interlocutors, apparently, argued from Genesis 17 that Abraham's "seed" is clearly defined in terms of circumcision, so that if Gentiles want salvation they must first become part of Abraham's family — which means that they must be circumcised. Paul's response, however, is interesting on two counts: (1) He accepts the premise of his interlocutors that Gentiles need to become full members of Abraham's "seed" (Rom 4:16; Gal 3:29), though he insists that the means of membership is faith and not circumcision. The latter qualification, of course, puts Paul in considerable tension with Gen 17:9-14, where circumcision is the *sine qua non* for membership in Abraham's "seed."

(2) If Paul had wanted to emphasize a "righteous Gentiles" approach, he could have opted to use Genesis 18 instead of Genesis 17. That is, he could have taken the "softer" approach to bring Gentiles into relationship with Abraham by simply identifying Gentile believers with "all the nations of the earth" who were to be "blessed in him" (Gen 18:18). The fact that Paul ignores this softer option — which was tailor-made for a "righteous Gentile" approach — and insists, against the clear statement of Genesis 17, that uncircumcised but believing Gentiles are full members of Abraham's "seed," weighs heavily against any attempt to account for Paul's Gentile concern along "righteous Gentile" lines.

Gentile Proselytism

But this observation leads naturally to our final pattern of Jewish universalism, that is, proselytism. As the preceding comments demonstrate, Paul's description of his Gentile converts corresponds in formal terms to the language of proselytism: Gentiles are members of Abraham's family or "seed"; they are members on the same terms as Jews, and so can call Abraham "father"; they are grafted into the stock of Israel; and so on. The difference is that Christ has replaced Torah as the boundary marker and condition of membership in the family of Abraham.

The observation that, for Paul, Christ has replaced Torah becomes especially significant when taken in conjunction with another, namely, the suggestion of Gal 5:11 that there had been a time when Paul had "preached circumcision." In the context of Galatians, "to preach circumcision" means "to encourage Gentiles to be circumcised as a condition of entry into Abraham's family." If we are to take this statement seriously (and I believe we must), it suggests that there was a time when Paul had encouraged Gentiles to convert to Judaism. If this is a correct reading of the statement, it almost certainly is to be taken to refer to a pre-Damascus stage in Paul's life. It is difficult, as noted earlier, to imagine some post-conversion phase when Paul had preached such a different "gospel." And if Gal 5:11 refers to a pre-Damascus stage in Paul's life, then Paul's Gentile mission may be understood as the christological transformation of a proselytizing concern already present in his pre-conversion days.

Such an approach can only be summarized here (for a detailed treatment, see my *Paul and the Gentiles*). On such an understanding, the three biographical points with which we began this essay can be lined up as follows:

(1) Paul's pre-Damascus framework of meaning was provided by the pattern of religious life and thought that Sanders has described as "covenantal nomism." Within this broad framework, Paul is to be located more specifically among those who took the strict line that Gentiles had to become proselytes in "This Age" if they wanted to share in the salvation of the "Age to Come." In addition, Paul had evidently played some active role in the making of proselytes. This is not to say that he was involved in any full-scale "mission." Instead, his role may have been akin to that of King Izates' adviser Eleazar (Josephus, *Antiquities* 20.34-48), who urged those already drawn to Judaism to become full proselytes. Furthermore, his objection to the early Christian movement, and so his persecuting activity, arose out of his perception that the Christ of the kerygma was functioning as a rival to the Torah in its role of defining the boundary of the covenant people (i.e., of "the righteous"). This tension between Christ and Torah was produced by the peculiar "already–not yet" eschatological structure of the kerygma — a tension that Paul may have seen more clearly than many of the early believers.

(2) Paul's Damascus experience convinced him that God had raised Jesus and that Jesus was indeed Messiah and Savior. This experience necessitated a fundamental reconfiguration of his set of world-structuring convictions, with Christ replacing Torah as the means by which membership in the people of God was to be determined. While some convictions were abandoned in this process and others added, it can be assumed that many of Paul's native convictions were carried over into his new world of meaning, being similar in form but organized around a new material center.

(3) In particular, Paul continued to believe that in order to share in the fulfillment of God's promises of salvation, Gentiles needed to become full and equal members of the family of Abraham. The difference was that membership in that family was now determined by Christ, not by Torah. This is not to say that Paul's Gentile mission was merely a continuation of his former patterns of belief and activity, Torah having simply been replaced by Christ. His encounter with the risen Christ released a whole new source of energy into the equation. Still, this energy flowed along channels of belief and activity that were already present.

5. Conclusion

The convictional reconfiguration being proposed here is not without its loose ends. In particular, it requires that we see Paul as working with two different definitions of "Israel" — one based on the traditional ethnic markers; the other on Christ. Still, this is not an insurmountable problem. For the fact that he lived in the first Christian generation — which he also believed to be the last — meant that the two definitions were not as mutually exclusive for him as they might have been for subsequent generations. Nevertheless, on the whole, this proposal provides a consistent and satisfactory accounting of the evidence: Paul was (1) a zealous Jew and a proselytizer, who (2) had a world-transforming encounter with the risen Christ, and (3) as a result felt himself called to invite Gentiles to become Christ-proselytes — that is, full and equal members of the family of Abraham, with membership in that family having been reconfigured around Christ.

Selected Bibliography

Boyarin, D. *A Radical Jew: Paul and the Politics of Identity.* Berkeley: University of California Press, 1994.

Davies, W. D. *Paul and Rabbinic Judaism.* London: SPCK, 1948.

Donaldson, T. L. "The 'Curse of the Law' and the Inclusion of the Gentiles: Galatians 3.13-14." *New Testament Studies* 32 (1986) 94-112.

————. *Paul and the Gentiles: Remapping the Apostle's Convictional World.* Minneapolis: Fortress, 1997.

Dunn, J. D. G. "The New Perspective on Paul." *Bulletin of the John Rylands Library* 65 (1983) 95-122.

————. "'A Light to the Gentiles': The Significance of the Damascus Road Christophany for Paul." In *The Glory of Christ in the New Testament,* ed. L. D. Hurst and N. T. Wright. Oxford: Clarendon, 1987, 251-66.

Gaston, L. *Paul and the Torah.* Vancouver: University of British Columbia Press, 1987.

Kim, S. *The Origin of Paul's Gospel.* Grand Rapids: Eerdmans, 1982.

Räisänen, H. *Paul and the Law.* Philadelphia: Fortress, 1986.

Sanders, E. P. *Paul and Palestinian Judaism.* Philadelphia: Fortress, 1977.

————. *Paul, the Law, and the Jewish People.* Philadelphia: Fortress, 1983.

Stendahl, K. *Paul Among Jews and Gentiles and Other Essays.* Philadelphia: Fortress, 1976.

Stewart, J. S. *A Man in Christ.* London: Hodder & Stoughton, 1935.

Tomson, P. J. *Paul and the Jewish Law: Halakha in the Letters of the Apostle to the Gentiles.* Assen: Van Gorcum; Minneapolis: Fortress, 1990.

Watson, F. P. *Paul, Judaism and the Gentiles.* Cambridge: Cambridge University Press, 1986.

Wright, N. T. *The Climax of the Covenant: Christ and the Law in Pauline Theology.* Minneapolis: Fortress, 1991.

Paul and Justification by Faith

JAMES D. G. DUNN

1. Introduction

How does Paul's teaching on justification by faith relate to his conversion? The question is an important one because justification by faith has so often been regarded within both Christian tradition and New Testament scholarship as the quintessence of Paul's gospel and theology. And precisely because the subject matter is so vital, as touching the raw nerve of personal faith, disagreement in answering the question can easily become fractious. Furthermore, the discussion can run aground on undeclared presumptions or trigger hidden sensitivities, with disastrous consequences for constructive debate.

The parameters of the debate may be sketched as follows. On the one hand, for a variety of reasons, it is logical to assume that Paul's theology of justification was a direct result of his encounter with the living Christ on the Damascus road. At the heart of the logic is the conviction that what Paul *experienced* on the Damascus road was justification by faith, and that his theology of justification was in large part simply the working out of his experience. The key supporting text is Phil 3:7-9, where the discovery of Christ is linked directly to a new appreciation of what the righteousness of God through faith really means. In the light of the interpretation of that passage, it is natural to link in other texts like Rom 4:4-5 and 10:4 as further expressions of what Paul found in his encounter with the risen Christ (so, e.g., Stuhlmacher, "End of the Law," 139-41; Kim, *Origin of Paul's Gospel*, 269-311; Westerholm, *Israel's Law and the Church's Faith*).

85

To be noted is the fact that this approach does not require or depend on a detailed analysis of Paul's internal experience or thought process. It is not necessary, for example, to argue that Paul already had a severe guilt problem before his conversion. For the key passages in which Paul refers to the buildup to his conversion (Gal 1:13-14; Phil 3:5-6) give no hint of a tortured conscience (whether regarding Stephen, or whatever). Likewise, Paul never mentions "repentance" in the context of talk about conversion or justification. Nor does this approach depend on a detailed account of how Paul's attitude to the law changed in the process — in some such stages as (1) the law condemned Christ, (2) God raised Christ, (3) therefore the law is wrong, and (4) so justification is not by the law.

The meaning of Gal 2:19 ("I through the law died to the law") has, of course, to be unpacked. But that particular unpacking is not attested by any of Paul's writings on the subject. The traditional exposition of the correlation between Paul's conversion and his teaching on justification, in fact, does not even depend on a text like 1 Tim 1:15-16 (Paul's conversion was his receiving mercy as "the foremost of sinners"), whose lack of correlation again with Gal 1:13-14 and Phil 3:5-6 leaves its witness problematic as a testimony to how Paul's own self-understanding was transformed by the Damascus road event.

On the other hand, a minority of voices has repeatedly drawn attention to two features of what Paul says on these two subjects about his conversion and justification. The one is that Paul's doctrine of justification through faith seems to arise directly out of and/or within the context of his Gentile mission. It emerges as his answer to the question: How may Gentiles be accounted acceptable to the God of Israel and of Jesus (cf., e.g., W. Wrede, *Paul* [London: Green, 1907] 122-28; Stendahl, *Paul Among Jews and Gentiles*, 1-7)? This is the clear implication of the primary expositions of justification by faith that Paul provides in Galatians 2–3 and Romans 3–4. The other feature of what Paul says on these subjects is that the primary significance of his encounter with the risen Christ seems to have been, for him, that it commissioned him as an apostle or missionary to the Gentiles (Gal 1:15-16; 1 Cor 9:1; 15:8-10; cf. Acts 9:15; 22:10; 26:16-18). The echoes of Isa 42:7; 49:1, 6; and Jer 1:5 in some of these passages underscore the point that whereas we think most naturally of the Damascus road encounter as a conversion, Paul thought of it more as a prophetic calling (cf., e.g., J. Knox, *Chapters in a Life of Paul* [Macon: Mercer University Press, 1987]

97-98; Stendahl, *Paul Among Jews and Gentiles,* 7-12; Räisänen, "Paul's Conversion," 406-08).

On this reading of the data, the sequence of Paul's theological rethinking following his Damascus road experience is somewhat different. It was not so much a personal experience of acceptance by God (though a sinner), leading to the conclusion that Gentiles could share directly in this same experience for themselves, through faith (alone). It was rather the conviction that God was commissioning him to fulfill Israel's calling (to be a light to the nations), leading to the conclusion (crystallized for him particularly by the Antioch incident of Gal 2:11-16) that this was possible of realization only if justification was through faith (alone).

I have attempted to make my own contribution to this debate elsewhere, and so will not repeat myself unnecessarily here ("Light to the Gentiles"; *The Partings of the Ways;* and "Paul's Conversion"). Suffice it to say that my emphasis has been on the latter of the two approaches sketched out above — principally because it has seemed to me that there are clear expressions of Paul's own summation of the significance of the Damascus road encounter, particularly in Gal 1:13-16, that have been too much ignored by the more traditional view. At the same time, I see no reason to dispute — indeed, I wish strongly to affirm — what the more traditional approach highlights and underscores as a theological assertion of fundamental significance, expressed particularly in Rom 4:4-5: that justification by faith is at the core of Paul's gospel and theology. What is rather at stake in the continuing debate on this subject is to secure a properly rounded and integrated grasp of Paul's teaching, and to clarify, so far as possible, how much and in what way Paul's conversion contributed to this fundamental element of his thought.

In what follows, therefore, I will attempt to sketch out the heart of Paul's theology of justification, why it was as contentious as it evidently was, and how the particular antithesis of "justification from faith and not from works" ties back into his conversion.

2. Justification — A Fundamental Scriptural (Jewish) Doctrine

As is well known, discussions of "justification" suffer from some terminological problems. I refer not only to the fact that English uses two different words, "justify" and "righteousness," to translate what are cognate terms in

Greek (*dikaioō* and *dikaiosynē*), thus causing some unavoidable confusion for those who think in English (the issue is nicely pointed out by E. P. Sanders, *Paul*, 44-47). There is also the fact that the underlying Hebrew thought in both cases is different from the Greek. For in the typical Greek worldview, "righteousness" is an idea or ideal against which the individual and individual action can be measured. Our contemporary English usage reflects this ancient mind set when it continues to use such expressions as "Justice must be satisfied." In contrast, however, "righteousness" in Hebrew thought is a more relational concept — that is, "righteousness" in Hebrew thinking has to do with the meeting of obligations that are laid on an individual by the relationship of which he or she is a part (cf., e.g., G. von Rad, *Old Testament Theology*, vol. 1 [Edinburgh: Oliver & Boyd, 1962] 370-76; K. Kertelge, *"Rechtfertigung" bei Paulus* [Münster: Aschendorff, 1967, 1971], 15-24). A classic example is 1 Sam 24:17, where King Saul says he is unrighteous in that he failed in his duty as king to his subject, while David is more righteous because he refused to lift his hand in violence against the Lord's anointed. A key factor in gaining a secure hold on Paul's teaching on justification, therefore, and one whose ramifications are too little appreciated in much of the discussion about Paul's teaching, is the recognition that the thought-world that comes to expression in our English term "justification" is through and through Hebraic/biblical/Jewish in character.

The relevance of this observation begins to become clear when we recall Paul's thematic statement about justification in Rom 1:16-17 as being "the righteousness of God . . . from faith to faith." For the righteousness of God, in line with the Hebraic understanding of "righteousness" referred to above, denotes God's fulfillment of the obligations he took on himself in creating humankind, and particularly in his calling of Abraham and choosing of Israel to be his people. Fundamental to this conception of God's righteousness, therefore, is the recognition of the prior initiative of God, both in creation and in election (for an emphasis on God's righteousness as creator, see C. Müller, *Gottes Gerechtigkeit und Gottes Volk: Eine Untersuchung zu Römer 9–11* [Göttingen: Vandenhoeck & Ruprecht, 1964]; P. Stuhlmacher, *Gerechtigkeit Gottes bei Paulus* [Göttingen: Vandenhoeck & Ruprecht, 1965] 228-36). As Deuteronomy repeatedly points out, it was nothing that Israel was or had done that caused God to choose them as his people and to enter into covenant with them; it was only his love for them and his loyalty to the oath he had promised to their fathers (4:32-40;

6:10-12, 20-23; 7:6-8; etc.). It should be equally evident why God's righteousness is repeatedly understood, particularly in the Psalms and second Isaiah, as God's faithfulness to his people — that is, the fulfillment of his covenant obligation as Israel's God in delivering and vindicating Israel, despite Israel's own failure (e.g., Pss 51:14; 65:5; 71:15; Isa 46:13; 51:5-8; 62:1-2).

The point here is threefold. First, Paul's teaching on justification is drawn immediately from this Old Testament understanding about God's righteousness. That the language of Romans stems directly from such Old Testament usage is well appreciated and not in dispute (cf. S. K. Williams, "The 'Righteousness of God' in Romans," *Journal of Biblical Literature* 99 [1980] 241-90; also my *Romans,* vol. 1 [Dallas: Word, 1988] 40-42). Second, and fundamental to Jewish self-understanding and covenant theology, is the recognition and affirmation that Israel's standing before God was due entirely to the initiative of divine grace. The same point is implicit in a covenant system that provided atonement for sin through repentance and sacrifice. Third, Paul's teaching on justification did not first emerge as a reaction against his Pharisaic past or any "judaizing" opponents, but was simply a restatement of the first principles of his own ancestral faith — that is, his emphasis on the initiative of divine grace within his teaching on justification was a central part of his religious thought even before his Damascus road experience.

All this needs to be restated against a still prevailing assumption that the Judaism of Paul's day was inherently and thoroughly legalistic, teaching that individuals had to earn acceptance by God by their works of merit. Indeed, it has been a deeply disquieting feature of Christian apologetics — first clearly attested in Ignatius, steadily strengthened since then, and reinforced by Reformation polemics — that Christianity has tended to understand itself in antithesis to Judaism, and so to portray Judaism as the polar opposite of Christianity. In such a scenario, Christianity as gospel is set over against Judaism as law. So it needs to be said clearly: justification by faith is at heart a Jewish doctrine; dependence on divine grace remains a consistent emphasis throughout Jewish thought, at least up to the time of Paul (we need take the discussion no further here); and there is no clear teaching in pre-Pauline Jewish literature that acceptance by God has to be earned (Sanders, *Paul and Palestinian Judaism;* Dunn, "New Perspective on Paul").

There is, of course, an emphasis in Judaism on the need for Israel's obedience — that is, on Israel's law-keeping as its response to God's saving initiative (as classically expressed in Exod 20:2-17), with covenant life being ordered and directed by reference to the law (cf. Lev 18:5). But at its heart, that is no different from the Christian/Pauline emphasis that faith must expresses itself in obedience, for faith that does not work through love is not faith (Rom 1:5; Gal 5:6; cf. Hooker, "Paul and 'Covenantal Nomism,'" 47-56). Hence the highly Jewish character of Rom 2:6-16.

In any discussion of justification vis-à-vis Judaism, there are also questions of definition to be clarified, such as "Who is Israel?" and "What is Judaism?" — not to mention the relation of this ancestral faith to the various Jewish sectarian groups and documents that emerged during the two hundred years prior to Paul (for an attempted clarification of these issues, see my "Judaism in the Land of Israel in the First Century," in *Judaism in Late Antiquity. Part 2: Historical Syntheses,* ed. J. Neusner [Leiden: Brill, 1995]). But the basic point remains, that God's righteousness first in choosing Israel to be his people, and then in sustaining Israel in that covenant relationship, is a theologoumenon fundamental to Jewish religion and identity. The proposition that relationship with God is first and foremost a gift and not something earned — an act of grace and not a reward for merit — would be axiomatic to any Jew who took the Torah and the Prophets seriously (see further my "In Search of Common Ground").

3. From Faith — A Reaffirmation of the Universal Outreach of God's Grace

The more we stress the continuity between Paul's teaching on justification and Paul's Jewish heritage, the more pressing becomes the question: Why, then, is Paul's teaching formulated in such a polemical manner, as in Gal 2:16 and Rom 3:20? If he was not reacting against his inherited Jewish convictions, and if he was not reacting (precisely as a result of his Damascus road experience) against his own past as a Pharisee, what was he reacting against? If he was not opposing Jewish legalism — at least in the sense of being able to claim salvation as a right, as a wage rather than a gift — what was he opposing?

In a word, the primary answer seems to be that Paul was reacting not so much against Jewish legalism as against Jewish *restrictiveness* — that is, the tendency in Judaism to restrict the covenant grace of God and covenant righteousness to Israel. This protest or reaction comes to clear expression repeatedly throughout the argument of Romans.

It is evident, first, in the thematic emphasis on "all": the gospel is for "all who believe" (1:16); the righteousness of God is "to all who believe" (3:22); Abraham is father of "all who believe" (4:11); "Christ is the end *(telos)* of the law as a means to righteousness for all who believe" (10:4), and so on. "All" is one of the really key words in Romans, where it occurs seventy-one times. And as these same references make clear in context, the "all" consistently means "all" — Jew as well as Gentile, Gentile as well as Jew. In pressing this point so consistently, Paul must have intended to break down the presupposition on the part of his fellow Jews that they were in a privileged position before God over against the non-Jewish nations. This is manifestly the chief thrust of Romans 2, as the immediately provoked question in 3:1 demonstrates: "What then is the advantage of the Jew?" (see further my "What Was the Issue Between Paul and 'Those of the Circumcision'?"; also my "Yet Once More — 'The Works of the Law': A Response," *Journal for the Study of the New Testament* 46 [1992] 99-117, esp. 106-09). Paul insisted on "all, Gentile as well as Jew," because his Jewish interlocutor or opponents assumed "Jew and not Gentile."

That Paul's arguments are directed against Jewish restrictiveness is evident, secondly, in the way in which Paul immediately draws out what was, for him, the chief corollary to his central statement in 3:21-26 on the righteousness of God. For in 3:27-31 the polemical antithesis between the "law of works" and the "law of faith" (3:27) is elaborated by the antithesis between "God of Jews only" and "God also of Gentiles" (3:29). It is clear from the run of the argument that the first members of each antithesis go together: "Is boasting excluded through the law of works? No! . . . otherwise God is God of Jews alone" — that is, to affirm the "law of works" is tantamount to affirming that God is "God of Jews only." But that cannot be so, for "God is one" — which is Israel's own basic creed (Deut 6:4). Therefore he is "God of Gentiles also." Here, it should be noted, the basic antithesis in Paul's formulation of justification — by faith and not by works — is elaborated precisely as: "Gentiles also and not Jews only." So "faith alone" asserts the proposition "Gentiles also," whereas "works [of law]" asserts its restrictive counterpart "Jews only."

The passage in Romans that most closely echoes this central argument is 9:30–10:13, where we find the most intense clustering of "righteousness" terminology in the letter apart from 3:21–4:22. Here we need simply note in passing the same antithesis as in 3:27 between the "law of works" and the "law of faith" — or, more precisely, between "the law [of righteousness!]" misunderstood "as if it was from works" and the same law successfully pursued "from faith" (9:30-32). But more important at this point is the elaboration of this misunderstanding of righteousness in the second part of the paragraph: "not knowing the righteousness of God and seeking to establish their own [righteousness], they have not subjected themselves to the righteousness of God" (10:3). This has commonly been understood as a classic statement of Jewish legalism — that is, that the Jews thought of righteousness as "their own" in the sense of a righteousness achieved or accomplished by them (so, e.g., R. Bultmann, *Theology of the New Testament*, vol. 1 [London: SCM, 1952] 285; C. E. B. Cranfield, *Romans*, vol. 2 [Edinburgh: Clark, 1979] 515).

But the sense of the Greek is clear, denoting by the expression "their own" something that belonged to them or was peculiar to them; that is, righteousness as Israel's covenant prerogative, the privilege of Jews only and not of Gentiles (cf. my *Romans*, vol. 2, 587-88). Hence, once again, the repeated "all" — "for all who believe" (10:4) — and the climax of the paragraph reinforce the point with repeated strokes: "For the scripture says, 'Everyone who believes in him shall not be put to shame.' For there is no distinction between Jew and Greek, for the same one is Lord of all, rich to all who call upon him. For 'everyone who calls upon the name of the Lord shall be saved'" (10:11-13). The restatement of "the righteousness of God" as a protest against Jewish restrictiveness could hardly be clearer.

More or less the same point has to be made with reference to the passage that has been regarded as the chief basis of the view that Paul's doctrine of justification was the immediate outgrowth and expression of his own experience of grace on the Damascus road, that is, Phil 3:7-9. The language is strikingly similar to Rom 10:3: Paul expresses his ardent desire to be found in Christ "not having my own righteousness which is from the law but that which is through faith in Christ, the righteousness of God to faith" (Phil 3:9; on the contentious phrase *pistis Christou*, see my "Once More, *Pistis Christou*," *SBL Seminar Papers* [Atlanta: Scholars Press, 1991] 730-44). Here, however, the very personal terms in which Paul describes what was an intensely personal experience (his conversion) may have misled us. For in this case he does not speak of "their own" righteousness, as in Rom 10:3, where the corporate dimension of Israel is to the fore. Rather, he speaks of "my own righteousness," and so may have encouraged the individualist suggestion of a personal possession attained and defended by personal effort (so, e.g., G. F. Hawthorne, *Philippians* [Waco: Word, 1983] 141; P. T. O'Brien, *Commentary on Philippians* [Grand Rapids: Eerdmans, 1991] 394-96).

This traditional interpretation, however, has tended to ignore the line of personal confession that builds up to this affirmation of ambition in Phil 3:4-6. That passage is, indeed, a statement of personal confidence. But the confidence is not primarily, if at all, of personal achievement. It is rather, once again, the confidence of Paul as a member of Israel, the covenant people — confident in his ethnic identity, confident in his share in the covenant marked by circumcision, confident that he was living within the terms of the covenant as laid out in the law, confident not least that he was defending the distinctiveness of Israel and its separateness from the nations, like zealous Phinehas and zealous Mattathias of old (on the significance of the term "zeal," see my *Galatians* [London: Black, 1993] 62-68; also my "Paul's Conversion").

It was his standing before God as a devout member of God's chosen people that Paul had previously treasured so highly (Phil 3:7-8). As such, he had rejoiced in a righteousness that non-Jews knew nothing of. It was "his," as one who had been "circumcised the eighth day, of the people of Israel." The thought, in other words, is not essentially different from that of Rom 10:3. And though Paul does not press the "all" line (i.e., Gentile as well as Jew) in Philippians 3, the thought is just as much of the righteousness of God understood as operating through the openness of faith and no longer restricted as being Israel's sole privilege.

If this line of exposition brings us anywhere near to Paul's thinking on this subject, then we can indeed speak of Paul's doctrine of justification as the immediate expression of his own experience of grace on the Damascus road. But not in the usual terms. For evidently what Paul experienced was not so much his acceptance as one who had previously been without acceptance by God, but primarily the shattering of his assumption that righteousness before God was Israel's peculiar privilege and his corollary assumption that those who threatened Israel's set-apartness to God, by preaching Messiah Jesus to Gentiles, had to be persecuted.

This reversal is not so clearly mirrored in Philippians 3, where the acceptability of Gentiles to God is not to the fore. But it is clear in the before and after of the parallel passage in Gal 1:13-16, which sets out the contrast between (1) previously a persecutor to prevent a gospel for Gentiles from adulterating or infringing Israel's covenant holiness to God (1:13-

14), and (2) God's Christ revealed to him in order that he might preach him among the Gentiles (1:15-16). And it is evidently the same theological thrust that drives the exposition of Paul's principal statement of his teaching on justification in Romans — that is, that the righteousness of God is for "all," not for Jews only but for Gentiles as well as Jews.

As a final observation in this section, we may draw in a point made in passing at the beginning of the previous section: God's righteousness denotes God's fulfillment of the obligations that he took on himself in creating humankind, as well as in the calling of Abraham and the choosing of Israel to be his people. Fundamental here is the recognition that God has a righteousness to fulfill as creator as well as his righteousness as Israel's covenant God. What Paul does in both Romans and Galatians is, in effect, to go behind the more restricted covenant obligation to Israel back to the more basic covenant obligation to the creation and humankind as a whole. In Romans he goes behind Moses to Adam (Rom 5:12-21); and he portrays Abraham as the type of the nations, with no prior covenant to call on and only his trust in the creator God, "who gives life to the dead and calls things which have no existence into existence" (Rom 4:17). In Galatians it is the new creation that relativizes both circumcision and uncircumcision (Gal 6:15). Here, then, is another way in which Paul gets behind Israel's restrictiveness. For the conviction that there is only one God of both the Jew and the Gentile forces the corollary that God justifies each alike through faith (Rom 3:30). So the confession of God as creator requires the recognition that God's saving righteousness is open to all humankind — Jew first, but Gentile as well.

This we might say in summary, therefore, is what Paul's conversion brought home to him: It did not teach him of God's grace as though as a Jew he was learning of it for the first time. It did, however, bring home to him that his own typically Jewish attitude had obscured that grace and to a serious degree perverted it. But, again, not by prompting him to think he had a claim on God by virtue of his own merits. The error that came home to him on the Damascus road was that Israel's claim to a special relationship with God was perverting the more basic insight of God's grace: as free grace it was open to all and not restricted to Jews and their proselytes. In this way and in this sense Paul rediscovered justification by grace on the Damascus road.

4. And Not from Works — A Rebuke of Jewish (Christian) Separateness

The other half of Paul's polemical formulation — justification from faith and not from works — is "not from works." We have already touched on some of the key passages in Paul where it appears. But for the sake of completeness we need to clarify its meaning and function more fully. This requirement is laid on us principally because the phrase has been so central to the traditional view of the relation between Paul's conversion and justification, which we have been questioning above. In the traditional view, as no one will need reminding, "justification by works" is understood as shorthand for the conviction that acceptance by God is something that has to be achieved or merited by obedience to the law. That Paul was principally protesting against such a belief depends almost exclusively on a particular reading of Rom. 4:4-5. But what has been said above should already have put various question marks against that traditional view.

The full phrase is, of course, "works of the law." It refers to what the law requires. To be noted at once is the fact that we are not talking about just any law here. This is an observation of some importance. For the tendency in the traditional view is to push in that direction — to see in Paul's conversion a general revulsion against the thought that any human striving or achievement can be the basis of God's acceptance. But Paul is talking about the Torah, the Jewish law. To be more precise, therefore, we should define "works of the law" as what the law requires of Israel as God's people.

Works of the law, in fact, are what we earlier referred to as Israel's response to God's grace in first choosing Israel to be his people: the obedience God called for in his people, which means the way Israel should live as the people of God. This is what E. P. Sanders described as "covenantal nomism" (*Paul and Palestinian Judaism*, 75, 236; see also his *Judaism: Practice and Belief 63 BCE–66 CE* [London: SCM Press; Philadelphia: Trinity Press International, 1992] 262-78, 377-78, 415-17). It is a phrase regularly echoed in these discussions over the past few years. And it is a phrase where both words are important — law as functioning within and in relation to the covenant; law as expression of and safeguard for the covenant; law as indicating Israel's part of the agreement graciously initiated by God.

What has been too much ignored, however, is the way that the law, thus understood, came to reinforce the sense of Israel's privilege and to mark out this people in its set-apartness to God. For as God's choice of Israel drew the corollary that God's saving grace was restricted to Israel, so the law's role in defining Israel's holiness to God became also its role in separating Israel from the nations. In this way the positive sense of "works of the law," as equivalent to Paul's talk of the obedience of faith, became the more negative sense that we find in Paul — that is, works of the law as not only maintaining Israel's covenant status (this is Sanders's emphasis in his understanding of "covenantal nomism"), but as also protecting Israel's privileged status and restricted prerogative.

It was because of their status and prerogative that the horror of idolatry was so deeply rooted in the people of Israel's psyche. And thus, we might say, the avoidance of idolatry was the supreme "work of the law" (cf. Exod 20:3-6; Deut 5:7-10). Although avoidance of idolatry does not feature in Paul's references to the works of the law, Paul's hostility to idolatry was as implacable as any Jew's, and it was that "zeal" or "jealousy" for Israel's special relationship with God that fueled his earlier persecuting zeal.

There were, however, other works of the law that from early times marked out Israel's set-apartness to God and separation from the nations. The terms on which circumcision was first required of Abraham made circumcision a fundamental identity marker of the people of the covenant (Gen. 17:9-14). Failure to circumcise a male child meant, in fact, exclusion from the covenant and the covenant people. No wonder, then, that Paul in his own time could boil the distinction between Jews and Gentiles down to "circumcision" and "uncircumcision" (Rom 2:25-27; 3:30; 4:9-12; Gal 2:7-8).

Likewise, observance of the Sabbath became a touchstone of covenant identity and loyalty (Exod 31:12-17). The Sabbath was a sign of Israel's set-apartness, and failure to keep Sabbath law was a capital offense. So, for example, for Isa 56:6 the mark of Gentile participation in the covenant would be their keeping of the Sabbath. More archetypal still, in some ways, were the laws of clean and unclean, which marked not only a separation of clean and unclean birds and beasts but also a separation of Israel from the peoples (Lev 20:22-26) — an association (unclean foods, unclean nations) which, according to Acts 10, was only brought into question in emerging Christianity through Peter's encounter with Cornelius (Acts 10:10-16, 28).

As is well known, the Maccabean crisis reinforced both Israel's sense of distinctiveness and its focus on particular laws as make or break issues in defining and defending Israel's set-apartness. It was the distinguishing features of Israel's religion that the Syrians strove to eliminate, in order to submerge the Judeans into the Hellenistic religious syncretism by which they hoped to unify their declining empire. And, as the Maccabean literature emphasizes, it was the practice of circumcision and the laws on clean and unclean, in particular, that became the focal point of conflict:

> According to the decree, they put to death the women who had their children circumcised, and their families and those who circumcised them; and they hung the infants from their mothers' necks. But many in Israel stood firm and were resolved in their hearts not to eat unclean food. They chose to die rather than to be defiled by food or to profane the holy covenant; and they did die. (1 Maccabees 1:60-63)

This sense that the law's requirements (i.e., the "works of the law") had as their primary goals the preservation of Israel's covenant distinctiveness and the separation of Israel from the nations is highlighted in the Jewish writings from this period, particularly in *Jubilees* and the *Epistle of Aristeas:*

> Separate yourself from the nations, and eat not with them. . . . For their works are unclean, and all their ways are a pollution and an abomination and an uncleanness. (*Jubilees* 22:16)

> In his wisdom the legislator [Moses] . . . surrounded us with unbroken palisades and iron walls to prevent our mixing with any of the other peoples in any matter. . . . So, to prevent our being perverted by contact with others or by mixing with bad influences, he hedged us in on all sides with strict observances connected with meat and drink and touch and hearing and sight, after the manner of the law. (*Epistle of Aristeas* 139, 142)

For such a mind-set, the oracle of Balaam became paradigmatic: "a people dwelling alone, and not reckoning itself among the nations" (Num 23:9) — which Philo glossed by adding the explanation, "because in virtue of the distinction of their peculiar customs they do not mix with others to depart from the ways of their fathers" (*On the Life of Moses* 1.278).

Until recently the actual phrase "works of the law" was not attested prior to Paul, which naturally made many commentators wonder whether Paul was fighting against demons of his own creation. But the growing recognition that the Qumran sect seemed to have used such a phrase (cf. 4QFlorilegium 1:1-7; 1QS [*Manual of Discipline*] 5:20-24; 6:18) has been dramatically reinforced in the last few years by the publication of one of the most important of the Dead Sea Scrolls, which is known by the abbreviation 4QMMT. This document from cave 4 of Qumran, called *Miqṣat Maʿaśeh ha-Tôrah* ("some of the works of the law"), is a letter in which someone — presumably a leader of the sect, or, perhaps, even *the* leader — explains to others in Israel the sect's own distinctive interpretations of the laws that they regard as crucial to their fulfillment of Israel's obligations under the covenant. In this case, the laws have to do with rulings related chiefly to the temple, priesthood, sacrifices, and purity. And it is these rulings that the letter sums up toward the end as "some of the works of the law" *(miqṣat maʿaśeh ha-Tôrah),* from which the document has been given its name. More striking still, the letter makes it clear that these "works of the law" are the reason why the sect "separated" from the rest of Israel. And it is these "works of the law" whose practice requires them to maintain that separate existence (see further my "4QMMT and Galatians").

It is against this background that we can best make sense of Paul's use of the same phrase "the works of the law." It refers, of course, to all or whatever the law requires, and so to covenantal nomism as a whole. But in a context where the relationship of Israel with other nations is at issue, certain laws would naturally come more into focus than others. We have noted circumcision and food laws, in particular. In the Qumran sect, however, the sensitive issues were not those between Jew and Gentile, but those between Jew and Jew — and so focused on internal disagreements having to do with such matters as sacrifice and purity.

Elsewhere in the Jewish literature of the day, we are made aware of a violent disagreement about how to calculate the appropriate feast days, whether by the sun or by the moon. The disagreement was so sharp that each party regarded the other as failing to keep the feast — as observing the feasts of the Gentiles and not those of Israel's covenant (e.g., *Jubilees* 6:32-35; *1 Enoch* 82:4-7; see further my *Partings of the Ways,* 104). Today we might think of issues like abortion, or women priests, or inerrancy. None of the disputants in such internal controversies would regard the points at issue as the whole of their faith, or even as the most important element in their faith. But they have become foci of controversy to such an extent that the status of the opponent's Christian profession as a whole can, in fact, be called into question.

When we turn to Paul's first use of the phrase "works of the law" in Gal 2:16, it is precisely with this sort of issue that we are confronted. For Paul clearly uses the phrase to denote the attitudes he has opposed in the preceding verses. The "false brothers" who tried to secure the Gentile Titus's circumcision (2:4) were insisting on works of the law; faith in Christ was insufficient. So too Peter and the other Jewish believers who "separated" (the same verb as in 4QMMT) themselves from Gentile believers, presumably because the law required Israel to maintain such separation by observance of various food laws (2:12), were insisting on works of the law, faith alone being considered insufficient. Hence Paul's attempt to open Peter's eyes to see that "no human being is justified by works of the law, but only through faith in Jesus Christ," and his repeated insistence in 2:16 that it is faith and not works that is the sole basis of acceptance in Christ and should be likewise for mutual acceptance by those in Christ.

What is of relevance for us here is the way in which this particular formulation, the antithesis between faith and works, seems to emerge from the incident at Antioch (Gal 2:11-14). Why had it not emerged earlier? Paul had been converted for perhaps as many as seventeen years. He had been active in missionary work among Gentiles for most of that period. And yet the issue of Jew and Gentile fellowship and integration within the new house groups had not been posed. Even at the Jerusalem consultation, when the issue of circumcision, a primary work of the law, had been resolved, the question of these (other) works that had traditionally marked out Israel's separateness from the nations had not been raised. It looks very much, therefore, as though it took the particular confrontation at Antioch to bring out this fundamental declaration of principle from Paul. What had been thus far a gray area — an issue not perceived, a question not posed — suddenly had the spotlight turned on it. And Paul, in one of the great defining moments in Christian theology, pronounced what was to become his most memorable and telling principle: no one is justified by works of the law, but only through faith in Christ.

That is not to say, however, that this was a wholly new principle for Paul, first discovered, as it were, in and through the Antioch incident. It would be more accurate to say that the principle was implicit in the "revelation" made to him on the Damascus road. For that revelation, if we are right, came to focus in the realization that the God of Israel was also the God of the nations — that the good news of God's Son was not to be restricted to Israel, but was also for the Gentiles as freely as for the Jews (Gal 1:12-16); that the promise of Abraham was also of blessing for the nations (3:6-14). What his years of initial missionary work, climaxing in the Jerusalem consultation and the Antioch incident, brought home to him were the ramifications of this basic revelation. The controversies that his preaching of Christ among the nations provoked forced him to think through and to articulate in sharper and antithetical terms what that revelation amounted to — that is, what was at stake in the gospel itself. And he summed it up in the classic slogan: justification from faith and not from works.

5. Conclusion

In what sense, then, can we say that Paul's doctrine of justification by faith was part of the impact of his conversion? Not in the sense that Paul as an individual, long searching for peace with God, at last found peace for his troubled conscience. Not in the sense that he turned there from a legalistic Judaism that had lost all sense and sight of divine grace and found it exclusively in Christ and Christianity. But rather in the sense that on the Damascus road he discovered afresh the roots of his ancestral faith, based in the acknowledgment of God as creator, rooted in God's call and promise to Abraham, and growing out of God's saving act in the deliverance of the no-people Israel from slavery in Egypt. Rather, in the sense that the Damascus road confrontation brought home to him how much his people's and his own preoccupation with maintaining their set-apartness from the nations had become a perversion of that original call and promise and choice, and so a subversion of the fundamental character of that call and promise and choice as an act of free grace. It was that basic insight (revelation) and the call (to the Gentiles) bound up with it that he sought to implement. And in the success and controversy that ensued, it was that basic insight and call that he clarified and crystallized in his most memorable slogan: justification from faith and not from works.

Selected Bibliography

Dunn, J. D. G. "'A Light to the Gentiles', or 'The End of the Law'? The Significance of the Damascus Road Christophany for Paul." In *Jesus*,

Paul and the Law: Studies in Mark and Galatians, 89-107. London: SPCK; Louisville: Westminster, 1990.

————. "The New Perspective on Paul." *Bulletin of the John Rylands Library* 65 (1983) 95-122. Reprinted in *Jesus, Paul and the Law: Studies in Mark and Galatians.* London: SPCK; Louisville: Westminster, 1990, 183-214.

————. *The Partings of the Ways between Christianity and Judaism.* London: SCM; Philadelphia: Trinity Press International, 1991.

————. "What Was the Issue Between Paul and 'Those of the Circumcision'?" In *Paulus und das antike Judentum,* ed. M. Hengel and U. Heckel. Tübingen: Mohr-Siebeck, 1991, 295-317.

————. "Paul's Conversion: A Light to Twentieth Century Disputes." In *Evangelium — Schriftauslegung — Kirche* (*Festschrift* for P. Stuhlmacher), ed. O. Hofius et al. Göttingen: Vandenhoeck & Ruprecht, 1996, 77-93.

————. "4QMMT and Galatians." *New Testament Studies* 43 (1997), 147-53.

————. "In Search of Common Ground." In *Paul and the Mosaic Law,* ed. J. D. G. Dunn. Tübingen: Mohr-Siebeck, 1996, 309-34.

Hooker, M. D. "Paul and 'Covenantal Nomism." In *Paul and Paulinism: Essays in Honour of C. K. Barrett,* ed. M. D. Hooker and S. G. Wilson. London: SPCK, 1982, 47-56.

Kim, S. *The Origin of Paul's Gospel.* Tübingen: Mohr-Siebeck, 1981.

Räisänen, H. "Paul's Conversion and the Development of His View of the Law." *New Testament Studies* 33 (1987) 404-19.

————. *Jesus, Paul and Torah: Collected Essays.* Sheffield: Sheffield Academic Press, 1992.

Sanders, E. P. *Paul and Palestinian Judaism.* Philadelphia: Fortress; London: SCM, 1977.

————. *Paul.* London: Oxford University Press, 1991.

Stendahl, K. *Paul Among Jews and Gentiles and Other Essays.* Philadelphia: Fortress; London: SCM, 1977.

Stuhlmacher, P. "'The End of the Law': On the Origin and Beginnings of Pauline Theology." In *Reconciliation, Law, and Righteousness: Essays in Biblical Theology.* Philadelphia: Fortress, 1986, 134-54.

Westerholm, S. *Israel's Law and the Church's Faith: Paul and his Recent Interpreters.* Grand Rapids: Eerdmans, 1988.

God Reconciled His Enemy to Himself:
The Origin of Paul's Concept of
Reconciliation

SEYOON KIM

COMMENTATORS often observe (1) that reconciliation terminology is unique to Paul in the New Testament, (2) that Paul's use of "reconciliation" is quite different from that in Greek literature or the Hellenistic Jewish writings, and (3) that in 2 Cor 5:11-21, which is one of two passages in the major letters of Paul where "reconciliation" is a key term (the other being Rom 5:1-11), Paul seems at several points to be reflecting on his Damascus road experience. Yet contemporary scholarship has seldom brought these three matters together and so has not often discussed Paul's doctrine of reconciliation in connection with his Damascus road experience — whether that experience be understood as a "conversion" and/or a "call." Nevertheless, the question must be asked: Is it not plausible that these three observations should be considered together?

In what follows, my intent is to give detailed support for these observations. In the process I will discuss some of the suggestions that have been proposed for the origin and development of Paul's teaching on reconciliation. Ultimately and most importantly, however, my aim will be to set forth and substantiate the thesis that Paul's teaching about divine reconciliation grew out of his personal meeting with the risen Christ on the road to Damascus.

1. The Uniqueness of Paul's Reconciliation Terminology

It is well known that reconciliation terminology in the New Testament, when referring to the relationship between God and human beings, appears only in Paul's letters. The verb "to reconcile" *(katallassein)* occurs in Rom 5:10 (twice) and 2 Cor 5:18, 19, 20; the noun "reconciliation" *(katallagē)* occurs in the same contexts as the verb in Rom 5:11; 11:15 and 2 Cor 5:18, 19; and the intensive verbal form *apokatallassein* is to be found in Eph 2:16 and Col 1:20, 22.

Moreover, Paul's use of reconciliation terminology is unique not only in its pattern of occurrence but also in its usage. For Paul never says that God is reconciled (or, that God reconciles himself) to human beings, but always that God reconciles human beings to himself or that human beings are reconciled to God. It is not, in fact, God who must be reconciled to human beings, but human beings who need to be reconciled to God. Nor is it by people's repentance, prayers, or other good works that reconciliation between God and human beings is accomplished, but rather by God's grace alone. In such a usage, Paul has made, as we will see, a fundamental correction of the Hellenistic Jewish conception of spiritual reconciliation.

The distinctiveness of Paul's use of this terminology has led many to affirm that reconciliation is a uniquely Pauline category for interpreting God's saving act in Christ. Some scholars, however, think that Paul took over a pre-Pauline Christian conception. Ernst Käsemann, for example, argued that 2 Cor 5:18-21 is a "a pre-Pauline hymnic fragment," while Ralph P. Martin believes these verses (minus vv. 19b and 20c) represent a pre-Pauline "confessional statement" (*Reconciliation,* 94-95). Others take only the first part of verse 19 — that is, that "God was reconciling the world to himself in Christ, not counting people's sins against them" — to be a Pauline quotation of an earlier formulation (e.g., Breytenbach, *Versöhnung,* 118-20). But such "pre-Pauline" views with regard to this passage have been soundly overthrown by R. Bieringer (*Studies on 2 Corinthians,* 429-59) and Margaret Thrall (*Second Epistle to the Corinthians,* 1.445-49). So we may confidently reaffirm the generally accepted understandings (1) that reconciliation terminology in the New Testament is uniquely Pauline, and (2) that Paul's use of this terminology represents a real innovation in the history of religion.

2. Linguistic Background

On the basis of a thorough study of its linguistic background, C. Breyten-bach points out that the term "reconciliation" in the literature of the Greeks is never used in a religious context for the relationship between God and human beings, but that its most prominent use with respect to interpersonal relations is in connection with a peace-treaty process that takes place in a political or military context (*Versöhnung*, 40-83). So in light of parallels between the vocabulary of 2 Cor 5:20 and a Hellenistic military conception of "ambassadors" *(presbeis)* sent to "petition" *(deomai)* or "appeal" *(parakalein)* to warring parties for reconciliation, he suggests that Paul's reconciliation terminology must be seen against such a Hellenistic diplomatic background.

Howard Marshall, however, has pointed to several passages in 2 Maccabees where "reconciliation" *(katallagē)* is, in fact, used in a religious context for God being reconciled to his people ("Meaning of 'Reconciliation,' " 120-21, 129-30). For example, 2 Maccabees 8:29 states that when Israel's apostasy aroused the wrath of God the people prayed to God "to be reconciled with his servants" (cf. 1:5). In other places in 2 Maccabees it is said that when God has vented his wrath on his people, or on their representatives, then he will be reconciled with them (see 5:20; 7:32-33). Of importance here is to note the way in which reconciliation takes place in this Hellenistic Jewish writing — that is, that God is reconciled to humanity, rather than the reverse.

Breytenbach himself points out that, like the author of 2 Maccabees, both Philo (*On the Life of Moses* 2.166; *On Joseph* 11.18) and Josephus (*Jewish War* 5.415; *Jewish Antiquities* 7.153) also apply, though somewhat infrequently, the originally diplomatic sense of the verb "to reconcile" *(katallassein)* to relationships between God and human beings — that is, that God "is reconciled" to Israel or to David when they repent or pray. Nevertheless, being impressed by (1) the difference between the Hellenistic Jewish use of the term (i.e., that God is reconciled to human beings) and Paul's use (i.e., that God reconciles human beings to himself), as well as by (2) the close parallelism between a profane Greek diplomatic use and Paul's use in 2 Cor 5:18-20, Breytenbach insists that only the profane Greek use forms the background to Paul's use (*Versöhnung*, 70-81).

It must be stated, however, that Paul's application of terminology that was originally rooted in a diplomatic context for use in a religious context is, at least formally, a significant point of contact between Paul and the Hellenistic Jewish writings. Furthermore, Peter Stuhlmacher has justly criticized Breytenbach for failing to note that both Philo (*On the Life of Moses* 2.166; *Questions and Answers on Exodus* 2.49) and Josephus (*Jewish Antiquities* 3.315) present Moses as not only a "mediator" *(mesitēs)* but also a "reconciler" *(katallaktēs)* between God and Israel (Stuhlmacher, *Biblische Theologie*, 1.319). This complex of ideas may be reflected in 2 Cor 5:18–6:2, since Paul seems to compare and contrast his own ministry of the new covenant with Moses' ministry of the old covenant (cf. 2 Corinthians 3).

It seems necessary, therefore, to affirm that Paul does indeed reflect a Hellenistic Jewish use of "reconciliation" when he uses such terminology to speak about relations between God and human beings, even though he has made a fundamental correction of those Hellenistic Jewish authors in terms of how that reconciliation takes place. As we will see, though, Paul also reflects a profane Greek use of the same terminology in a political/military context.

3. Various Suggestions about the Origin of Paul's Concept

The conclusions above naturally lead to the question: How, then, did Paul come to develop the concept of reconciliation as a metaphor for God's saving work in Christ? Leonhard Goppelt proposed that its "material starting-point" was (1) in the Jesus tradition — specifically, in Jesus' offer of forgiveness to sinners on God's behalf and his teaching as expressed in parables like that of the prodigal son — and (2) in the early Christian confession of Jesus' death as a vicarious atonement (Goppelt, *Christologie und Ethik,* 152-53). This view is eminently plausible, for there can be little doubt about Paul's knowledge of and dependence on the Jesus traditions (see my "Jesus, Sayings of," *Dictionary of Paul and His Letters,* ed. G. F. Hawthorne and R. P. Martin [Downers Grove: InterVarsity, 1993] 474-92). It is insufficient, however, in terms of explaining how Paul came to use the term "reconciliation" itself.

According to Otfried Hofius, Paul developed his reconciliation concept chiefly from the fourth Servant Song of Deutero-Isaiah — that is, from Isa 52:3–53:12 (*Paulusstudien,* 11-13). Hofius points to parallels between the "sinless" Servant's suffering and death "for many," which serves to make them "righteous" and give them "peace," and Paul's presentation of Christ as the "sinless" one who died a vicarious death "for all," a death that now functions as the ground for God's "justification" of human beings and his "reconciliation" of them to himself (2 Cor 5:11-21). Hofius equates the "peace" of Isa 53:5 with Paul's concept of "reconciliation" in 2 Cor 5:19, and he argues that Rom 10:15-16 witnesses to Paul's appreciation of the concepts of "peace" and "gospel" in Isa 52:6-10. According to Hofius, the combination of Isa 52:13–53:12 and 52:6-10 led Paul to affirm in 2 Cor 5:18-21 "that God's saving act includes *both* the cross-event as the *act* of creating the universal 'peace' and the cross-preaching as the *word* that proclaims 'peace' worldwide." And Hofius's demonstration of Paul's reflection on Isaiah 52–53 in 2 Cor 5:11-21 has been supported by Otto Betz in his study of 2 Cor 5:16 ("Fleischliche und 'geistliche' Christuserkenntnis").

Yet it is a questionable whether it is adequate to point to the concept of "peace" in Isa 52:7 and 53:5 as the basis for how Paul came to understand God's saving act in Christ's death and his own apostolic ministry in terms of reconciliation. For the term "reconciliation" itself is lacking in those Isaianic passages.

Marshall speculates that the Jewish martyr tradition represented in 2 Maccabees may have been the catalyst for Paul's development of his concept of reconciliation ("Meaning of 'Reconciliation,' " 129-30). That is, while interpreting Jesus' death as an atoning sacrifice in the light of the martyr tradition of 2 and 4 Maccabees, Paul may have formulated his reconciliation doctrine in deliberate contrast to the Jewish view of a martyr's death, which was interpreted as moving an angry God "to be reconciled" to his people. It is possible, of course, that the Hellenistic Jewish tradition represented in 2 Maccabees exerted some influence on Paul's concept of reconciliation. But a theory about the origin of the concept must be able to explain not only how Paul came to apply reconciliation terminology to God's saving act in Christ's death but also how he came to designate his own career as a "ministry of reconciliation" (2 Cor 5:18). And Marshall's conjecture seems to fall short of doing the latter.

According to Bieringer, it was the conflict situation between the Corinthian church and Paul that led Paul to use reconciliation terminology in his portrayal of Christ's death in 2 Corinthians 5 (*Studies on 2 Corinthians*, 454-55). But this view is unlikely, since in this passage Paul speaks only of God's reconciliation of human beings to himself and not also of a reconciliation between himself and the Corinthian church.

Several of these suggestions, taken separately, may be deemed plausible for a partial explanation of the origin of Paul's concept of reconciliation — that is, that Paul was influenced by a primitive Christian confession regarding Christ's vicarious death, or by the Jesus tradition having to do with forgiveness, or by the Servant Song of Isaiah 52–53, or by a Hellenistic Jewish tradition of reconciliation as represented in 2 Maccabees, or by a Greek diplomatic use of reconciliation language. None of them, however, can be claimed to be the basis or sole catalyst for the use of this terminology in his thought and expression.

Hofius's conclusion represents the best approach for understanding the origin and development of Paul's doctrine of reconciliation:

> The Pauline idea of "reconciliation" is . . . shaped decisively by the message of [Deutero-Isaiah]. Its *foundation,* however, lies elsewhere: in [Paul's] encounter with the Risen One, in which God disclosed to the persecutor the cross as his *act* of reconciliation and called him to be the envoy of the *word* of reconciliation. What had been revealed to Paul in this event, he then found confirmed and interpreted through the prophetic witness of Scripture. Thus he obtained from the OT the language by which he was able to express the saving act of God in Jesus Christ.

But Hofius provides no exegetical support for such a thesis. Rather, he seems to speak only intuitively, being aware of various possibilities and having a feel for the situation. What is needed, however, is a firmer exegetical analysis of Paul's thought regarding reconciliation, which is provided in what follows.

4. An Exegetical Analysis of 2 Corinthians 5:11-21

Of the five passages in the Pauline letters where the doctrine of reconciliation appears, 2 Cor 5:11-21 is the earliest and seems to provide the best access to determining the origin of Paul's teaching. Reconciliation terminology is concentrated in vv. 18-21, and since our exegetical analysis will focus on these verses, it will be helpful to cite them here in full:

> [18]All this is from God, who reconciled us to himself through Christ and gave us the ministry of reconciliation [19]because God was reconciling the world to himself in Christ, not counting people's transgressions against

them. And he has entrusted to us the message of reconciliation. [20]We are therefore Christ's ambassadors, as though God were making his appeal through us. We implore you on Christ's behalf: Be reconciled to God. [21]God made him who had no sin to be sin for us, so that in him we might become the righteousness of God.

The Structure of Verses 18-19

A cursory glance at verses 18-19 reveals that the term "reconciliation" appears four times, twice as a noun and twice as a participle. In addition, a certain structure seems evident in these verses, though it has been variously set out. Within verses 18-21, verse 19 is clearly a disturbing element.

Among the various problems presented by this verse, we are here principally concerned with the mutual relationship of the three participles "reconciling" *(katallassōn)*, "counting" *(logizomenos)*, and "entrusted" *(themenos)*. Some commentators take the two participial phrases that start respectively with "not counting" and "and entrusted" (v. 19b and 19c) as being intentionally linked together, with both also being subordinated to the main statement of verse 19a, that "God was reconciling the world to himself in Christ." But a "not . . . and" *(mē . . . kai)* construction seems strange. Furthermore, the paralleling of a present participle *(logizomenos)* with an aorist participle *(themenos)* produces an illogical sense, making "the entrusting of the 'word of reconciliation' prior in time to the reconciling act itself" (Thrall, *Second Epistle to the Corinthians,* 1.435). Most commentators, therefore, take the phrase "reconciling the world to himself in Christ" as periphrastic, with "not counting" *(mē logizomenos)* seen as being subordinate to the main sentence and "has entrusted" *(themenos)* as equivalent to the finite form "he entrusted" *(etheto)*. Yet this analysis also has the difficulty of combining in an unnatural fashion the periphrastic imperfect "was . . . reconciling" *(ēn . . . katallassōn)* and the aorist "entrusted" *(themenos)*.

Some commentators take this incongruity between verse 19ab and 19c to be a sign that 19ab is a citation of a pre-Pauline formulation and that 19c is Paul's own addition. They further point out (1) that the change from the aorist in verse 18 to the imperfect in verse 19ab is also incongruous; (2) that the transition from "against them" *(autois)* in verse 19b to "to us" *(en hēmin)* in verse 19c is not smooth; (3) that the content of verse 19ab has the function of elaborating and substantiating the statement of verse 18; (4) that the "as/because" *(hōs hoti)*, which begins verse 19, can well be understood as an introductory formula for a citation; and (5) that there is a logical consistency if we take verse 18bc and verse 19c together, leaving out verse 19ab (cf., e.g., Breytenbach, *Versöhnung*, 118-19; Furnish, *II Corinthians*, 320).

All these points clearly suggest that verse 19ab should be considered to be an insertion. But since there is little reason to regard it as being pre-Pauline, we propose that it is best to take it as a Pauline parenthesis. The aorist participle "entrusted" *(themenos)* of verse 19c clearly belongs with the substantival participles of verse 18bc: "the one who reconciled" *(katallaxantos)* and "the one who gave" *(dontos)*. And the three participial clauses together make up a logically coherent statement whose structure can be laid out as follows:

> 18All this is from God,
> > who *reconciled (katallaxantos)* us to himself through Christ
> > and who *gave (dontos)* us the ministry of reconciliation
> > > 19ab[because *(hōs hoti)* God was reconciling the world to himself in Christ, not counting people's transgressions against them].
> > 19cAnd he has *entrusted (themenos)* to us the message of reconciliation.

What is particularly significant about this structure is that reconciliation terms are highlighted in the three participial clauses, as well as in the parenthetical comments of verse 19ab. In each case, also, God is shown to be the author of reconciliation.

Two further grammatical questions arise, which can be dealt with more briefly. First, Why does the nominative form appear in *themenos* rather than the genitive, as in *katallaxantos* and *dontos?* It is most likely due to the influence of the nominative *theos* in verse 19a, though perhaps also because of the *os*-endings of *katallaxantos* and *dontos*. Second, What is the meaning of the opening two words *(hōs hoti)* of verse 19? These words should probably be seen as a combination of the comparative "as" *(hōs)* and the causal "because" *(hoti)*, which together introduce a parenthetical statement that provides the ground for what Paul has declared in verse 18.

A final significant point in this passage is that the three main participial clauses, as outlined above, each refer to "us": God reconciled *us (hēmas);* God gave *to us (hēmin)* a ministry; and God entrusted *to us (hēmin)* a message. It is most likely, then, that Paul is talking about God's grace to him personally — that is, that God reconciled the apostle *himself* to God, gave *him* the ministry of reconciliation, and entrusted *him* with the message of reconciliation. The next question to be answered, then, is: When did Paul consider these events to have occurred in his life?

Allusions to the Damascus Experience in Verses 13-19

Not only the "us" phrases of verses 18-19, but also the three aorist participles in these verses *(katallaxantos, dontos,* and *themenos)* clearly allude to Paul's personal experience — in particular, his sense of forgiveness/reconciliation, his call to apostleship/ministry, and his being entrusted with the gospel message of reconciliation. And each of these aspects must be seen as having occurred on the road to Damascus.

Otfried Hofius rightly observes (1) that Paul's "entrustment with the gospel message" of verse 19c corresponds to Paul's testimony in Gal 1:12, 15-16a about his reception of God's revelation of the gospel, and (2) that Paul's "ministry of reconciliation" of verse 18c corresponds to Paul's words in Gal 1:16b about his apostolic commission to preach to the Gentiles ("Erwägungen," 29). We may add (3) that there is a correspondence between "God's reconciling action" mentioned in verse 18ab and what is implicit in Gal 1:13-14 about God's grace to Paul, despite his previous persecution of the church. These close correspondences between Gal 1:12-16 and 2 Cor 5:18-19, therefore, put in sharp relief the interpretation that the three participial clauses in the latter allude to Paul's Damascus experience, which is explicitly referred to in Gal 1:12-16.

The three participial clauses, however, are not the only allusions to Paul's Damascus experience in 2 Cor 5:11-21. Verse 16, which refers to "knowing Christ from now on" in a new way, is almost universally recognized as alluding to Paul's conversion. The phrase "from now on" signals a fundamental turning point in Paul's life, which took place as a consequence of the proper recognition of the eschatological saving event of Christ's death and resurrection (vv. 14-15). Paul now has a completely new perspective on Christ — as well as, for that matter, on every other person. There is no doubt that Paul is here speaking about his Damascus experience when he abandoned his prior "fleshly" estimate of Christ in the face of the divine revelation of Christ as the one who had died for humankind and been raised from the dead.

Verse 17, which speaks of the "new creation" that obtains "in Christ," also alludes to Paul's Damascus experience. The "new creation" certainly is rooted in the eschatological event of the death and resurrection of Christ. But as the individualizing "anyone" *(tis)* makes clear, Paul is here thinking of an individual's participation in that new creation through coming to be "in Christ." Although verse 17 is formulated gnomically (i.e., in general terms), the context indicates that Paul is speaking mainly of himself by way of an apostolic defense, and so the verse must be taken to refer to Paul's own experience.

On the Damascus road Paul came to perceive Christ correctly. In particular, he came to understand that Christ's death was a vicarious act and that faith in Christ somehow placed him "in Christ." Earlier in 2 Cor 4:6 he referred to his encounter with the risen Christ on the Damascus road as an appearance of the shining light of divine glory — that is, describing that encounter in terms of a light shining in his heart that was analogous to God's command at the first creation to let light shine out of darkness. And so, with respect to 2 Cor 5:17, Paul has already implied that on the Damascus road God's act of new creation took effect on him personally.

The fact that Paul speaks of a "new creation" in connection with his conversion experience (vv. 13-16) reminds us of similar language in the Hellenistic Jewish writing *Joseph and Aseneth,* where Joseph in blessing Aseneth speaks of God as the one who "gave life to all [things] and called [them] from darkness to light" and asks of God to "renew her [Aseneth] by your spirit, and form her anew by your hidden hand, and make her alive again by your life" (8:10-11). By the same token, Paul's connection of this "new creation" with the idea of "reconciliation" to God (vv. 18-21) reminds us of the rabbinic tradition that compares forgiveness on the Day of Atonement with a new creation.

In addition, it needs to be pointed out that two words in 2 Cor 5:14 also seem to allude to Paul's conversion near Damascus. First, when the apostle says, "Christ's love compels us, having judged this *(krinantas touto)*, that one died for all, and therefore all died," the Greek aorist participle *krinantas* along with the demonstrative pronoun *touto* suggests the sense of "having once reached the conclusion." If we ask when Paul reached the conclusion in question, the answer must be that he came to a new and correct "judgment" about Christ's death as a vicarious death "for all" *at his conversion* on the Damascus road. For it was there that he realized the magnitude of Christ's love for him and for humankind.

The word "compels" *(synechei)* is the second word in verse 14 that probably alludes to Paul's Damascus experience. It appears here in the context of verses 11-21, which, as we will see in some detail in the following section, concerns Paul's apostolic ministry. "Compels" is a strong term that brings to mind similar strong terms used by Paul in connection with his apostolic ministry — for example, that he was "enlisted" *(katelēmphthēn)* by Christ (Phil 3:12); that he was "called by God's grace" to "preach Christ among the Gentiles" (Gal 1:15-16); that he considered himself a "debtor" *(opheiletēs)* to the Gentiles (Rom 1:14); and that he sensed that a "fateful necessity" *(anangkē)* had been laid on him to preach the gospel (1 Cor 9:16). Since these other passages refer not only to Paul's apostolic ministry but also to his apostolic call on the Damascus road, it is likely also that "compelled by the love of Christ" refers to what Paul felt for the first time on the Damascus road.

Finally, there is the phrase in 5:13, translatable as either "if we were in ecstasy" or "if we were out of our mind" *(eite . . . exestēmen),* that also probably alludes to Paul's Damascus experience. A number of commentators argue that *exestēmen* refers to Paul's own ecstatic religious experiences and that Paul is here responding to certain criticisms by his Corinthian opponents — arguing against accusations either (1) that he was illegitimately appealing to his own ecstatic experiences in support of his apostolic ministry or (2) that he was deficient with respect to such ecstatic experiences. Without getting into the details of this debate, it is evident that Paul's opponents prized ecstatic religious experiences as one authentication of their own "apostolic" claims (cf. 2 Corinthians 10–13). Also, it is certain that Paul is referring here to some ecstatic experience that caused controversy among the Corinthians. The natural reading of verse 13 clearly suggests that here Paul is being defensive of his own ecstasy. So Margaret Thrall, who is one of the champions of the latter view (i.e., that he is speaking against criticism about his deficiency of ecstatic experiences), proposes that Paul responds, in effect, that his ecstatic experiences (which he does have) "are no concern of his readers but concern God only" (*Second Epistle to the Corinthians,* 407).

It must be pointed out, however, that the juxtaposition of *exestēmen* with *sōphronoumen* ("we are in our right mind") indicates that *exestēmen* carries not only the idea of ecstasy but also the pejorative sense "we were out of our mind." In addition, the juxtaposition of the aorist *exestēmen* with the present tense *sōphronoumen* suggests that the former points to a completed event in Paul's past. What, then, might we identify as the ecstatic experience in Paul's life that was disputed by his opponents? The apologetic context of 5:11-21 directs us to think of Paul's Damascus experience of conversion and call. The most natural interpretation of verse 13a, therefore, is as follows: Paul is responding to his opponents' criticism that he was basing his apostolic claim on his visionary experience of Christ on the Damascus road (cf. 1 Cor 9:1; 15:8-10) rather than on a proper appointment by Jesus and on the proper doctrine of Christ that his apostles taught. Perhaps the opponents ridiculed his Damascus vision as nothing but "madness," just as Festus did in hearing Paul's account of his Damascus vision (cf. Acts 26:24-25).

In conclusion, 2 Cor 5:11-21 is highly significant for what it says about Paul's conversion/call experience on the Damascus road, even though the words "conversion," "call," and "Damascus" are nowhere used. But what is more significant for our purposes is that Paul here seems to link his conversion/call experience with his experience of reconciliation — which leads us to believe that the basis for his thinking about reconciliation was his vision of the risen Christ on the road to Damascus. And while all of this is illuminating, there is still more going on "behind the scenes" in 2 Cor 5:11-21. For Paul's allusions to his conversion and his choice of reconciliation terminology are also conditioned by the fact that throughout chapter 5 he is defending his apostolic ministry against the assertions of certain opponents.

5. Paul's Opponents in the Social Context of Corinth

In 2 Cor 5:11-21 Paul defends his apostolic ministry against "those who boast in what is external rather than what is in the heart" (v. 12c). That Paul's Corinthian converts had been influenced by these opponents is evident from such statements as: "What we are is plain to God, and I hope it is also plain to your conscience" (v. 11), and "We are not trying to commend ourselves to you again, but are giving you an opportunity to take pride in us" (v. 12). But who were Paul's opponents at Corinth? And what can we learn about them that would help us understand why Paul alludes to his Damascus experience and why he speaks so forcefully about reconciliation?

The Opponents' Identity

Various passages in 2 Corinthians suggest that Paul's opponents came to Corinth from outside the ranks of the Corinthian believers (11:4) and that they were masquerading as "apostles of Christ" and as "ministers of righteousness" (11:13, 15, 23). They boasted of their Jewish heritage, being Hebrews, Israelites, and descendants of Abraham (11:22). What motivated them to infiltrate Paul's Gentile mission field (10:12-18) was apparently their desire to correct Paul's "gospel" — his preaching about "Jesus," his doctrine of the "Spirit," and his understanding of Christian ministry (11:4-12). Evidently they gloried in the Mosaic covenant and the Torah (3:1–4:6). But they also boasted about their visions and revelations (12:1-10), their signs, wonders, and miracles (12:12), and their knowledge and rhetorical powers (10:5, 10; 11:6, 18).

These characteristics of the opponents have led scholars to differing views about their identity. Some emphasize their corruption of Paul's gospel, believing that they must have been Palestinian Judaizers who, as in the Galatian context, were seeking to force Gentile Christians to conform to the Mosaic covenantal obligations. Others, however, stress the visionary, miraculous, and rhetorical features of the opponents' stance, and so postulate that they were Hellenistic pneumatics or Hellenistic Jewish Christians.

The dual character of these opponents has made identifying them rather difficult. G. Friedrich, for example, noted similarities between the party of Stephen and Philip in Acts, on the one hand, and the opponents of 2 Corinthians, on the other, and so suggested (1) that Paul's Corinthian opponents were Hellenistic Jewish Christians of Stephen's party, and (2) that this group had been driven out of Judea into the Diaspora, with some taking up residence at Corinth ("Gegner des Paulus," 181-215). More recently, P. W. Barnett has argued (1) that Judea had already been considerably Hellenized by AD 44-66, and (2) that during the political upheavals of this period there existed a religious milieu of prophetic inspiration and miraculous signs. So if such pneumatic Palestinians made their way to Corinth, this would account for the Hellenistic features being mixed together with Judaizing tendencies evident in Paul's opponents ("Opposition in Corinth," *Journal for the Study of the New Testament* 22 [1984] 3-17).

Other than listing those features by which he has characterized them, an exact identification of Paul's Corinthian opponents seems unattainable. Nonetheless, it is possible, to some extent, to ascertain their criticisms of Paul, which fall into two categories: (1) criticism of his apostolic qualification, and (2) criticism of his "gospel."

Criticism of Paul's Apostolic Qualification

Paul's opponents took issue with his "qualification" or "competency" (*hikanotēs*) to be an apostle (2 Cor 3:5-6; cf. also 2:6, 16; 1 Cor 15:9). Actually, two matters in this regard seem to have come to the fore, being present in 5:11-13 but also elsewhere in 2 Corinthians. And a third set of more general criticisms appears particularly in chapters 10–13.

The first of these matters is that the opponents denigrated Paul for having no "letter of recommendation" (3:1-6). When Paul says in 5:12, "We are not trying to commend ourselves to you again," he is reacting to his opponents who considered that without the proper documentation Paul had not been officially recognized as an apostle by the (Jerusalem?) church. Instead, they believed that he was a self-made apostle who engaged in self-commendation (cf. 3:1, 5; 4:2; 5:12; 6:4; 10:12, 18; 12:11).

The second matter relating to Paul's apostolic qualification concerned his visionary experience on the road to Damascus. As already noted, Paul's opponents evidently accused him of "being out of his mind" (5:12) for claiming to have seen the risen Christ. No doubt they also cast aspersions on him for having persecuted the church (cf. 1 Cor 15:9) — with suspicions still lingering about his present motives. But the focus of their attack seems to have been the "vision of Christ" to which he kept referring: Was it valid as a criterion for claiming apostleship?

The argument against Paul's apostleship, as based on his Damascus vision, comes to expression in the Pseudo-Clementine *Kerygmata Petrou* (*Preaching of Peter*), where Peter is portrayed as rejecting Paul's appeal to a vision as a means of validating a revelation from God or Christ. In fact, Peter attributes Paul's vision to a demon. Peter's own experience of God's revelation of his Son (cf. Matt 16:13-17) was a revelation between friends and from mouth to mouth. But Peter in the *Kerygmata Petrou* is presented as claiming that visions reveal only God's wrath, for visions are a means of revelation to an "enemy" (cf. Num 11:6-9). So Peter concludes:

> And if our Jesus appeared to you also and became known in a vision and met you as angry with an enemy, yet he has spoken only through visions and dreams or through external revelations. But can anyone be made competent to teach through a vision? And if your opinion is, 'That is possible', why then did our teacher spend a whole year with us who were awake? . . . But if you were visited by him [the Lord Jesus] for a space of an hour and were instructed by him, and thereby have become an apostle, then proclaim his words, expound what he has taught, be a friend to his apostles and do not contend with me, who am his confidant. . . . But if you really desire to cooperate with the truth, then learn first from us what we have learned from him and, as a learner of the truth, become a fellow-worker with us. (H XVII 19.1-7; trans. E. Hennecke, *New Testament Apocrypha*, ed. W. Schneemelcher, trans. R. McL. Wilson [London: Lutterworth, 1965] 2.123)

If Paul's opponents were somehow connected with Peter, and if the *Kerygmata Petrou* genuinely reflects a Petrine tradition, then the attack on Paul's visionary experience could be legitimately traced to a Petrine faction at Corinth. But even if we cannot be certain of either of these scenarios, this material from the *Kerygmata Petrou* still adds support to the suggestion that the Jewish Christian community at Corinth disputed Paul's claim to apostleship on the basis of his visionary revelation.

Even prior to the writing of 2 Corinthians, however, two passages in 1 Corinthians, namely, 9:1-3 and 15:8-10, give evidence that Paul's opponents had disputed his claim to apostleship on the basis of his Damascus revelation. Both passages imply that the opponents were not willing to grant his vision of the risen Lord as being equal to the resurrection appearances of the risen Lord to his (true) apostles. 1 Cor 15:8-10 is distinctive in that only here does Paul apologetically refer to his past persecution of the church, explicitly admitting it as his guilt, and claim apostleship alongside the other apostles as one who had seen the risen Christ (though see also 1 Tim 1:12-14). While Paul accepts criticism for his past persecution, stressing that God's grace had effected a dramatic change in his life, he adamantly refuses to give in to arguments against his apostolic authority. So the opponents' dispute about Paul's apostleship, as seen in 2 Cor 2:14–7:4, appears to have been merely a continuation of what had already existed at the time when 1 Corinthians was written.

A third set of criticisms related to Paul's apostolic qualifications appears in chapters 10–13, which catalogue a number of points that were likely used against Paul: (1) that he was "timid" when face to face, but "bold" when away (10:1); (2) that he was "weak" in general (11:21, 29, 30; 12:9-10; 13:3-4, 9); (3) that he had unimpressive rhetorical powers (10:10; 11:6); (4) that he lacked spiritual visions and revelations (12:1-10); (5) that he lacked the spiritual power to perform signs and wonders and miracles (12:12); and (6) that he made a living with his own hands rather than claiming the privilege the Lord had given his apostles to live on the church's support (11:7-12; 12:13-18).

What led Paul to recount these criticisms and to reply to them? Was it because he had to counter his opponents' "glory" christology, on which basis they not only defended their understanding of "glory" apostleship but also discredited Paul's gospel of "Christ crucified" and his apostleship of weakness and suffering? If it were just for that, did he need to admit his mistaken perspective in his pre-conversion days (cf. Breytenbach, *Versöhnung*, 130)? And why did he need to go on recounting that he was made "a new creation," had been "reconciled" to God, and was commissioned with the "ministry/word of reconciliation"? This latter consideration seems to suggest that what really led Paul to this line of apologetic was his opponents' insinuation that in his past as a persecutor of the church he was an enemy of Jesus Christ and of God, as well as their rejection of his claim to apostleship on the basis of the Damascus revelation of Christ (cf. 1 Cor 9.1; 15.8-10; so Friedrich, "Gegner des Paulus," 214; Breytenbach, *Versöhnung*, 130).

Criticism of Paul's Gospel

A second major criticism of Paul concerned his "gospel." The opponents criticized his gospel as being "veiled" (2 Cor 4:3). From Paul's apology in 11:4 it is clear that they were preaching "another gospel" and "another Jesus" — at least from Paul's perspective.

Two other passages taken together, namely, 4:10-14 and 5:14-21, shed some light on the nature of the opponents' "gospel." First, we should note the repeated use of the singular name "Jesus," without the title "Christ," in

4:10-14 (six times; cf. also 4:5), in contrast to the repeated use of "Christ" in 5:14-21 (seven times). The former usage is unusual. But it is even more unusual in a passage on the death of Jesus, where the title "Christ" is normally used. A comparison of these verses with Gal 6:17 ("I bear on my body the marks of Jesus") and 1 Thess 4:14 ("We believe that Jesus died and rose again"), where "Jesus" also appears without "Christ" in a passage on Jesus' death, suggests that Paul is thinking of the historical Jesus and the historical event of his death. But of more significance for us here is that Paul's unusual usage of "Jesus" alone in 4:10-14 seems to reflect the *language of his opponents,* who lauded the historical Jesus but attached a deficient interpretation to his death.

For Paul, the meaning of "Jesus" was determined entirely by his vicarious death and resurrection, something his opponents apparently rejected since they preached "another Jesus." In 4:10-14, therefore, Paul corrects his opponents' misinterpretation of "Jesus," and then in 5:14-21 he expresses the true significance of Jesus' death using the title "Christ" throughout. Two powerful formulations in these two passages attest to Paul's view of Christ's death: "We always carry around in our body the dying *(nekrōsis)* of Jesus, so that the life of Jesus may also be revealed in our body" (4:10), and "God made him who had no sin to be sin for us" (5:21). It is probable, then, that Paul's opponents rejected what was so central to Paul — that is, the vicarious death of Jesus. And this is what, as noted earlier, was revealed to Paul on the Damascus road (cf. 5:13-15).

The opponents' deficient interpretation of Christ's death also appears to be the focus of Paul's comments in the difficult text of 5:16. Here Paul seems implicitly to criticize that christology as "knowing Christ according to the flesh." It is now commonly agreed that the phrase "according to the flesh" *(kata sarka)* in 5:16 is an adverbial phrase modifying the verbs in that verse, and that Paul is here talking about knowing or estimating Christ according to a "fleshly" criterion or from a "fleshly" perspective. But what exactly is meant by this "fleshly" perspective? Since the phrase "to boast according to the flesh" *(kata sarka)* in 11:18 seems to correspond to the phrase "to boast in face" *(en prosōpǭ)* in 5:12, "according to the flesh" likely has to do with an emphasis on outward appearance. Moreover, in 11:18ff. Paul specifies what he means by his opponents' "boasting according to the flesh," for he implies that they were boasting about being Hebrews, Israelites, and Abraham's descendants (11:22), about their apostolic accomplishments (11:23), and about their visions and revelations (12:1). These reasons for boasting again suggest that "according to the flesh" refers to a perspective that values impressive external appearances — particularly with regard to spectacular charismatic manifestations.

Paul's statements here remind us of Phil 3:2-10, where he also accuses his opponents of having "confidence in the flesh" *(en sarki)* on the ground of their being Israelites, Hebrews, etc. And in Phil 3:2-10, as in 2 Cor 5:11-21, Paul contrasts a "fleshly" perspective with a perspective that is determined by the knowledge of Christ as one who died and rose again (cf. also Gal 6:12-16). So, again, it seems that "according to the flesh" in 5:16 refers to a human perspective that bases value on Jewish particularism (cf. also Rom 4:1; 9:3-5; 1 Cor 10:18; Gal 4:21ff.). And the opponents' boasting of the Mosaic covenant, against which Paul has just argued in chapter 3, supports this reading.

What, then, was the christology of the opponents that Paul implicitly designated "according to the flesh"? As already noted, their emphasis on the name "Jesus" rather than on his atoning death seems to suggest that they focused on the historical Jesus. In view of their stress on the charismatic gifts of visions and miracles, it is possible that they proclaimed Jesus mainly as a powerful miracle-worker (so Georgi, *Gegner des Paulus*, 254ff., 290ff.). Likewise, in view of their emphasis on the glory of the Mosaic ministry (3:7-18), they may have preached Jesus more specifically as the second Moses or the eschatological prophet like Moses (cf. Deut 18:15; so Friedrich, "Gegner des Paulus," 191, 204). Or, in view of their Jewish nationalistic emphasis, they may even have presented Jesus as the Davidic national Messiah (so F. F. Bruce, *Paul and Jesus* [Grand Rapids: Baker, 1974] 22-25). Whatever may have been the case, all of their perspectives about Jesus, in Paul's view, were still merely human, earthly, and entirely external in orientation — and so were on the same level as his pre-conversion estimation of Christ.

At his conversion, as stated in 5:14, Paul had "reached the conclusion" *(krinantas touto)* that Jesus' messianic work consisted in his vicarious death for all. Thus while in v. 16 Paul does not set out his new and correct estimation of Christ, this has already been given in vv. 14-15 and is recapitulated in v. 21. Paul's apologetic tone in 5:16, however, is evident in his repeated use of the particle "now" *(nyn)* and his use of the conditional phrase "even though" *(ei kai)*, both of which indicate a turning point in his perspective about Christ in contrast to his opponents who maintained a "fleshly" perspective.

6. Paul's Apologetic Response to His Opponents

Once the social context of 2 Cor 5:11-21 has been determined, it is not difficult to reconstruct the background and purpose for Paul's *apologia* and to appreciate the function of the metaphor "reconciliation" in that *apologia.*

Though Paul does not explicitly mention his past hostility to Christ and the church in 2 Cor 5:11-21, he plainly acknowledged it earlier in 1 Cor 15:9. And the thought is implicit in his allusions to his Damascus experience throughout 2 Cor 5:11-21. For in verse 16b he explains that he had misjudged Christ, knowing him only from a "fleshly" or earthly perspective. Like his contemporary Jewish colleagues, he had been a zealous Pharisee (Phil 3:5) and probably expected a nationalistic Messiah like David or Moses. From such a vantage point, Jesus of Nazareth could not have been the Messiah. His death by crucifixion only indicated that he had been accursed by God (Deut 21:23; Gal 3:13; 1 Cor 12:3). So Paul became hostile to Jesus and persecuted his followers. On the road to Damascus, however, God revealed the crucified Jesus to be, indeed, both Messiah and Lord. This experience led Paul to a new "judgment" about Jesus Christ, specifically, that he died vicariously for the sins of humanity and was raised by God from the dead (2 Cor 5:14-15, 21).

This conversion gave Paul not only new knowledge about Christ (5:16), but also a sense that he had come to be "in Christ" and was "a new creation" (5:17). Unlike the Jewish conception of "new creation," which was thought to be brought about annually on the Day of Atonement, God's eschatological act of new creation through his Messiah had individual application to Paul himself. Paul's point, therefore, in recounting his Damascus conversion in terms of being "a new creation" was to underscore his liberation and forgiveness from the burden of his past hostility to Christ and the church, and so to imply to his opponents that their insinuations about his past were futile. Perhaps when Paul confessed his new status in Christ (5:17b) he was thinking of a text like Isa 43:18-19 (LXX): "Do not remember the former things, and do not discuss *the old things.* Behold I make *new things*" (also Isa 66:17; cf. Beale, "Old Testament Background," 553-54).

It is in this context of "new things" that Paul introduces the concept of reconciliation (5:18-21). The Jewish tradition of applying the metaphor of "new creation" to the idea of atonement on the Day of Atonement may stand in the background. But what directly leads Paul to introduce the idea of reconciliation here is his opponents' criticism of his past opposition to Christ and his church, which formed part of their repudiation of his apostolic claim. Against such a criticism Paul asserts that God forgave him on the Damascus road, reconciling him to himself. Paul was, indeed, an enemy of Christ and of God. But God reconciled his enemy Paul to himself.

Though Paul does not use the term "enemy" in 2 Cor 5:11-21, it appears in Rom 5:8-11 where "sinners" and "reconciliation" appear: "While we were still sinners, Christ died for us. . . . For if, when we were enemies, we were reconciled to God through the death of his Son, how much more, having been reconciled, shall we be saved through his life!" Thus Paul regarded sinners as "enemies" of God.

Yet there seems to be more than a hint of this idea in 2 Cor 5:21, even though "enemies" is lacking. For the statement here is about God making Christ, who had no sin, to be sin for us, so that in Christ we might become the righteousness of God. This statement is often seen in terms of an "exchange curse" — that is, that the sinless Christ took humanity's sin in exchange for which sinful humanity receives the righteousness of God. But in the context of Paul's discussion of reconciliation, Paul also means to suggest that the purpose of divine reconciliation was to bring together sinners and a righteous God, which, of course, was accomplished through "him who had no sin." The gap between sinful humanity and a righteous God that is implied here, therefore, is not far from the idea of "enmity between God and humanity." In Rom 11:28, Jews who reject the gospel are "enemies" of God; in Phil 3:18, those who do not live in a manner consistent with the gospel are "enemies of the cross of Christ." So in light of such descriptions, it is likely that Paul also viewed his own pre-conversion life of hostility to Christ as being at "enmity" with God.

That Paul took the concept of enmity with God quite literally seems to be suggested by the imagery in 2 Cor 2:14 of "being led in a triumphal procession" *(thriambeuesthai)*. This description of the Christian life comes from Roman military practice where a general would lead his conquered enemies as slaves in a triumphal procession through the city, usually to their death. So Paul's use of this imagery presupposes his own conversion, which he understood to be his defeat as an "enemy" of God and his having been captured as a "slave" of Christ (cf. Hafemann, *Suffering and Ministry,* 31-32).

As with any metaphor, however, this image can be taken only so far by way of analogy. For Paul is no longer God's enemy. On the Damascus road God reconciled him to himself. Nevertheless, the military imagery of "being led in a triumphal procession" seems to confirm that Paul's use of reconciliation terminology in 2 Cor 5:18-21 is, as Breytenbach insists, derived from — or, at least, echoes — its usual military-diplomatic usage in the Greco-Roman world (*Versöhnung*, 40-83).

In 2 Cor 5:18-21, therefore, Paul argues (against his opponents) not only that he is now a "reconciled enemy," but also that through God's grace he has been appointed as an "ambassador" for Christ and has been sent to the rebellious world to "petition" and "appeal" that people be "reconciled to God" (v. 20). Thus Paul claims that God gave him the "ministry of reconciliation" and entrusted him with the "message of reconciliation" (vv. 18-19).

All of this "reconciliation talk" served to combat the criticism of Paul's opponents who referred to his past in order to dispute his claim to apostleship on the basis of God's Damascus call. How could they go on criticizing his past when God had conquered him as an enemy and reconciled him to himself? And how could they go on disputing his apostleship when God's "reconciliation" and "appointment" of him as an "ambassador of reconciliation" illustrated so perfectly the gospel of reconciliation that was accomplished through Christ's atoning death?

7. Conclusion

It is impossible to determine whether Paul developed his soteriological concept of reconciliation at the time of his writing 2 Corinthians or prior to that time. In any case, it is most likely that his use of the metaphor of reconciliation grew out of his own theological reflections on his Damascus road conversion experience. This thesis explains, more plausibly than any other, the fundamental innovation that Paul made in the Jewish idea of reconciliation — that is, that it is not human beings who reconcile an angry God to themselves through their prayers, repentance, or good works; rather, it is God who reconciles human beings to himself through the atoning death of Jesus Christ. For on the Damascus road, Paul, who came to see himself as God's enemy in his activities before Damascus, experienced God's reconciling action, which brought forgiveness of sins and the making of a new creation by his grace.

But after his personal revelatory experience, Paul no doubt felt the need to substantiate his new understanding of God's work through the

Scriptures. For this he turned to the fourth Servant Song of Isaiah 52–53, which is a marvelous prophecy of God's work of reconciling sinners through the vicarious death of Christ. So, as Otfried Hofius, Otto Betz, and Gregory Beale have clearly demonstrated, Paul's presentation in 2 Cor 5:11-21 bears all of the marks of his reflection on Christ and God's work in him in the light of that Servant Song.

In addition to Scripture, Paul could very well also have been influenced in his understanding of reconciliation by his own reflections on the church's Jesus tradition, which included such teachings as Jesus' offer of forgiveness to sinners on God's behalf, his parable of the prodigal son who received forgiveness, and his eucharistic saying about the blood of the covenant poured out for the forgiveness of sins.

In this way, the metaphor of reconciliation, which is one of the most significant categories of preaching the gospel of Christ, came into being. How its effectiveness as a soteriological category has been rediscovered in recent theology is a topic for another study. If the present thesis is correct, the way in which Paul developed the doctrine of reconciliation has a paradigmatic significance for our theologizing today. For as our own personal experience of being encountered by Christ leads us to confirm the truth of the apostolic kerygma, we will interpret that kergyma by means of a new category drawn from our own experience, thereby making the kerygma more relevant to our situation today. Furthermore, to substantiate that new interpretive category, we will turn not only to the Old Testament but also to the traditional materials that come from Jesus.

Selected Bibliography

Beale, G. K. "The Old Testament Background of Reconciliation in 2 Corinthians 5–7 and Its Bearing on the Literary Problem of 2 Corinthians 6.14–7.1." *New Testament Studies* 35 (1989) 550-81.

Betz, O. "Fleischliche und 'geistliche' Christuserkenntnis nach 2. Korinther 5,16." *Theologische Beiträge* 14 (1983) 167-79. Reprinted in his *Jesus, der Herr der Kirche: Aufsätze zur biblischen Theologie II*. Tübingen: Mohr-Siebeck, 1990, 114-28.

Bieringer, R. "2 Korinther 5,19a und die Versöhnung der Welt." *Ephemerides Theologicae Lovanienses* 63 (1987). Reprinted in R. Bieringer and J. Lambrecht, *Studies on 2 Corinthians*. Leuven: Leuven University Press, 1994, 429-59.

Breytenbach, C. *Versöhnung. Eine Studie zur paulinischen Soteriologie.* Neukirchen-Vluyn: Neukirchener Verlag, 1989.

Friedrich, G. "Die Gegner des Paulus im 2. Korintherbrief." In *Abraham unser Vater: Juden und Christen im Gespräch über die Bibel. Festschrift für Otto Michel zum 60. Geburtstag,* ed. O. Betz et al. Leiden: Brill, 1963, 181-215.

Furnish, V. *II Corinthians.* Garden City, NY: Doubleday, 1984.

Georgi, D. *Die Gegner des Paulus im 2. Korintherbrief.* Neukirchen-Vluyn: Neukirchener Verlag, 1964.

Goppelt, L. *Christologie und Ethik.* Göttingen: Vandenhoeck & Ruprecht, 1969.

Hafemann, S. J. *Suffering and Ministry in the Spirit. An Exegetical Study of 2 Cor. 2:14–3:3 within the Context of the Corinthian Correspondence.* Tübingen: Mohr-Siebeck, 1986; Grand Rapids: Eerdmans, 1990.

Hofius, O. "Erwägungen zur Gestalt und Herkunft des paulinischen Versöhnungsgedankens." *Zeitschrift für Theologie und Kirche* 77 (1980) 186-99. Reprinted in his *Paulusstudien,* 1-14. Tübingen: Mohr-Siebeck, 1989.

————. " 'Gott hat unter uns aufgerichtet das Wort von der Versöhnung' (2 Kor 5,19)." *Zeitschrift für die Neutestamentliche Wissenschaft* 71 (1980) 3-20. Reprinted in his *Paulusstudien,* 15-32. Tübingen: Mohr-Siebeck, 1989.

Kim, S. *The Origin of Paul's Gospel.* Grand Rapids: Eerdmans, 1982; 2d ed. Tübingen: Mohr-Siebeck, 1984.

Marshall, I. H. "The Meaning of 'Reconciliation.'" In *Unity and Diversity in New Testament Theology: Essays in Honor of G. E. Ladd,* ed. R. Guelich. Grand Rapids: Eerdmans, 1978, 117-32.

Martin, R. P. *Reconciliation: A Study of Paul's Theology.* Atlanta: John Knox, 1981.

Stuhlmacher, P. *Biblische Theologie des Neuen Testaments. Band I: Grundlegung von Jesus zu Paulus.* Göttingen: Vandenhoeck & Ruprecht, 1992.

Thrall, M. E. *The Second Epistle to the Corinthians,* vol. 1. Edinburgh: Clark, 1994.

Contours of Covenant Theology in the Post-Conversion Paul

BRUCE W. LONGENECKER

1. Introduction

The extent to which Paul should be considered a covenant theologian is a matter of dispute. Some believe "covenant" to be inadequate as a description of both Paul's theological perspective and the subject of his deliberations. Others find his basic convictions and theological reflections to be both animated and permeated by covenantal structures and content. Still others argue that the truth lies somewhere in-between.

While this matter cannot be treated fully here, two theses seem fairly obvious and so commend themselves widely. First, while Paul after his conversion drew on a wide range of motifs, traditions, and stories in his theological deliberations, a theology of God's covenant relationship with Israel was certainly an important theological resource — indeed, in some contexts a primary resource for his thought and expression. Second, if this was the case for Paul after his encounter with the risen Christ, no doubt it would not have been any less so for him prior to that encounter. With some confidence, therefore, one can posit that God's covenant relationship with Israel had been the principal focus of Paul's theological reflection and practical instruction prior to his conversion.

My investigation of Paul's use of covenantal motifs and theology in his letters will focus on a number of case studies, almost in snapshot fashion. I will not attempt to trace out Paul's use of the term "covenant" itself, as found in Rom 9:4; 11:27; 1 Cor 11:25; 2 Cor 3:6, 14; Gal 3:15, 17; 4:24; and Eph 2:12. That has been adequately done by others (e.g., Campbell, "Covenant and New Covenant"). Nor is it my intention to examine specifically the question of "Israel" in Paul's letters. Rather, my investigation will seek to identify (1) ways in which Paul's theological reflection takes its cues from the arena of covenant theology, and (2) how Paul revised and reformulated those covenantal motifs in the light of his conversion.

My starting point for this essay will be an analysis of 1 Cor 8:6. For in that single verse Paul exhibits in remarkable fashion how a central strand of traditional Jewish covenant theology has been reworked in the light of his own Christian convictions. From there I will move on to examine Paul's reformulation of covenantal motifs, using Galatians and Romans as the primary texts and focusing on a number of other matters where covenantal motifs play an important role.

2. The Covenant God and Jesus the Lord

In any investigation of how Paul's understanding of the covenant was affected by his conversion, we do well first to consider 1 Cor 8:6. Here Paul writes that "for us"

> there is one God, the Father,
> > from whom are all things
> > and for whom we are;
> and there is one Lord, Jesus Christ,
> > through whom are all things
> > and through whom we are.

This verse exhibits an almost poetic quality, due especially to a structure in which its first and second halves operate in balanced parallel. Such careful crafting is important to note, since it follows from and gives expression to a bold conviction about the covenant God of Israel, as we will see.

Paul's affirmation that there is but "one God" (cf. also v. 4) lies at the heart of Jewish monotheistic faith and practice, in contrast to beliefs within the pagan world that posited (in a variety of heavenly scenarios) a plethora of divinities, each of whom was deemed worthy of allegiance for one reason or another. Such a plethora of gods, of course, could be conceived of as a

126

form of monotheism, in that the various divinities were all thought to be aspects of the ultimate divinity. But monotheism of this sort was a far cry from Jewish monotheism (cf. Wright, *People of God*, 248-59).

Most forms of Judaism have assumed a fundamental theological connection between monotheism and election, with the confession that there is one, sovereign, and universal God being seen to go hand in hand with the affirmation that that same God was Israel's God, who had chosen her to be his people. This connection is evident in the *Shema* — the traditional prayer recited morning and evening by pious Jews, which takes its name from the Hebrew word *šema'* ("Hear") that begins Deut 6:4 and is constructed from Deut 6:4-9; 11:13-21; and Num 15:37-41. Deut 6:4 reads: "Hear, Israel, the LORD, our God, the Lord is one." Not only is this one God identified as Israel's own God ("the LORD, our God"), but there immediately follows the injunction to love God and obey his commandments in order that Israel might live pleasingly before him, in distinction from the other nations (Deut 6:5ff.). Monotheism (i.e., the God whom Israel worships is "one") and covenant election (i.e., God is "our God," we are his people) were, therefore, integrally associated in the Jewish piety of Paul's day.

With this background in mind, Paul's affirmation of monotheism in 1 Cor 8:6 is notable for two reasons. First, Paul's starting point in this pastoral situation is the central theological affirmation of Jewish covenant theology: God is one. This is especially significant since Paul was addressing a community made up mostly of Gentiles who had been immersed in paganism only a few years earlier. Thus when considering the practical needs of these recently converted Gentiles in relation to food sacrificed to idols and other "so-called gods" (1 Corinthians 8–10), Paul takes his theological stand in familiar territory — that is, in a theology of the covenant, creator God.

Second, in this verse Paul refashions, in the light of Christ, the traditional portrait of the one, sovereign, and covenant God. The *Shema* is reconfigured according to Christian convictions about the centrality of Christ. Thus "Jesus Christ" appears at the heart of an axiomatic Jewish affirmation concerning God, who is known as the sovereign creator of the world and the one who has elected Israel in covenant relationship. Before his conversion, Paul would have prayed the *Shema* every day and understood "God" and "LORD" as two terms referring to Israel's sovereign and covenant God. At some point after his conversion, however, Paul began to understand all this differently, taking "God" as referring to "the Father" and

"Lord" as referring to "Jesus Christ" (cf. esp. Phil 2:9-11; so also throughout the Pauline corpus).

In effect, then, the *Shema* was split into two parts, with the second of those parts focusing on Jesus Christ. And if the *Shema* had the practical effect of bolstering one's commitment to Israel's sovereign God and consolidating a consciousness of one's membership within God's chosen people, Paul's revised and "Christianized" form of that most distinctive Jewish confession has the effect of transforming one's awareness of God and his people, with Jesus Christ as the focal point of the whole theological and corporate enterprise. Likewise, this same kind of transformation is evident in other contexts in Paul's writings — as, for example, in Rom 3:29-30 where he again cites the *Shema* in a way that displaces Jewish ethnocentrism (cf. also Gal 3:20).

Much more could be said about 1 Cor 8:6. In particular, the relationship between "God the Father" and "Lord Jesus Christ," both in this passage and elsewhere in the New Testament, would require greater articulation and more careful nuancing (see further Wright, *Climax of the Covenant*, 120-36; also more broadly Hurtado, *One God, One Lord*). The point here is simply that in this passage there appears a dramatic revision of a cardinal tenet in the traditional Jewish understanding of the God of the covenant — with the essence of that revision being that Jesus of Nazareth, a Judean itinerant teacher of humble origin and means, who died a humiliating and disgraceful death, is referred to, in a text written only twenty-five years (or so) after his crucifixion, in a fashion that puts him at the center of traditional Jewish devotion to the sovereign God of the covenant.

3. Paul's Reformulation of Covenantal Motifs

A number of other "case studies" where covenantal motifs play an important role in Paul's thought and expression need also to be noted. In the main, these appear in Galatians and Romans. And all of them have to do, in one way or another, with covenant identity and lifestyle vis-à-vis relationship with the one whom Paul came to know in his conversion as the risen Lord.

The Marks of Covenant Identity

The literature of Early Judaism demonstrates repeatedly, though not necessarily in every case, that an awareness of Israel as God's covenant people was the principal foundation on which much of Jewish thought and practice was based. Definitions of covenant membership, however, varied from one situation to the next, and the notion of covenant did not function in the same way or mean the same thing across the spectrum of Early Judaism. That God had called unto himself a people was rarely questioned. But how that people was to be identified became a pressing matter of debate and interpretation.

Those who constituted his people identified themselves by a number of expressions, such as "the Elect," "the Saints," "the Sons of Light," etc. One term that is especially important in Paul's letters in this regard is "righteousness" *(dikaiosynē)* and its cognates ("the righteous," etc.). This term, firmly rooted in the soil of Jewish covenant theology, is a shorthand way of speaking about membership within God's covenant people (Hays, "Justification"). Moreover, when "righteousness" or "righteous" is ascribed to God, it connotes God's fidelity to his covenant promises (as in the Psalms and Deutero-Isaiah; cf. Zech 8:8; *Jubilees* 1:5-6; see Dunn, *Romans,* 1.40-42) — that is, his saving activity in relation to his people, which ultimately is to result in the establishment of his eschatological reign of justice.

A text like Paul's letter to the Galatians depicts the way in which many early Christians understood the notion of covenant membership or "righteousness." For just as pious Jews of the Maccabean period viewed circumcision and food laws to be fundamental test cases of covenant fidelity in the face of intruding Hellenism (cf. 1 Maccabees 1:60-63), so some first-generation Christians thought such "nomistic" practices as circumcision (Gal 2:2-10; 5:2-11; 6:12-15), Jewish dietary observances (2:11-14), and Jewish festivals (4:10) to be necessary for full participation in the covenant. Paul himself seems to have held similar convictions prior to his encounter with Christ — or so we are led to believe from the depictions of his "previous way of life within Judaism" in Gal 1:13-14 and Phil 3:4-6, with both passages highlighting his abundant "zeal" that led him to "excel in Judaism" and to "persecute the church of God." Prior to his conversion, it seems, Paul understood righteousness, or membership within the covenant people of God, to be a matter of observing the law and considered himself to have been blameless in observing that law (so Phil. 3:6, where "blameless" does not mean "morally perfect").

A similar constellation of ideas appears in Rom 9:30–10:3, where Paul speaks of Israel's pursuit of the "law of righteousness" (9:31) in connection with their "zeal for God" (10:2) and where he identifies the problem for the people of Israel as residing in their unenlightened efforts to "establish their own righteousness" (10:3). In this passage Paul does not mean to say that Israel's problem was "legalism" in a negative sense of the term — that is, that they were trying by means of strenuous effort to prove their own worthiness before God by performing more good actions than bad actions, thereby putting God under obligation to effect their salvation. In such a legalistic scheme, salvation can be figured out simply with a calculator. But although various forms of legalism have come under attack at numerous times in history — and although Paul's writings have rightly played a healthy part in those attacks — the target of Paul's attack here in Rom 9:30–10:3 seems to have less to do with legalism than with an understanding of the covenant as being the exclusive privilege of the ethnic people of Israel. So, expansively paraphrasing Rom 10:3, we may say that the failure of the people of Israel lay not in some attempt to "justify" themselves by legalistic means, but in their attempt to establish a righteousness that was exclusively theirs, thereby defining covenant membership along national lines.

The word "zeal" in Rom 10:2 supports such an understanding, for "zeal" was recognized to have characterized and motivated all of those famous Jews of Israel's history who sought to preserve — even to the point of death and against the influence of external pagan forces — the distinctiveness of Israel's covenant identity in conformity to the law (cf. Num 25:10-13, esp. v. 11; Judith 9:4; *Jubilees* 30:1-20, esp. v. 18; Sirach 45:23-24; 1 Maccabees 2:19-28, esp. vv. 24, 26-27; 2:49-68, esp. vv. 50, 54, 58; Josephus, *Jewish Antiquities* 12.271; 4 Maccabees 18:12). Zeal of this sort is sometimes glossed further as "zeal for the Law." It is also frequently associated with issues of Israel's righteousness, and so has to do with the nation's fidelity to God in covenant relationship by preserving Israel's ethnic character in conformity to the law.

Accordingly, "righteousness," "law," and "zeal" form a self-defining cluster of concepts that usually expresses an understanding of the covenant in terms of ethnic identity. This helps to explain Paul's meaning when he uses the same terms to depict both Israel's unenlightened view (Rom 9:31–10:3) and his own pre-Christian view (Gal 1:13-14; Phil 3:4-6; for further discussions of Jewish covenantalism as the primary background of Paul's thoughts, see Dunn, "Justice of God"; also my *Eschatology and the Covenant*, 23-35.)

This matter of covenant membership is frequently addressed in Paul's letters in connection with the notion of "righteousness." In his Christian career, however, Paul maintained a different view of covenant membership than had previously been the case, and he often addressed the matter by means of a contrast between "works of the law" and "faith." The meaning of the phrase "works of the law" (Gal 2:16; 3:2, 5, 10; Rom 3:20, 28) has been a matter of some dispute. It seems best, however, to take it as a shorthand way of signifying the requirements of the law on those who would be God's covenant people — that is, the legal obligations placed on Israel as a demonstration of her covenant fidelity before God, which served to preserve her identity as distinct from other nations. The Qumran community referred to "works of the law" (and related terms) in a similar fashion, although nuancing that expression in a more restricted sense to cohere with its own sectarian self-definition (cf. 1QS 5:21, 23; 6:18; 4QFlor 1:7; 4QMMT 113). Those who propagated the covenantal necessity of "works of the law" would have pointed to various Old Testament passages to support their view, such as Exod 19:5-6, where God directs Israel:

> If you obey me fully and keep my covenant, then out of all the nations you will be my treasured possession. Although the whole earth is mine, you will be for me a kingdom of priests and a holy nation.

A similar sentiment appears repeatedly throughout the Old Testament (e.g., Lev 20:26; Deut 7:6; 14:2, 21; 26:19; 28:9-14; 1 Kgs 8:53) and in other Jewish writings.

Such a view of the identity of the covenant people seems to have been adopted by some of the first Christians, who considered a proper lifestyle before God to be associated with a distinctively Jewish lifestyle. The concern of some Christians "to separate" themselves *(aphōrizein,* Gal 2:12) and "to live as Jews" *(Ioudaizein,* Gal 2:14) is challenged by Paul's consistent emphasis on "faith" as the exclusive mark of the true heirs of Abraham. Nomistic practices, which previously had marked out the identity of God's covenant people along ethnic lines, are relativized in the light of Christ. The people of God are now to be identified exclusively by their faith — a faith evident already in Abraham (Rom 4:1-24; Gal 3:6-9) and enlivened more recently by God's activity in Christ. The covenant people of God are to comprise a diverse and worldwide assembly identified by their faith in Christ and united in him. To cite only one of many passages to this effect, Rom 3:21-22 is clear: "The covenant righteousness of God *(dikaiosynē theou)* has now been manifest apart from the law . . . to all who have faith."

This group of people, identified by faith, inherits a variety of designations that connote its identity as the covenant people of God. These designations include such expressions as:

1. "the church of God" (*hē ekklēsia tou theou,* Gal 1:13; *ekklēsia,* from the Greek *kalein,* "to call," appears throughout the LXX in reference to the called/elected congregation of Israel; see Deut 23:2; 1 Chr 28:8; Neh 13:1; Mic 2:5; etc.);
2. "the [true] circumcision" (Phil 3:3; cf. Rom 2:25-29);
3. "sons of God" (e.g., Rom 8:14-15; Gal 3:26; 4:6-7; etc.; on "sonship" as a designation of Israel or the righteous remnant of Israel, see Rom 9:4; Exod 4:22-23; Deut 14:1; Jer 3:22; 31:9, 20; Hos 11:1; Wisdom of Solomon 18:13; *Psalms of Solomon* 17:26-27; 18:4; *Sibylline Oracles* 3.702; etc.); and,
4. "the Israel of God" (Gal 6:16, though this is a disputed reading of that verse; the term is consistently applied to the ethnic people [or a subgroup thereof] in Romans 9–11).

Prior to his encounter with the risen Lord, Paul would have reserved designations of this sort for (the faithful members of) ethnic Israel. In the wake of that encounter, however, he viewed such terms as being applicable to the new social group of those who have faith in God apart from ethnic identity.

Jesus and Covenant Faithfulness

If faith excludes "works of the law," how is it that faith itself leads to "righteousness," understood as "covenant membership"? What are the mechanics involved that allowed Paul to relate faith and covenant righteousness?

This matter can be addressed by considering the Greek phrase *pistis Christou* (and its variations), the meaning of which has been, of late, extensively debated. Many take *Christou* to be an objective genitive, thereby translating the phrase "faith *in* Christ." A growing number of scholars, however, understand *Christou* to be a subjective genitive, thereby translating the phrase "the faith/faithfulness *of* Christ." The intricacies of this issue are complex and cannot be considered here (cf., e.g., Hays, *Faith of Jesus Christ;* also others cited in my "Defining the Faithful Character"). In my opinion, it is better to take the phrase to refer to "the faithfulness of Christ" and to see it playing an important role in Paul's Christianized form of covenant theology.

While Paul often speaks of the importance of faith in his letters, at times he also speaks of faith in relation to the faithfulness of Christ. So, for instance, in a passage already cited, Paul writes in Rom 3:21-22: "The covenant faithfulness *(dikaiosynē)* of God has now been manifested apart from law . . . through *the faithfulness of Jesus Christ* to all who *believe*." This translation understands Paul to be saying that God's faithfulness to his covenant promises (i.e., his righteousness) has been fulfilled in, and operates through, Christ's own faithful life for the benefit of those who have faith.

There is an implicit contrast here with the covenant fidelity of Israel. For throughout Rom 2:17–3:20, one of Paul's concerns is to demonstrate that Israel's corporate life was characterized by "faithlessness" (*apistia,* 3:3) due to her position "under [the power of] sin" (3:9), as was also the case of the Gentiles (cf. 1:18-32). The result of Israel's covenant election (2:17-20) had not been, as it should have been, the affirmation of the sovereignty of God throughout the world, but instead the dishonoring of God and the mockery of his name among the Gentiles (2:23-24). This disastrous result was the outcome of Israel's disobedience (2:21-24) — that is, her lack of covenant fidelity.

In contrast, Jesus' faithfulness serves as the embodiment of covenant fidelity, through which God's covenant fidelity flows to the whole world. So rather than the Gentiles blaspheming the name of God because of Israel's disobedient faithlessness, Gentiles can now enter into the salvation offered by the covenant God of Israel because of the obedient faithfulness of Jesus Christ (cf. Rom 15:8-9).

This might be compared with a long-established (though not unanimously held) Old Testament set of convictions that Israel was to be (1) a light to the Gentiles in testifying to the sovereignty of the God of Israel (cf. Isa 42:6-7; 43:10-21; 44:8; 49:6), (2) the locus of divine splendor in the world (Isa 49:3), and (3) the channel through which all people of the earth would process to worship God in obedience (Isa 2:1-4; Mic 4:1-3; Zech 2:11; 8:20-23; many extrabiblical Jewish sources also depict these same convictions). In the faithful ministry of Jesus, Israel's commission has been fulfilled — salvation is now available to all people through the one who embodies the faithfulness expected of God's covenant people. So, as Paul continues in Rom. 3:25-26 (expansively translated), God has put Jesus forward as:

> an atoning sacrifice through his [Jesus'] faithfulness by means of his blood . . . in order to demonstrate his [God's] own covenant faithfulness *(dikaiosynē)* in the present time of eschatological dawning *(en tō nyn kairō)*, thereby proving that he (God) is faithful *(dikaion)* to his covenant promises and brings into covenant relationship *(dikaiounta)* those who live on the basis of the covenant faithfulness of Jesus *(ton ek pisteōs Iēsou)*.

It is probable that much of this passage stems from a confessional formula that existed within early Christian communities as an expression of their understanding of the ways of God in Christ. Nonetheless, Paul restates that formulaic material here without hesitancy, affirming the conviction of the early Christians concerning the establishment of God's covenant fidelity through Christ's covenant fidelity for the benefit of all who believe (cf. further my "PISTIS in Romans 3.25"). Informing this conviction is a view that can be found in many of the writings of Early Judaism, namely, that the authentic fulfillment of the covenant between God and Israel would result in the eschatological dawning of a rightly ordered world under the sovereignty of Israel's God (cf. Wright, *People of God,* 268-79). So with such an expectation in view, Rom 3:25-26 should be seen as proclaiming that a new world order of divine sovereignty is emerging from the context of Jesus' covenant faithfulness.

A similar view can be found in Gal 2:15-16. References to "righteousness" and its cognates appear here and in the following verses five times (three times in v. 16 and once each in vv. 17 and 21), highlighting how Paul's statements in this passage are set in a covenantal context. Moreover, he writes as if all believers in Christ were agreed that covenant righteousness is through the faithfulness of Jesus Christ. Thus while there were disagreements among Christians in Galatia as to the implications of Christ's work of faithful obedience, all the parties in the dispute affirmed (note the word *eidotes,* "know," in 2:16) that the basics of Christian identity have first and foremost to do with the covenant fidelity of Jesus Christ (*dia pisteōs Iēsou Christou*, "through the faithfulness of Jesus Christ").

Covenant relationship with God, therefore, is operative not by means one's own practice of covenant "works of the law," but through "the faithfulness of Jesus Christ." In Paul's view, Christians participate in Jesus' covenant fidelity simply by faith. This is why Paul says in 2:16b: "we believed in Christ Jesus, in order that his covenant faithfulness might be effective for us." And this same thought appears in Gal 3:22, where God's promise to bless the nations through Abraham (3:15-22) is grounded in the assurance that the promise "has been given through the faithfulness of Jesus, to those who have faith" (*ek pisteōs Iēsou Christou dothē tois pisteuousin*). By faith people enter into covenant relationship with God, which relationship is based on and emerges from Jesus' own covenant faithfulness.

Paul's "faith" language in these verses is fundamentally a language of participation. For just as he speaks of being crucified with the crucified one, of dying with the one who died in order to live with the one who lives, and of "sonship" arising out of participation in the "sonship" of Jesus, so he can talk of participation in the faithfulness of Christ (*pistis Christou*) through faith (*pistis*). If God's in-breaking into the world has emerged from the covenant faithfulness of Christ — with the result of deliverance from "the present evil age" (Gal 1:4) and the establishment of a "new creation" (Gal 6:15) — Christian faith in the faithful Messiah is the means of participation in that eschatological event, with an accompanying anticipation of its future culmination.

Paul's comments in Phil 3:7-9 need also to be noted in this regard. Prior to these verses, Paul has listed reasons why he might boast in his Jewish identity (vv. 4-6). Now, however, he finds these things to be worthless. For now as one who is in Christ, Paul recognizes that he does not have "covenant membership" (*dikaiosynē*) on the basis of the law, but only through "the faithfulness of Christ." This re-interpretation of covenant dynamics focuses on Christ and his faithfulness, in contrast to Paul's previous law observance. A new sphere of existence has emerged (cf. 3:10) that is operative only through Christ — arising out of a faithfulness (i.e., Christ's faithfulness) that qualitatively surpasses all other expressions of covenant faithfulness. In fact, with Christ's faithfulness in view, Paul regards his own faithfulness to the law to be worthless (note the contrast between "blameless" and "rubbish" in vv. 6 and 8) and considers only Christ's faithfulness to be the mark of his covenant membership before God.

Jesus and the Situation of Israel

While Jesus is contrasted with Israel in terms of faithfulness, Paul locates the coming of God's Son within the milieu of Israel's own historical context. Jesus' faithfulness, while distinctive and the locus out of which eschatological transformation arises, transpires not in some sphere beyond Israel's situation but from within it.

Such seems to be the case, for instance, in Gal 3:13-14, where Paul writes: "Christ redeemed us from the curse of the law, having become a curse for us . . . that the blessing of Abraham might come upon the Gentiles in Christ Jesus, that we might receive the promise of the Spirit through faith." While it is not wholly clear just who Paul had in mind when referring to "us" and "we" in this passage, it can be argued that, in the first two cases, he was thinking of Jews who had put their faith in Jesus. If so, these verses envision a scenario in which Christ (1) takes on himself the Jewish condition of being cursed by the law (3:13b), (2) redeems that condition for those who have faith (3:13a), in order that (3) a new age might be established in which salvation is extended to all (3:14; see esp. Donaldson, "'Curse of the Law'"; Scott, "Works of the Law"; and Wright, *Climax of the Covenant,* 137-56).

Gal. 4:4-5 envisages the same kind of process. For in these verses God's eschatological activity is set out in terms of Christ, who "was born under law in order to redeem those under law." God's universal redemption, it seems, required that the Messiah come "under law," where Israel herself had been (3:23; cf. 4:21; 5:18), rectifying that situation (i.e., "to redeem those under law") in order that the effect of Jesus' sonship might be available to others beyond that situation. The situation of Israel, therefore, (1) is the situation into which God's Son was "sent," in order that (2) that same situation might be redeemed, with the result that (3) salvation might be offered on a universal scale, beyond the boundaries of the people of Israel.

Perhaps Paul has the same thing in mind when he writes in Rom 15:8-9: "Christ has become a servant of the circumcised to reveal the covenant trustworthiness of God *(alētheias theou),* in order to confirm the promises given to the patriarchs, and in order that the Gentiles might glorify God for his mercy." The extension of God's covenant faithfulness to the Gentiles has passed through, by necessity, the terrain of Israel, whose "servant" Jesus became.

These three passages cohere around a common emphasis: the situation of the people of Israel is the historical context out of which, once that situation has been redeemed, a new eschatological sphere of existence arises. The redemption of Israel's situation is the prerequisite for the expansion of salvation to an unlimited, universal extent. These passages may not explicitly outline a progressive development in salvation history that leads up to a final eschatological conclusion in Christ. They do, however, set out a scenario in which Israel's situation has been, and needed to be, first of all addressed and remedied. So Gal 4:4-5 seems to have been constructed along the lines of a carefully balanced *chiasmus* in which the structural focus and centerpiece is Israel — that is, first Israel's situation (B) and then Israel's redemption (B¹):

A   God sent his *Son,* born of a woman
B   born under the *law*
B¹ in order that he might redeem those under the *law*
A¹ in order that we might receive adoption as *sons*

God's salvation in Christ did not avoid, trivialize, or render irrelevant Israel's situation. Instead, the situation of Israel was the arena wherein God's transforming power was initially operative before being extended to universal proportions. The rectification of Israel's predicament stands as the prerequisite for the inauguration of the "new creation." God's unrestricted salvation begins in and issues from Israel's own situation. This was the place where God had already been at work (e.g., in giving the law), and it became the locus for God's eschatological initiative (i.e., in sending his Son) in order to transform Israel's situation and inaugurate a new age. Eschatological deliverance from "the present evil age" (Gal 1:4) required the metamorphosis and transformation of Israel's situation, rather than its substitution or displacement.

From what we know of Jewish covenant expectations of the day (cf., e.g., Wright, *People of God,* 268-79, 331-34), it is likely that, in his pre-Christian career, Paul would have maintained this same inseparable connection between the restoration of Israel and the emerging of the eschatological age. After his conversion, however, Paul's expectations in relation to these two intertwined phenomena were refocused. For after his conversion he focused on Jesus Christ as the risen Lord who had effected the means for Israel's redemption and so inaugurated a new age of salvation. In this way, God's promises to Israel "find their 'Yes' in him" (2 Cor 1:20).

Further Modifications in Covenant Definition

The distinctiveness of Paul's Christian covenant theology vis-à-vis his pre-Christian theology is evident in four further ways. First, an inversion in Paul's understanding is evident in the way in which he came to think of Jesus as the one who embodied covenant righteousness. Prior to his conversion, Paul considered Jesus to have played no part in God's redemptive activity, not least because of the manner of his death on a cross as one cursed by God (cf. Gal 3:13; Deut 21:23). This is a part of what Paul has in mind when he speaks of a crucified Messiah as a "stumbling block for Jews" (1 Cor 1:23), and when he says in 2 Cor 5:16 that "even though we previously appraised Christ according to human standards, we now no longer appraise him in that fashion." The reversal in Paul's regard for Christ is evident in his recognition of Jesus as the obedient one (e.g., Rom 5:12-21; Phil 2:6-11) who solely embodied the covenant faithfulness acceptable to God. This reversal is most likely rooted in Paul's own experience of encountering the one whom he had previously thought of as a sinner, but who is now revealed to him as God's Son (Gal 1:12, 16), the Lord in heavenly splendor (cf. Acts 26:15).

Second, this inversion of categories applies not only to Jesus, but also to the identification of "the righteous." In Early Judaism, whereas "the righteous" signified those who were members of God's covenant people, the term "sinners" was frequently a signifier for "those outside the boundaries of the covenant" — and who were, therefore, in some form of fundamental opposition to God and his ways. Notions as to who was to be numbered among "the righteous" and who among "the sinners," however, varied from situation to situation, according to the needs of self-definition within particular groups.

For many, the category of those within the covenant was quite large and included most of the Jewish people, who were designated "the righteous." They were distinguished from "the sinners" — that is, from Gentiles and those Jews who had blatantly sinned by intentionally disregarding or scorning covenant obligations, thereby breaking out of the boundaries of the covenant people. For others, such as the covenanters at Qumran, the category of "the righteous" was far more restricted, encompassing a much smaller number of Jews who thought that they alone had been faithful before God. In such a restricted understanding, the large majority of Jewish people were looked on as having abandoned their covenant status, thereby joining the ranks of "the sinners" along with the Gentiles.

In this way, terms like "righteous" and "sinner" operated in Early Judaism in relation to particular convictions about covenant fidelity (see Dunn, "Pharisees, Sinners and Jesus"). And the same was true of Paul. Thus, for example, in Gal 2:15-17 he follows the same simple rules of covenant definition in referring to these diverse categories — although in his view the embodiment of covenant faithfulness is to be found neither in an ethnic people (i.e., Israel), nor in a sub-group within that people (e.g., the covenanters at Qumran), but in a single individual: Jesus Christ. It is Christ's covenant faithfulness alone that is the basis of relationship with God and the vehicle through which God's covenant righteousness is creating a new sphere of existence, a "new creation." For Paul, the consequence of restricting the boundaries of covenant faithfulness to a single individual is that all others find themselves to be "sinners," and so outsiders to the covenant. The result is a redefinition of "sinners." And such a redefinition may very well be what Paul had in mind when he wrote in Gal 2:17: "If, seeking covenant relationship 'in Christ', we ourselves were found to be sinners. . . ."

Prior to his conversion, Paul's understanding of "sinner" would probably have coincided with his comments in Gal 2:15, where he refers in a tongue-in-cheek manner to "Gentile sinners" *(ex ethnōn hamartōloi)* in distinction from "Jews by nature" *(physei Ioudaioi)*. Such an attitude and definition of covenantal boundaries seems to have marked out Paul's pre-Christian career, in common with many other Jews of his day (cf. my *Eschatology and the Covenant,* 27-31 for documentation of this attitude within Early Judaism). After his conversion, however, a radical redefinition occurred. For when the covenant boundaries are defined as exclusively encircling a single individual, the category applicable to all others is that of a covenant outsider, or "sinner."

It is little wonder, then, that Paul evaluates his "blamelessness in the law" (Phil 3:8) to be of no worth, and that he fiercely chastises those who would supplement the efficacy of the covenant faithfulness of Christ with their own nomistic practices. Ethnic identity ("Jews by nature," Gal 2:15) and nomistic practices ("works of the law," Gal 2:16) fail to remedy the primary category of self-identity apart from Christ — that is, that of "sinner." Christ's covenant faithfulness alone, appropriated solely on the basis of faith, is the means whereby one is transferred out of the ranks of "the sinners" and included among the people of God in covenant relationship as "the righteous."

A third modification in Paul's post-conversion understanding is evident in his depiction of nomistic observance after the appearance of Christ. A distinction might helpfully be made here between the phenomenon that Paul is concerned to undermine, on the one hand, and how he came to understand that phenomenon, on the other hand — or, to state the matter somewhat differently, a distinction between *what* Paul is fighting against and *how* he fights against it.

Thus, on the one hand, it appears that the target of Paul's attack is often (particularly in Galatians and Romans) the attempt to define the covenant according to ethnic or national lines. Paul's words in Rom 3:29-30, for example, are more easily understood to be undermining an ethnocentric covenantalism than a form of legalism:

> Is God the God of Jews only? Is he not the God of Gentiles also? Yes, of Gentiles also, since God is one, and he will bring into covenant relationship *(dikaiōsei)* the circumcised on the basis of faith and the uncircumcised through faith.

Echoing the words of the *Shema,* with its strongly nationalistic import ("Hear, Israel, the LORD, our God, the LORD is one"), Paul's depiction of the one true God, who is able to be approached by all people and every nation through faith, wrestles the central affirmation of Jewish piety from its ethnic context and turns it into support of his attack on an ethnocentric definition of the people of God. Here, the target of his attack seems to be ethnocentric covenantalism (cf. 2:17-20).

On the other hand, there are other passages where Paul does seem to suggest that nomistic observance can be a form of legalism. (It needs to be noted here, however, that Paul saw nothing wrong with nomistic observance in and of itself, for Jewish Christians could still be law-observant if they so desired. What he opposed was the view that nomistic observance is *necessary* for either salvation or a proper Christian lifestyle.) So just a few verses after reworking the significance of the *Shema* in Rom 3:29-30, Paul gives an analogy concerning a worker who expected to be rewarded according to his labors, trusting in his own works rather than in God (4:4-5). While some have argued that this analogy does not include a charge of legalism (so, e.g., Dunn, *Romans,* 1.203-04), such a charge seems nonetheless evident here. And the same seems to be true of passages such as Rom 9:32 and 11:5-6 (cf. also 9:11-12), where Paul contrasts the Jewish interest in "works" with divine "grace." For works apart from grace is a sure formula for legalism.

With that said, however, a charge of legalism should not necessarily lead to the conclusion that legalism is what Paul is attacking. Instead, this charge against traditional forms of Judaism seems to arise as a consequence of Paul's conversion perspective. Once God's covenant grace is defined in exclusive reference to Christ (as in Rom 3:21-31 and throughout), Jews outside of that sphere of grace who expect God to look favorably on their nomistic observance can nonetheless be depicted legalistically. Even if, in their own minds, their observance of the law is being carried out as a response to God's gracious election of Israel, in Paul's mind they are guilty of acting by their own efforts in order to gain their reward from God.

Most Jews would probably have shunned such a view of salvation, understanding their nomistic observance much differently (as Paul did of his own earlier observance; cf. Phil 3:6). In Paul's eyes, however, outside of the community of God's eschatological people, any Jew who considers nomistic observance to be a response to divine grace in covenant relationship is, for all intents and purposes, attempting to earn salvation through works apart from grace, and is thereby cut off from the people who enjoy God's eschatological bestowal of grace (a view that Paul qualifies in Rom 11:26-31; cf. my *Eschatology and the Covenant,* 251-65). In this way, whenever a charge of legalism arises in Paul's critique of the necessity of nomistic observance, it arises out of his own transformed view and functions as a strategy for discrediting an attitude of ethnic privilege (cf. again my *Eschatology and the Covenant,* 211-14; also Westerholm, *Israel's Law and the Church's Faith,* 152, 163, 220).

Fourth, Paul's new perspective not only considers traditional forms of Judaism to be legalism, it also portrays them as a form of paganism since the coming of Christ. This is evident when, in Gal 4:1-11, Paul identifies those who would observe the law as being under "the elements of the world" (*ta stoicheia tou kosmou,* see vv. 3 and 9). Although the origin and precise meaning of this phrase may be debated, it is clear that, with the turning of the ages (1:4), Paul lumps together Jewish nomistic practices (when thought to be salvific) and pagan religion. The interest of the Galatian Christians in observing the law represents, for Paul, a potential return to the enslavement of "the elements" from which Christ has already redeemed them. They would, as Paul sees it, be trading an intimate relationship with God for enslavement to "beings who, by nature, are not gods" (4:8). For now that Christ has come, nomistic observance — when considered necessary for acceptance by God or as the only proper Christian lifestyle — is characterized by Paul as nothing short of paganism, since relationship with God is exclusively through Christ. Paul considers the religion of nomistic practice to be one of many forms of religion enslaved to "the weak and beggarly elements" (4:9). Needless to say, such a view seems not to have been maintained by Paul prior to the revelation of God's Son to him.

It is notable, moreover, that concern to obey the law for either salvation or a proper Christian lifestyle is associated in Galatians with "the flesh" (e.g., 3:2-5; 4:29). Paul, in fact, links nomistic practices and the flesh together in a way that flies in the face of the whole Jewish tradition, where the law was thought to be the corrective to what Paul calls "the flesh." No doubt the pre-Christian Paul would have maintained the same traditional view as those who were stirring up interest in nomistic obedience at Galatia. But Paul as a Christian associates "law" and "flesh" in a manner wherein they both stand in opposition to the Spirit (e.g., 5:16-18).

Therefore, claiming that to be led by the Spirit results in not being under law (5:18), Paul goes on to produce a catalogue of "the works of the flesh" (5:19-21) — as if his reference to the law paved the way for this "fleshly" list. The list of "the works of the flesh" reinforces the point that Paul is making, for it depicts qualities that, to many a Jewish mind, were thought to mark out the decadence of the pagan world (e.g., fornication, impurity, licentiousness, idolatry, sorcery, etc.), in contrast to the obedience of God's covenant people. In so doing, Paul's purpose is to unmask the value system of those who would observe the law. In effect, he shows that system to be nothing but a web of corruption and perversity, in contrast to the work of God in Christ, who has delivered us from "the present evil age" (1:4).

Along with this we need to compare the way in which Paul depicts the character of life that is fostered within those who observe the law. For in Galatians, those who promote the necessity of nomistic observances are characterized in terms of manipulating and exploiting others (2:4; cf. the pre-Christian Paul himself in 1:13) and in terms of self-promotion and enhancing their own reputations (4:17; 6:13). And if the Galatian Christians follow that road, they will manifest attitudes of fierce competitiveness and cut-throat rivalry (5:15, 26).

It is clear, therefore, that the issue about law observance involves more than simply a dispute about social boundary markers and group membership, although that dimension is certainly included. For Paul the converted Christian, an ethnic definition of covenant relationship has become a full-blown case study of something far more fundamental within the human condition. For him it has become a nationalistic example of the basic human problem — that is, the tendency toward egocentrism and self-interest. Any community characterized by these fleshly qualities has little hope for health or longevity, because its fabric becomes torn apart by chaotic internal forces (cf. Gal 5:15, 26). Such a community fails to exhibit the transforming power of God, who makes all things alive in a new creation.

Paul envisages the community of God's people — which knows and is known by God (Gal 4:9), and which even in its diversity is to be marked out by unity and solidarity (3:28) — to consist of those who consider the needs of others, bearing other people's burdens, and serving them in love (5:13-14, 22-23; 6:2). To understand the gospel in terms of "works of the law" is to incorporate matters of "flesh" into it, thereby denuding the gospel of its testimony to the power of the sovereign God who brings into existence a united community transformed into the image of the self-giving Christ (cf. 3:26-28; 4:19). On such an understanding, the gospel becomes a tool testifying to the power of those who would perpetuate their own self-interests by transforming others into their image (cf. 4:17; 6:13). No doubt this view would have been quite foreign to Paul's perceptions prior to his encounter with the one whose gospel he now preached.

The Foundation of Covenant Ethics

In passages like Exod 19:5-6 and in most forms of traditional Judaism, one of the purposes for observing God's commands was to ensure that God's treasured people might be distinctive in their holiness. Accordingly, for many Jewish Christians of his day, Paul's case against the necessity of observing the law would have seemed deficient theologically and dangerous practically, since it appeared to lack any guidance for, or any external restraint on, everyday behavior. If the law is salvifically irrelevant, as Paul believed, then the way is open to ethical antinomianism and self-indulgence without restriction. Paul indicates that precisely this charge has been laid against him when he tells the Christians at Rome that he himself has been accused of saying, "Let us do evil in order that good might result" (Rom 3:8; cf. 6:1, 15) — that is, "The worse our behavior, the greater God's grace is shown to be."

Christians in Galatia seem to have been concerned about this same "deficiency" in Paul's understanding and to have seen the law as both the means whereby one was included among Abraham's heirs and the standard by which ethical behavior was to be managed and regulated. Paul's letter to them addresses this issue initially in relation to the faithful life of Christ that is embodied within the lives of Christians. So in Gal 2:19 (or 2:20, as in some English translations), Paul claims that Christ lives in him — a notion that he develops further in 2:20 in terms of the faithfulness of Christ: "The life I live in the mortal body, I live by the faithfulness of the Son of God" *(en pistei zō tē tou huiou tou theou)*. In Paul's understanding, everyday life is marked out neither by nomistic observance nor by ethical antinomianism, but by the covenant faithfulness of the Son of God that is being lived out in the life of the believer. Paul fills out the content of Jesus' faithfulness further in 2:20 in terms of the Son's love for others and his giving himself up for their benefit (cf. 1:4).

Paul's ethic in Galatians develops from this christological point and in relation to the Spirit, who is identified as the Spirit of Christ (4:6). The Spirit's activity nurtures characteristics within the Christian community that resemble the character of Jesus, being little more than dynamic extensions of the qualities that he exhibited in his earthly life. The christological model of covenant faithfulness, which is manifest in love and self-giving (1:4; 2:20), is for Paul the paradigm of Christian character (see Hays, "Christology and Ethics"; also my "Defining the Faithful Character"). The result of such an ethic is that social relationships between those in Christ are to be defined not by such things as circumcision or dietary regulations, or any other "works of the law," but by "faith working practically through love" (5:6).

So as Paul describes "the fruit of the Spirit," love heads the list as the primary characteristic of a Christian lifestyle (Gal 5:22-23). This Christ-like character is to be formed within the corporate life of the believers (4:19). And it is to be formed as its members are "clothed with Christ" (3:27), just as an actor puts on the costume of another in order to "be" that person within the context of a play. In this analogy, the whole of life is the theater wherein Christians "embody" and "perform" Christ by means of their Christ-like character, which is brought to life by the Spirit. The covenant faithfulness of Christ is the context out of which arise the characteristics of the new world order of Spirit-enabled love and self-giving.

Paul brings all this to bear on the question of antinomianism when, in Gal 5:13-14, he identifies this eschatological character as the manner in which the law is fulfilled. Those who walk by the Spirit in love and service to others "fulfill" *(plērein)* or "meet the standard of" the Mosaic law by that Christ-like love, even without observing the law's prescriptions (cf. 6:2; Rom 8:4; 13:8-10). Although the period of law observance has come to an end, the Mosaic law nonetheless comes to its fullest and proper expression in the loving service of those who are being transformed by the Spirit of Christ into conformity with the character of Christ. Despite all that Paul says against living in accordance with the prescriptions of the law, in the end he demonstrates that his gospel not only excludes the charge of anti-nomianism but also provides the only possible avenue of "fulfilling" the law for God's people.

Here Paul compares well with other Jewish covenantal theologians of his day, for whom definitions of "law" and "covenant people" were to dovetail and cohere. It is little wonder, then, that Paul applies, as he most likely does in Gal 6:16, the term "Israel of God" to the community of those in Christ, wherein the law finds its fulfillment.

4. Conclusions

From this survey of aspects of Paul's presentation (particularly in Galatians and Romans), attention has been drawn to the way in which matters of covenant self-definition and theology frequently emerge in Paul's concerns. In the end of the day, it may be that covenantal categories of thought are simply one of many features in Paul's theological reserves. But even if that be the case, they are significant nonetheless.

Yet whenever Paul explores matters of faith and practice in relation to a covenantal perspective, Jesus Christ permeates every aspect of that perspec-tive — whether it be Paul's understanding of God, of covenant identity markers, of faithfulness, of history, of ethics, or of Jewish nomistic practice. If the focus of Paul's life prior to his conversion was the covenant between God and his people Israel (as his comments in Gal 1:13-14 and Phil 3:4-6 have led us to believe), the focus of his later life is on what God has done in Christ.

Paul often explores the meaning of what God has done in Christ by exploiting the rich resources of the covenant theology of his Jewish heritage. And he frequently demonstrates a proficiency in using covenantal motifs and patterns of thought as a metaphorical context in which to probe the significance of salvation in Christ. So in his letters, Paul's repertoire of covenantal motifs is consistently put in the service of articulating the riches of God's saving action in Christ.

Selected Bibliography

Campbell, W. S. "Covenant and New Covenant." In *Dictionary of Paul and His Letters*, ed. G. F. Hawthorne and R. P. Martin. Downers Grove/Leicester: InterVarsity, 1993, 179-83.

Donaldson, T. L. "The 'Curse of the Law' and the Inclusion of the Gentiles: Galatians 3.13-14." *New Testament Studies* 32 (1986) 94-112.

Dunn, J. D. G. *Romans*. 2 vols. Dallas: Word, 1988.

――――. "Pharisees, Sinners and Jesus." In *Jesus, Paul and the Law*. London: SPCK; Louisville: Westminster, 1990, 61-88.

――――. "The Justice of God: A Renewed Perspective on Justification by Faith." *Journal of Theological Studies* 43 (1992) 1-22.

Hays, R. B. *The Faith of Jesus Christ: An Investigation of the Narrative Substructure of Galatians 3:1–4:11*. Chico, CA: Scholars Press, 1983.

――――. "Christology and Ethics in Galatians: The Law of Christ." *Catholic Biblical Quarterly* 49 (1987) 268-90.

――――. "Justification." In *The Anchor Bible Dictionary*, ed. D. N. Freedman et al. New York: Doubleday, 1992, 3.1129-33.

Hurtado, L. W. *One God, One Lord: Early Christian Devotion and Ancient Jewish Monotheism*. London: SCM, 1988.

Longenecker, B. W. *Eschatology and the Covenant: A Comparison of 4 Ezra and Romans 1–11*. Sheffield: JSOT Press, 1991.

――――. "PISTIS in Romans 3.25: Neglected Evidence for the 'Faithfulness of Christ'?" *New Testament Studies* 39 (1993) 478-80.

――――. "Defining the Faithful Character of the Covenant Community: Galatians 2.15-21 and Beyond." In *Paul and the Mosaic Law*, ed. J. D. G. Dunn. Tübingen: Mohr-Siebeck, 1996, 75-97.

Scott, J. M. " 'For as Many as Are of Works of the Law Are under a Curse' (Galatians 3.10)." In *Paul and the Scriptures of Israel*, ed. C. A. Evans and J. A. Sanders. Sheffield: JSOT Press, 1993, 187-221.

Westerholm, S. *Israel's Law and the Church's Faith: Paul and His Recent Interpreters*. Grand Rapids: Eerdmans, 1988.

Wright, N. T. *The Climax of the Covenant: Christ and the Law in Pauline Theology*. Edinburgh: Clark, 1991.

――――. *The New Testament and the People of God*. London: SPCK, 1992.

Sinai as Viewed from Damascus:
Paul's Reevaluation of the Mosaic Law

STEPHEN WESTERHOLM

IMAGINE yourself, if you will, among the readers of a novel with a startling ending. As you make your way through the book's opening chapters, you find yourself — subconsciously, perhaps, but inevitably — conceiving and testing various understandings of what takes place, all more or less plausible in the light of what you have read thus far. As the book nears its end, however, the number of possible constructions is gradually reduced. Perhaps most readers, on beginning the last chapter, will have settled on a single interpretation.

But then comes the unexpected ending. If the novel is well crafted, its conclusion, however surprising, will both make perfect sense in the light of everything that preceded it and, at the same time, allow you as the reader to come to a better understanding of the earlier chapters than you achieved by reading those chapters alone. Details overlooked in your initial reading are now seen to be significant. The perfection of the "perfect ending" lies partly in its capacity to release whatever emotional tensions the book may have roused in its readers, but also partly in the sense of appropriateness with which it leaves them. Rightly understood, they will feel, the book *could* not have ended in any other way.

For Paul, the revelation he received of God's Son (Gal 1:15-16) provided just such a surprising climax to the drama of divine redemption, requiring him to reassess and reconstrue a story he thought he had understood. The earlier protagonists in the story remained the same: Adam,

Abraham, Moses, the prophets, and so on. What he understood them to have said and done did not change — after all, that part of the story had long since been fixed in holy writ. But his understanding of their roles and their significance needed rethinking now that the mystery of redemptive history had been resolved and Jesus revealed as the one "who dunnit." Paul's reconstruction of the drama of divine redemption has proven so compelling that millions of people — including a number of the most influential figures in the religious history of the western world — have come to interpret the significance of their own lives within that drama as Paul came to construe it.

My focus in this essay is on the shift in Paul's perspective regarding the law of Moses. How did he understand it prior to the epiphany of God's Son? What were his views after the reevaluation that that revelation provoked? In what follows I will set out eight theses that are intended to sum up the essential features of Paul's *Christian* view of the law. (It is only Paul's *Christian* view, after all, to which we have direct access — primarily in his letter to the Romans, though other Pauline letters will be drawn upon as well.) In each case, I will (1) note the major Pauline texts from which the thesis is derived, (2) query to what extent the thesis reflects convictions that Paul might have held prior to his conversion, and (3) ask to what extent the thesis was the product of Paul's subsequent reevaluation.

THESIS ONE: *Human beings find themselves in an ordered world not of their making, with the capacity to acknowledge or deny their dependence on the creator, to conform to or defy the wise ordering of his creation. Life and divine favor are enjoyed by those who fear the Lord and do good. Those who reject what is good and do what is "right in their own eyes" court disaster.*

Students of Paul will immediately think of Rom 1:18–2:11. The eternal power and deity of God, Paul argues, may be inferred from his created order. When, therefore, people refuse to acknowledge him or give him thanks — when they focus their devotion on creatures rather than on the creator — their conduct is both willful and inexcusable. Divine judgment is at work when those who thus close their minds to the most basic truth about their existence proceed to further violations of nature's order: they must live with the consequences of their deeds in a world marred by human violence, insolence, and irresponsibility. Nor is judgment confined to the bane of sin in this world. Still to come is the day of God's righteous judgment, when life everlasting will be bestowed on all who do what is good, but wrath poured out on those who do evil. The sanctions apply, Paul insists, to Jews and Gentiles alike.

For our purposes, the absence of any reference to the law in Rom 1:18–2:11 is significant. Merely to be a moral creature in God's world, Paul believes, is to be bound to do what is good and to avoid evil (2:6-10). Most fundamental is the duty of giving God his due, an obligation clearly rooted not in any arbitrary divine decree but in the very conditions of human existence. Those who receive life from the hands of God respond appropriately with thanks and praise. To refuse to do so, and thereby to suppress knowledge of human dependence on God, is senseless, perverse, and the precursor of other acts that are "contrary to nature" and "unfitting" (1:26-28).

The terms "fitting" and "unfitting," as well as "according" and "contrary to nature," are expressions that were shared by many in antiquity. For Paul, they serve in this passage to define the "good" to be pursued and the "evil" to be shunned. Human beings are born into an already ordered cosmos. Non-human creation instinctively conforms to its order. For their part, humans are faced with the moral choice of patterning their behavior in accordance with nature's order, thus doing what "befits" them, or of defying it. Since even the defiant inevitably participate in, and depend on, the wise ordering of the cosmos, such would-be declarations of independence are both preposterous and highly "unfitting."

They are also, in Paul's view, inexcusable. Paul attributes to human beings a basic awareness of good and evil — that is, of what, in the light of the conditions of human existence in God's world, is appropriate behavior and what is inappropriate behavior. Those who act perversely and applaud the perverse do so, he claims, in deliberate defiance of the judgment of God (1:32). Those who do what is good, however, he goes on to say, act in accordance with an inner awareness of what is right (2:14-15). So all are subject to the demands of the good — demands that are inherent in their status as moral creatures in God's world — and their waywardness cannot be excused by ignorance.

This first Pauline thesis, though fundamental to Paul's thinking as a

Christian, was doubtless one he picked up in Tarsus or Jerusalem rather than on the road to Damascus. Its clearest expression in the Hebrew Bible is to be found in the book of Proverbs: "The fear of the LORD is the beginning of wisdom" (9:10); "Do not be wise in your own eyes; fear the LORD and turn away from evil" (3:7); "Those who find [wisdom] find life and obtain favor from the LORD; those who miss [wisdom] harm themselves; all who hate [wisdom] love death" (8:35-36). Much in Rom 1:18–2:11, in fact, simply restates themes found already in Proverbs.

Indeed, as suggested above, the perspective in this passage has close parallels in pagan thought as well. The language of "fitting" and "unfitting" behavior, of conduct "according" or "contrary to nature," echoes, for example, Stoic formulations. A major difference between the thinking of most ancients and that of many in the modern West, however, is that, whereas the former saw it as a human responsibility to *discover* what is good, many moderns imagine they must themselves *decide* what is good. The shift is fundamental. Implicit in the ancient posture is the perception that humans are not the source of the order of the cosmos, though it is their vocation to discern and affirm it. Implicit in the modern posture is the conceit that non-human creation has no inherent goodness of its own, that value and meaningful order were not introduced to the cosmos prior to the (rather tardy) appearance of *homo sapiens* (or, perhaps, the even tardier appearance of the western post-Enlightenment strain of that species), and that humans are therefore free to impose whatever shape they please on their lives and environment. The ancient perspective is demonstrably that of Paul.

THESIS TWO: *The law of Moses articulates the appropriate human response to life in God's creation. Its gift to Israel represents a signal token of divine favor.*

If our first thesis is most explicit in Rom 1:18–2:11, the second finds its primary support in Rom 2:12-29. The underlying assumption appears to be that, though all people possess some nagging awareness of the demand to do good and avoid evil, their moral perceptions have been clouded by their predilection for evil (cf. 1:21). Certainly humanity is thought to be well served by a direct reminder, given by God, of its fundamental responsibilities.

Such a reminder, providing plain guidance of what is at the same time God's will and appropriate behavior for all human beings, has been given to Jews in the law of Moses. So favored, Jews are in a position to instruct Gentiles of things that Gentiles, too, need to know — to be "guides for the blind, lights for those in darkness, instructors of fools, teachers of the young." Thus the "knowledge and truth" that Paul sees embodied in the Mosaic law (2:19-20) are manifestly thought to be of universal application, though Jewish apprehension of the truth has been facilitated by the gift of the law. Yet Paul can envisage Gentiles who observe the law's requirements without being exposed to its precepts, by acting in accordance with their own inner awareness of what is right (2:14-15, 26).

From Romans 2 alone, no reader would suspect that the Mosaic law contains precepts peculiar to Israel. All people, Paul insists, will be judged by their deeds, whether those deeds are "good" or "evil." Nothing in the passage suggests that "good" and "evil" have differing contents for different people. In this passage, at least, it is primarily the form in which people encounter the universal moral demands that separates Jews from Gentiles. Jews learn them from the law of Moses.

Nor is this passage unique in Paul. Elsewhere, too, we find the Mosaic law spoken of where the only commands in view are moral demands thought to be binding on all people. Sin is said to have been present in the world before the law was given and among those to whom it was not given. The law merely spells out pre- and proscribed behavior for human beings, thereby creating the possibility of human "transgression" of an explicit code (Rom 2:12; cf. also 4:15; 5:13). When Paul develops the relation between the law, sin, and the "flesh" in Romans 7, the command he cites by way of illustration is the moral prohibition of covetousness (7:7). The goodness of the law and of its individual commands is repeatedly conceded (7:16, 19; cf. 7:12) — that is, the law's commands are seen, not as arbitrary divine demands, but as articulations of human requirements whose appropriateness and goodness compel human recognition. Again, it needs to be noted, prescriptions confined to Israel are not in view.

Paul goes on in Romans to insist that, in those who "walk . . . according to the Spirit," "what the law ordains is fulfilled" (8:4); still later, that the law's individual commands are all summed up in the words: "You shall love your neighbor as yourself" (13:9). In this latter verse the Mosaic law is certainly intended, as is evident from the selection of commandments in the first part of the verse. But the Mosaic law is treated as the concrete embodiment of demands that are inherent in the terms of human existence and that are susceptible of recognition and compliance even without the law's tutelage.

In our second thesis, too, there is nothing specifically Christian. Already in Deuteronomy the "statutes and ordinances" given to Israel were thought to be recognizably righteous in the eyes of other nations (Deut 4:5-8). If Proverbs prescribes the pursuit of wisdom for all people without reference to the Mosaic law, later wisdom literature identified Torah with the wisdom of the created order — for example, in Sirach 24, where, as in Romans 2, Jews are seen as having priviieged access to "universal" norms. And Philo repeatedly makes the claim that the "law of nature," which is binding on all people, finds perfect expression in the "laws" of the Jews (cf. *On the Creation of the World* 3; *On the Life of Moses* 2.52). Not yet, then, do we see signs of a Pauline reevaluation.

THESIS THREE: *The law of Moses contains ordinances binding only on Jews, whose observance marks them off from other nations as God's covenant people of old.*

Though Paul, like many Jews, could speak of Torah as the embodiment of what is God's will and appropriate behavior for all people, he could also insist, as did other Jews, that it contained precepts required only of Israel. In 1 Cor 9:20-21 he claims that he lives among Jews who are "under the law" as though he himself were "under the law," whereas when he is among Gentiles who are "outside the law" he lives as one "outside the law." In this passage Jews, but not Gentiles, are thought to be subject to demands contained in the law — demands whose observance or nonobservance is, for Paul, a matter of effective missionary strategy rather than moral right or wrong. Food laws, festival observance, and the like must be in mind.

Similarly, those to whom Paul writes in his Galatian letter show their eagerness to be "under law" (4:21; cf. 3:2) by contemplating circumcision and observing "days, months, seasonal festivals, and years" (4:10). The "works of the law" that Paul insists do not justify (2:16) are hardly to be confined to ritual observances of the sort explicitly mentioned, but they certainly include them. Paul's point in stressing the limitations of the law and warning against submission to its demands is to insist that Gentiles ought not to be compelled to "live as Jews" (2:14), to whom such distinctive laws had been given.

Nowhere in his extant letters does Paul explicitly express the conviction that the Mosaic law combines demands binding on all humankind with other precepts required only of Israel. The absence of such a clarification is, presumably, to be attributed to the nonsystematic character of his writings. Both halves of the conviction are amply attested in his letters. And both halves are traditional.

THESIS FOUR: *Adamic humanity does not, and cannot, submit to God's law.*

In Rom 1:18–3:20 Paul declares that all humanity is culpable before God for concrete acts of wrongdoing, which are rooted in people's refusal to give God due glory and thanks. All are, in Paul's terms, "under sin" (3:9) and liable to divine judgment (3:19-20).

Only a short parenthesis can be devoted here to the problem of the apparently "righteous" Gentiles spoken of in Rom 2:14-15, 26. If Paul intended to affirm that some Gentiles apart from Christ satisfactorily fulfill God's demands and are therefore acknowledged as righteous, the affirmation contradicts his own conclusions in 3:9-20 and elsewhere. We can do no more here than note the two most common alternative interpretations.

1. Paul does not mean to say that some Gentiles can be approved by God as being righteous on the basis of their own consistently righteous behavior, but only that the righteous deeds that Gentiles on occasion do perform attest to their awareness of the demands of goodness, their responsibility to carry them out, and their potential for highlighting the shortcomings of Jews whenever Gentiles but not Jews comply with God's requirements.

2. Paul has in mind Gentile Christians, as is perhaps suggested by the claims that what God's law ordains is "written on their heart" (Rom 2:15; the language is reminiscent of the promise of "new covenant" righteousness in Jer 31:33) and that their "circumcision" is spiritual (or perhaps "by the

Spirit," Rom 2:29; cf. 7:6; Phil 3:3; Col 2:11). Why would Paul not make explicit their Christian identity? Perhaps because the focus of his argument at this point is not on the fulfillment of the law by those empowered by God's Spirit but rather on the conviction that possession of the law without adherence to its demands can only lead to divine condemnation. The appropriateness of such judgment is the sole point in drawing a contrast between the transgressions of those entrusted with the law and the behavior of others who fulfill the law's demands.

Whatever stance one might take regarding the "righteous" Gentiles of Rom 2:14-15, 26, the argument of Romans 1–3 concludes that Jews and Gentiles alike are guilty of specific acts of wrongdoing. In Romans 5, however, Paul's depiction of human sinfulness goes further. When Adam sinned, his descendants were all "made sinners" (5:19). They remain personally responsible for the concrete acts of sin that they commit. But in such acts they are merely giving expression to the pretensions of autonomy and the underlying hostility toward God that Paul sums up in the term "flesh" and that he sees as endemic in Adam's race. When "flesh" that is hostile to God encounters the wisdom of God in his created order or in the Mosaic law, the issue is inevitable: human rebelliousness is provoked into sinful actions (Rom 7:7-13). "Flesh" does not find within itself a capacity to submit to God's law (Rom 8:7-8; cf. 7:14-25). Discussion of the roots of this thesis will be postponed until we have considered the next one.

THESIS FIVE: *For Adamic human beings, the law cannot serve as the path to righteousness and life.*

This fifth thesis appears to run counter to several texts in Paul's letters that speak of the "righteousness of the law" or of the law as having been given with the promise of life for its adherents (Rom 2:13; 7:10; Phil 3:9). Lev 18:5 is twice quoted to this effect by Paul, in Rom 10:5 and Gal 3:12. Numerous parallels from Deuteronomy could also have been cited. There is no reason to suspect that Paul understood the point of these texts from the Hebrew Scriptures differently than did his Jewish contemporaries: God had chosen and redeemed Israel as his "peculiar" people, had granted them the gift of Torah, and had promised continued life in his favor as they kept his "statutes and ordinances."

Nonetheless, for Paul humanity as it is constituted in Adam does not — and effectively cannot — submit to God's law. Even in the case of Adam's most favored descendants, the gift of the law elicits only stiff-necked rebellion, not humble submission. Admittedly, the sanctions accompanying the institution of the law were dual in nature: life and blessing for all who obey its precepts, cursing and death for those who defy them. Only the latter sanctions, however, can be operative among those in the "flesh." So Paul says that all who are "of the works of the law" are subject to the curse it pronounces on transgressors (Gal 3:10).

Paul sums up the "ministry" of the law as being "glorious" (because of its divine origin), but also as being one of "condemnation" and "death" (2 Cor 3:7-9). The commandment that was given with the promise of life has proved, for those in the "flesh," a tool in the hands of sin leading to death (Rom 7:10-13). The law may spell out how Adamic human beings ought to behave, but it has no power to impart life to the dead (Gal 3:21). In itself, the law is "holy" and "spiritual," and its demands "holy, righteous, and good" (Rom 7:12-14). Yet it is utterly unable to elicit obedience from sinful "flesh" (Rom 7:18; 8:3). The notion that divine favor could be secured by Adamic human beings through their compliance with God's law is simply unthinkable, given Paul's understanding of the "flesh." Indeed, the contrary conviction is a Pauline axiom (Rom 3:20, 28; Gal 2:16, 21; 3:21). "In Adam all die" (1 Cor 15:22).

What are the roots of Paul's anthropological pessimism? A number of texts from the Hebrew Scriptures can be cited that speak of the universality of human sin. In Genesis 3, Adam and Eve are undoubtedly thought to be in some way representative of all humankind. The chapters that immediately follow are designed to show how sin intrudes upon and corrupts all inter-human relations, as well as relations between humans and the non-human creation — and, of course, between humans and God.

From among the nations, the Hebrew Bible goes on to say, Israel has been sovereignly chosen and redeemed to be God's covenant people. But neither before nor after Israel's election is it suggested that Israel is more righteous than other nations (cf. Deut 9:4-6). On the contrary, the Pentateuch, Deuteronomistic history, and prophetic literature uniformly depict Israel as stubbornly resistant to God's demands, in spite of extraordinary displays of God's goodness on its behalf. Prophetic texts view Israel's recalcitrance as being so deeply rooted that only a divine transformation of Israel's heart — a heart transplant, as Ezek 36:26-27 puts it — could render them submissive to God's ways (cf. Jer 13:23; 31:31-34). There are, in short, numerous texts in the Hebrew Scriptures that could be cited in support of this fifth Pauline thesis.

That being said, however, it must also be conceded that most Jews did not construe the human predicament — or, at least, the predicament of Israel — in terms as bleak as Paul's. The gift of Torah was commonly seen as the linchpin in God's dealings with human weakness and propensity for sin. Its laws, marking out the path on which Israel would enjoy life and divine blessing, were not considered to be beyond human achievement. In any case, its institutions provided atonement for those who repented of their shortcomings.

That Paul does not mention Jewish understandings of repentance and restoration is often thought remarkable. From his own perspective, however, effective repentance must surely lie beyond the capacities of a "flesh" that "does not, and cannot, submit to God's law." Paul's exclusion of Jewish notions of repentance is, therefore, quite consistent with his anthropology, as sketched out above. Still, the source of so pessimistic a judgment demands explanation, for it remains unusual in the context of Jewish thought.

To be sure, Paul's pessimism is not unprecedented. Some interpreters have suggested that his anthropological understanding had its roots in the more pessimistic strands of rabbinic teaching (e.g., H. J. Schoeps), or, perhaps, in Hellenistic Jewish thought (e.g., S. Sandmel). The difficulty with such views, however, is that — to judge from his own testimony about his pre-Christian experience — Paul must have been among the more optimistic Jews in his assessment of at least his own capacity to meet the standards required by the "righteousness of the law" (Phil 3:4-6). The evidence for Paul's "robust conscience," to which Krister Stendahl has drawn attention, does not suggest a mind schooled to doubt humanity's capacity to please God.

Here, then, it seems, we must speak of a post-conversion reevaluation. If the crucifixion of God's Son was required to redeem humankind — a conclusion that Paul could not doubt once Jesus had been "revealed" to him as "God's Son" (Gal 1:15-16) — then the sinfulness of humankind must be both radical in itself and beyond the capacity of existing (and less drastic) measures to overcome. To this extent, E. P. Sanders is certainly correct in insisting on the movement of Paul's thought "from solution to plight." The notion that "in Adam all die" may well have become fundamental to Paul's thinking first when he saw it as presupposed in the affirmation that "in Christ shall all be made alive" (1 Cor 15:22).

Not that Paul, the Christian apostle, had to create a crisis *ex nihilo* to correspond to and legitimate his understanding of redemption in Christ Jesus. The positing of a relationship between Adam's sin and human death was no Pauline innovation. The Hebrew Bible, as we have noted, is replete with denunciations of human waywardness. And Frank Thielman has quite properly reminded us that the movement "from plight to solution" is repeatedly traced in both biblical and post-biblical Jewish tradition. Nonetheless, it seems likely that Paul was first moved to draw extensively on that tradition, and to mold it in the way he did, by reflecting on the disclosure of the human predicament implicit in the cross of Christ. Like the reader of a novel with an unanticipated ending, Paul may well have felt that he first grasped the seriousness of scriptural appraisals of human sinfulness when he returned to ponder them in the light of the story's climax.

THESIS SIX: *The giving of the law served to highlight, at the same time as it exacerbated, human bondage to sin.*

Why did God institute a law that, on Paul's reading, people would not and could not keep? Perhaps the first point to be remembered is that the law, for Paul, merely spells out the moral requirements inherent in the terms of human existence in God's world. If moral creatures are completely dependent on God for their life and well-being, then they simply cannot live rightly without acknowledging God and giving him his due. This is not an arbitrary decree permitting adjustment to human predilections or capacities any more than solutions to mathematical problems can be altered to suit students' inclinations or abilities to deduce them. The occurrence of murder, adultery, theft, and false witness has doubtless been a feature of human society ever since humans were banished from Eden. But neither practice nor law can make them morally acceptable. That humans do not live up to moral standards that they themselves acknowledge is a truth to be confronted, not clouded over by the suppression or falsification of the standards. Ezekiel was to bear witness to the truth whether Israel heeded him or not (Ezek 2:3-5). In the same vein, Paul clearly believed, the law rightly attests to what is required of humankind, whether or not it is obeyed.

Paul sees, then, the primary purpose of the law to be to compel recognition of the nature and extent of human sinfulness (Rom 3:20; 7:8). Given his understanding of human nature, the reminder of human responsibility can only be thought to exacerbate human rebellion (Rom 5:20; 7:8-11). The law is viewed as transforming sin into deliberate transgression of God's stated will (Rom 4:15; 5:13). It highlights human unwillingness and incapacity to do what is right, but it is not itself equipped to overcome human sinfulness (Rom 7:14; 8:3). It is sufficient for the law if it shows human sinfulness to be "exceedingly sinful" (Rom 7:13). The roots of this Pauline thesis will be considered after our discussion of the next one.

THESIS SEVEN: *The "righteousness of God" revealed in Christ Jesus is operative "apart from law." Those who continue to pursue the "righteousness of the law" mistakenly attribute to the "works" of their unredeemed "flesh" a role in securing divine approval.*

A law that accentuates but cannot overcome human sinfulness can play no role in humanity's redemption. It rightly demands compliance with God's will, but it places its demands on creatures who are hostile to God and incapable of pleasing him. Their transformation must be brought about by other means to which they themselves, the "weak" and "ungodly" (Rom 5:6), are patently in no position to contribute.

Of the nature of divine redemption as Paul perceives it, we need note here only its utter *dependence* on divine grace and its *independence* from the law and its works. The insistence on both counts is consistent with Paul's anthropology, as sketched out above. After depicting in Romans 3 humanity as being "under sin" (3:9), culpable and without excuse before God (3:19), Paul then underlines the gratuity of redemption: those who believe "are justified freely by [God's] grace through the redemption provided in Christ Jesus" (3:24). The "ungodly" are approved, not by any of the things they do, but by believing in the one who "justifies the ungodly"

(4:5). Rom 5:15-21 is a paean of praise of the "grace of God and the gift that abounds to many through the grace of the one man, Jesus Christ" (5:15). The "free gift" or "grace" is operative to secure divine approval in a situation where "many transgressions" prevail (5:16). Death reigns until people are enabled to "reign in life" by "receiving the overflow of grace and of the gift of righteousness" (5:17).

In fact, Paul insists in Romans 9–11 that at each stage in the long history of redemption, God has achieved his purposes with rebellious humankind through interventions of divine grace initiated according to his own sovereign will, without regard to human "works." Isaac, for example, was *born* a child of promise (9:7-9). Even before his twins started fighting, before either had done anything — good or bad — to warrant divine intervention, God designated Jacob, not Esau, to further his redemptive purpose (9:10-13). All is dependent, not on human willing or achieving, but on God showing mercy (9:16). Where divine grace is the operative principle, there, by definition, nothing that humans do can be a factor (11:6). If God was long gracious to Jews while excluding Gentiles from his people, the tables have now turned; now Gentiles experience God's mercy at the cost of Israel's disobedience (11:30-31). Ultimately, however, God's purpose is to show mercy to all, since all have proved disobedient (11:32).

Nonetheless, Paul concedes — even in the midst of his discussion of God's operation in history by sovereign grace without reference to human works — that there are those who ignore God's righteousness and continue to try to establish their own (Rom 10:3). There are those who try to attain the righteousness that the law demands by doing the works prescribed by the law, rather than realizing that God's approval can only be gained by responding in faith to what God has done in Christ Jesus (9:30-32).

In a number of recent studies, Paul's critique of "works" is thought to be directed solely at Jewish particularism. Jews are held to be wrong in insisting on particular "works" (such as circumcision and the observance of food and festival laws) that distinguish them from other nations. Indeed, the suggestion is at times made that only those who read Paul through the eyes of Luther understand him as intending to deny human activity as such a part in justification. The suggestion, one would have thought, could only come from those who have never read Augustine's *The Spirit and the Letter* — and, moreover, who fail to see Eph 2:8-10 and Tit 3:4-7 as reflections of Pauline thought.

More to the point, such a suggestion, it seems to me, also fails to do justice to the clear relation between, on the one hand, Paul's exclusion of human "works" and, on the other, (1) the Pauline anthropology that insists that "flesh" cannot please God, (2) the Pauline soteriology that insists on the gratuity of redemption, (3) the Pauline understanding of redemptive history that insists that God always operates sovereignly without consideration of anything humans might do, and (4) the Pauline moral vision that insists that humans have no grounds for boasting before God (Rom 3:27–4:5; 1 Cor 1:26-31; Gal 6:14). As the pendulum of academic fashion has swung away from systematic portrayals of Pauline theology, even the obvious relation between these fundamental features of his thought, I would contend, has been lost to view.

Two objections to this traditional reading of Paul must be briefly noted. First, is not human faith itself a "work" that contributes to the process of justification? To this objection, the obvious answer must be that Paul does not see it so. The very texts in Romans that insist on the gratuity of the "gift of righteousness" also insist that it is "reckoned" to those who believe (Rom 3:22-24; 4:1-5; 5:1-11). If that "reckoning" were in response to some "work," Paul reasons, it would be a wage, not a gift of grace. But it is, he claims, clearly the latter, in that it is granted to those who "do *not* work but *believe* on him who justifies the ungodly" (4:4-5). This text, in particular, presupposes a fundamental distinction between "working" (that is, performing deeds that merit recognition) and "believing." Later in Romans, Gentiles who obtain the "righteousness of faith" are explicitly said *not* to be active in pursuit of righteousness — unlike Jews who pursue it but do not obtain it, thinking it to be a matter of works, not faith (9:30-32). That the law demands "works" is precisely what shows, for Paul, that its operative principle is not that of "faith" (Gal 3:12; cf. Rom 4:16; 10:5-8).

Why does Paul distinguish in this way between the "faith" that is necessarily involved in justification and "works" that cannot justify? Again, we need to turn to Paul's anthropology. No product of Adamic humanity can be pleasing to God, because the underlying orientation of Adamic humanity is that of hostility toward God. Even deeds that outwardly conform to the law's commands can only be acceptable as expressions of faith in God, and the mind-set of the "flesh" is the opposite to that of faith. The human faith essential to justification cannot, then, be a characteristic or product of the "flesh." Rather, it is for Paul a response to the divine word of salvation (Rom 10:17). It is a response that is first aroused in the hearts of believers by God in an act of divine illumination parallel to that by which the old creation had its beginnings: "The God who said, 'Let light shine out of darkness,' has shone in our hearts to bring the light of the knowledge that the glory of God is displayed in the person of Jesus Christ" (2 Cor 4:6). Thus faith, for Paul, does not — in fact, cannot — originate in a movement of the "flesh." Rather, it is a gift of God that is effective in bringing about a new, and necessarily divine, creation (Phil 1:27; cf. 2 Cor 5:17-18).

A second objection is often raised to the traditional reading of Paul given above: Does not Paul himself require "works" of believers? Indubitably. But such works, for Paul, are scarcely the products of the unredeemed "flesh." Those restored by grace to a right relationship with God and granted his Spirit to empower their living must express the reality of their new life in suitable behavior. They are to live in a manner worthy of the God who has called them to be his own (Phil 1:27; 1 Thess 2:12). Their faith is to be active in love (Gal 5:6). At the same time, Paul believes, they will sense, as he himself patently did, that God is "at work" within them, granting them both the desire and the ability to do what he approves (Phil 2:13; cf. 1 Cor 15:10; 2 Cor 12:9; Gal 2:20). The presence of God's Spirit *must* bear fruit in the lives of believers who are redeemed by divine grace. But this Pauline conviction hardly contradicts the thesis that "flesh" cannot be "justified" by its "works."

Paul cites Scripture in support of each component of this seventh thesis: that the "righteousness of God" revealed in Christ Jesus is operative "by faith" and "apart from the law" (cf. Gal 3:11-12; Rom 10:5-13); that "righteousness" is "reckoned" to those who "have faith . . . without works" (Rom 4:1-8); and that God operates at the initiative of his sovereign and gracious will without regard to human actions (Rom 9:10-18; 11:5-7). But Paul himself, by his own testimony, was once in pursuit of the "righteousness of the law" (Phil 3:6). So the distinction between such righteousness and that of faith, as well as the conviction that justification is ultimately a gift granted quite apart from the works of the law, can only have been the product of his Christian reevaluation. Scripture, when reconsidered from his Christian perspective, was found to support these convictions. But the convictions impressed themselves on Paul only when the crucifixion and resurrection of God's Son were believed to be both efficacious for human redemption and revelatory of the inadequacy of earlier institutions — even *divine* institutions — to achieve such an end.

The Christian Paul relegates the law to a minor role in the drama whose main protagonists are Adam and Christ (cf. Rom 5:12-21). Yet a divine law must nonetheless have had a divine purpose. The thesis that the Mosaic law served merely to highlight human bondage to sin must also be the product of Christian considerations.

THESIS EIGHT: *Believers in Christ are not "under law."*

Paul can say that believers have been "redeemed" (Gal 4:5) or "set free" (Rom 7:6) from the law — even that they have "died" to it (Rom 7:4, 6; Gal 2:19). The upshot is that they are not "under law" (Rom 6:14-15; cf. 1 Cor 9:20). The denial undoubtedly means, in part, that the curse that the law pronounces on its transgressors does not threaten believers. Christ absorbed that curse on their behalf, thereby freeing them from its effects (Gal 3:13). But Paul's language implies freedom as well from the law's demands. At times the law's ritual demands are specifically in mind (cf. 1 Cor 9:20-21; Gal 4:21). The Paul who insisted that neither circumcision nor uncircumcision amounts to anything (Gal 6:15), that no food need be avoided as "unclean" (Rom 14:14), and that, in the observance of holy days, the dictates of individual consciences may be followed (Rom 14:5-6), saw no obligation of Christians to the ritual demands of the law.

But when, as in Rom 6:15, Paul is concerned that Christian freedom from the law might be misconstrued as a license to sin, freedom from the law's ritual commands cannot be in view. A similar concern is addressed following declarations of freedom from the law in Gal 5:13-26. Indeed, none of the declarations of Christian freedom suggests a limitation of that deliverance to ritual demands. Nor, when Paul insists that the law was a temporary imposition, confining people under sin *until* the coming of Christ and faith, can the law of which he speaks be restricted to its ritual aspects (Gal 3:19–4:7). In Rom 7:6, Paul says flatly that believers now serve God, not in the old way of the letter, but in the new way of the Spirit. That Christians are not "under law" therefore implies a whole new way of life and mode of service, and not simply a deliverance from ritual demands.

Christian freedom, Paul insists, is freedom to serve God. It is a freedom that is denied to those in the "flesh," whose bondage to sin makes life in the service of goodness an impossibility (Rom 6:10–7:4). Law, for Paul, is God's way of getting the attention of those in the "flesh," reminding them of their obligations to God and goodness, and demonstrating the sinfulness of their sin. Its statutes can only encounter a rebellious "flesh," intent on its own autonomy, as foreign and vexatious. Christians, in Paul's understanding, have "crucified the flesh" (Gal 5:24), died to that old way of life (Rom 6:3-11), and received new life and the gift of the Spirit to enable them to live in the service of righteousness.

Of course, Christians still live within the terms prescribed by life in God's world, including the obligation of all humankind to do good and avoid evil. Paul tells Christians to "abhor what is evil and cleave to what is good" (Rom 12:9), to "overcome evil with good" (12:21), to be "wise when it comes to the good, innocent when it comes to evil" (16:11). The terms "good" and "evil" still represent appropriate and inappropriate responses to life in an ordered creation. Indeed, for Christians, the service of God involves responding "in a worthy manner" (Phil 1:27; 1 Thess 2:12), not only to the wise ordering of the old creation but also to the grace of God in the new. But no longer is that service experienced as an obligation to observe demands externally imposed on unwilling, hostile subjects. No longer are believers "under law." God's Spirit makes God's love a reality in their hearts (Rom 5:5) and enables them to serve God in the new way, filled with the fruits of the Spirit that no law condemns (Gal 5:23). Without faith, those "under law" cannot measure up to its commands. With faith that is active in love, believers not "under law" may, in fact, fulfill the righteousness that the law requires (Rom 8:4; 13:8; Gal 5:14).

What, finally, are the roots of this Pauline thesis? The hypothesis that Paul, already in his pre-Christian days, shared with other Jews a belief that Torah's validity would end with the coming of the Messiah has been tested, but found untenable. W. D. Davies searched valiantly for Jewish sources suggesting such an understanding. H. J. Schoeps proposed that Paul's views were so determined. But the parallels discovered are scanty and remote. The evidence that most Jews believed Torah's laws to be eternal proves so overwhelming that Paul could not have simply assumed a contrary position. Furthermore, Paul's arguments bear all the marks of a Christian reevaluation.

The belief that the Messiah had come would not itself have forced him to reassess the purpose and validity of Torah. Reevaluation, however, was required by the belief that, in order to fulfill God's redemptive purposes, the Messiah had been crucified. It followed that neither the Torah, nor the Sinaitic covenant of which it was a part, nor the institutions that it ordained, had served to effect redemption. Their role could only be seen as preparatory.

To be sure, Paul would have already read in the Hebrew Scriptures that true obedience to God will only be forthcoming when God writes his laws on people's hearts, replaces their hearts of stone with hearts more pliable to his purposes, and imparts to them his Spirit (so Jer 31:33 and Ezek 11:19-20; 36:26-27). Such texts may well have influenced the formulation of his Christian thought. But the notion that a preparatory age characterized by the service of the letter had given way to the age of the Spirit seems, again, Christian in its origins — its inspiration lying in the conviction that God's Son has died and risen, and his Spirit has been poured out, to bring about a new creation ruled by righteousness. The message of the cross was, for Paul, first and foremost redemptive. But it was also revelatory of God's purposes in the time of "the law and the prophets" as well as in the present "day of salvation" (2 Cor 6:2).

Selected Bibliography

Davies, W. D. *Torah in the Messianic Age and/or the Age to Come.* Philadelphia: Society of Biblical Literature, 1952.

Dunn, J. D. G. *Jesus, Paul and the Law: Studies in Mark and Galatians.* Louisville: Westminster/John Knox, 1990.

―――, ed. *Paul and the Mosaic Law.* Tübingen: Mohr-Siebeck, 1996.

Garlington, D. B. *'The Obedience of Faith': A Pauline Phrase in Historical Context.* Tübingen: Mohr-Siebeck, 1991.

Laato, T. *Paul and Judaism: An Anthropological Approach.* Atlanta: Scholars Press, 1995.

Räisänen, H. *Paul and the Law.* 2d ed. Tübingen: Mohr-Siebeck, 1987.

Sandmel, S. *The Genius of Paul.* 3d ed. Philadelphia: Fortress, 1979.

Sanders, E. P. *Paul and Palestinian Judaism.* Philadelphia: Fortress, 1977.

―――. *Paul, the Law, and the Jewish People.* Philadelphia: Fortress, 1983.

Schoeps, H. J. *Paul: The Theology of the Apostle in the Light of Jewish Religious History.* Philadelphia: Westminster, 1961.

Schreiner, T. R. *The Law and Its Fulfillment: A Pauline Theology of Law.* Grand Rapids: Baker, 1993.

Stendahl, K. *Paul Among Jews and Gentiles and Other Essays.* Philadelphia: Fortress, 1976.

Thielman, F. *From Plight to Solution: A Jewish Framework for Understanding Paul's View of the Law in Romans and Galatians.* Leiden: Brill, 1989.

———. *Paul and the Law: A Contextual Approach.* Downers Grove, IL: InterVarsity, 1994.

Westerholm, S. *Israel's Law and the Church's Faith: Paul and His Recent Interpreters.* Grand Rapids: Eerdmans, 1988.

———. *Preface to the Study of Paul.* Grand Rapids: Eerdmans, 1997.

Paul's Conversion as Key to His Understanding of the Spirit

GORDON D. FEE

The subject of this essay is full of inherent ambiguities. On the one hand, along with his encounter with the risen Christ, Paul's experience of the eschatological Spirit serves as one of the two key moments in his conversion. The Spirit, therefore, rather than being a truth to be understood in light of his conversion, is a primary datum of the conversion itself. This means that Paul's experience of the eschatological Spirit serves as a foundational datum for many of the other features of his theology that were affected by what happened to him at his entry point into the Christian faith.

On the other hand, Paul's understanding of the Spirit himself — including his role as the key element to the whole of the Christian life — almost certainly had its origin in his experience of the Spirit at the time of his conversion. Or at least that is what I hope to demonstrate in this essay. Thus the Spirit is for Paul both foundational to his theology and an integral part of his theologizing.

The difficulty of demonstrating that Paul's understanding of the Spirit had its origin in his experience of the Spirit at the time of his conversion, of course, has to do largely with the nature of our data. For Paul's letters are occasional letters written to address ad hoc situations in the lives of his congregations or his personal friends. This means that all of our direct knowledge of Paul personally and theologically comes by way of his responses to matters arising in the life of his churches — which means, in turn, that the agenda for those letters has been generally set by his addressees rather than by Paul himself. The net result is that not only do we have nothing close to a systematic setting forth of his theology, but that there are some matters that are simply not addressed in Paul's letters.

Theologizing on the basis of "silence" is an especially precarious procedure. One thinks immediately of the nonsense — repeated so often as to become fact for many — that Paul knew nothing of the "empty tomb" tradition because he never mentions it. What kind of strange Jew, one wonders, do scholars take Paul to be, who could imagine the bodily resurrection of Christ, "who was buried" (1 Cor 15:4), not to have included an empty tomb? Or who would believe that the Pauline churches celebrated the Lord's Supper if the Corinthians had not been messing it up?

This problem of silence is especially acute with respect to the present essay. For in the more than a score of autobiographical references in his letters, Paul seldom refers to his own conversion — and when he does, as in 1 Cor 15:8-10; Gal 1:13-16; Phil 3:4-11; and 1 Tim 1:12-16, he never mentions the role of the Spirit. How then, it may be asked, does one set about to show that Paul's experience of the Spirit at his conversion is the key to understanding the major role that the Spirit plays in his whole theological enterprise?

Yet despite the difficulties, I am convinced that such is the case and that the above thesis can be supported from Paul's letters. In what follows, therefore, I propose (1) to set forth in summary fashion the central features in Paul's understanding of the Spirit — a topic that is so pervasive in his theology and of such a nature as to demand an experienced reality as its origin; (2) to examine the texts where Paul refers to his readers' conversion experiences, and to point out how often he does so in terms of their having "received" the Spirit; and (3) to examine another series of "confessional" (usually soteriological) texts in which Paul includes himself along with his readers as a recipient of the Spirit. By this procedure I hope to demonstrate not only that one cannot understand Paul's theology without noting the key role played by the Spirit, but also that the source of this understanding of the Spirit stems from Paul's own experience of the eschatological Spirit in his Damascus road conversion.

1. The Spirit in Paul's Theology: A Summary

The following propositions set out in summary fashion the central features in Paul's understanding of the Spirit (cf. my *God's Empowering Presence*, where these propositions are spelled out in considerable detail):

1. The Spirit plays *the absolutely crucial role* in Paul's Christian experience, and therefore a crucial role in his understanding of the gospel. So significant is the Spirit to Paul's understanding of the Christian life that, in the final analysis, there is no aspect of his thought — at least, no basic feature of his theology — in which the Spirit does not play a leading role. To be sure, the Spirit is not *the* theological center for Paul. Christ is, ever and always! But the Spirit stands very close to the center, to empower all genuinely Christian life and experience. For this reason, the Spirit must be recognized to play a much more vital role in our thinking about Paul's theology than tends now to be the case.

2. Equally crucial to Paul's perspective is the *dynamic, experienced* way the Spirit comes into the life of the individual and into the ongoing life of the believing community. The experienced reality of the Spirit lies behind everything else that Paul says about the Spirit. And that experienced reality finds frequent expression not as something that Paul argues for, but as the reality he argues from. So in his letters: (a) the Spirit as an experienced reality is presupposed in both the Corinthians' abuse and Paul's correction of Spirit life in that community (cf. 1 Corinthians 12–14); (b) it is basic to his reminding the Thessalonians about the reality of their conversion (cf. 1 Thess 1:4-6); (c) it serves as primary evidence that life in Christ is based on faith and apart from Torah (cf. Gal 3:1-5; 4:6-7); (d) it is the assumption that stands behind the commands in 1 Thess 5:19-22 (cf. 2 Thess 2:2); (e) it serves as evidence confirming Paul's own ministry as an apostle (cf. Rom 15:18-19; 1 Cor 2:4-5; 2 Cor 12:12); (f) it is the basic truth on which Paul can argue for the sufficiency of life in the Spirit (cf. Gal 5:13–6:10); and (g) it is essential to his reminder to Timothy to fan Spirit life into flame in order to receive the necessary power and courage for ministry at Ephesus (cf. 1 Tim 1:18; 4:14; 2 Tim 1:6-7). Both Paul's direct and passing references to the work of the Spirit everywhere presuppose the Spirit as an empowering, experienced reality in the life of the church and the believer.

3. Pivotal to the Spirit's central role is the thoroughly *eschatological* framework within which Paul both experienced and understood the Spirit. The Spirit had played a leading role in his (and others') expectations about the end times, being crucial to at least two strands of expectation. The first of these strands is the promised new covenant. That covenant finds its first expression in the circumcision of the heart in Deut 30:6, is promised in Jer 31:31-34 in light of the failure of the former covenant, and then is tied explicitly to God's gift of his Spirit in Ezek 36:26-27, by whom his end-time

people shall live (37:14). The second of these two strands of expectation is the longed-for renewal of the prophetic gift among God's people, when the outpoured Spirit will, in effect, turn all of God's people into potential prophets (Joel 2:28-29).

Along with the resurrection of Christ, therefore, the outpoured Spirit radically altered Paul's eschatological perspective. For, on the one hand, the coming of the Spirit fulfilled these Old Testament promises as the sure *evidence* that the future had *already* been set in motion. All of God's people (may) now prophesy (1 Cor 14:24, 31; cf. 1 Thess 5:19-22). Likewise, the Spirit has fulfilled the promised new covenant through "circumcision of the heart" (Rom 2:29; cf. 2 Cor 3:3), thereby giving life to his people (2 Cor 3:6; cf. Gal 5:25). Yet, on the other hand, since the final consummation of God's kingdom had *not yet* taken place, the "eschatological" Spirit also serves as the sure *guarantee* of the final glory.

It is impossible to understand Paul's emphasis on the experienced life of the Spirit apart from this "already/not yet" eschatological perspective, which dominated his thinking. His primary metaphors for the Spirit are *down payment* (2 Cor 1:22; 5:5; Eph 1:14); *firstfruits* (Rom 8:23); and *seal* (2 Cor 1:22; Eph 1:13; 4:30). As "down payment" and "firstfruits" the Spirit is evidence that the future has already broken in on us, while at the same time "guaranteeing our inheritance until the redemption of those who are God's possession" (Eph 1:14). Thus by the Spirit God's people are "sealed for the day of redemption" (Eph 4:30).

4. Related to this critical eschatological framework are several converging data that demonstrate how for Paul the experience of the promised Spirit meant the return of *God's own personal presence* to dwell in and among his people. The Spirit marks off God's people individually and corporately as God's temple, the place of his personal dwelling on earth. Brought together here in terms of fulfillment are (a) the theme of the presence of God, which had been expressed in Old Testament times in the tabernacle and the temple; (b) the presence further understood in terms of the Spirit of the Lord (cf. Isa 63:9-14; Ps 106:33); and (c) the promised new covenant of the Spirit from Jeremiah and Ezekiel, wherein the Spirit would indwell God's people and cause them to live and to follow in his ways.

Paul not only sees these themes as fulfilled by the gift of the Spirit, but also understands the Spirit as God's *personal* presence. This best accounts for Paul's general reluctance to refer to the Spirit with such impersonal images as wind, fire, water, oil, or dove, as found in the Gospels and

Acts. On the contrary, he regularly refers to the Spirit's activity with verbs of personal action, as used elsewhere of God and Christ. The Spirit is, therefore, "the Holy Spirit of God" and "the Spirit of Jesus Christ" — that is, the way in which God is currently present with and among his people. The Spirit who knows God's own mind (1 Cor 2:11), and through whose presence we "have the mind of Christ" (2:16), also intercedes for us "in keeping with God's will [purposes]," inasmuch as God also knows the mind of the Spirit (Rom 8:26-27).

5. In this vein it is also important to note how absolutely fundamental to Paul's theology are his *presuppositions about the Trinity* — although that is neither his language nor his primary focus. What makes the Trinity foundational for him, without his ever discussing it as such, are the four ever-present realities (a) that God is one and personal, (b) that the Spirit is both the Spirit of God and the Spirit of Christ, and therefore personal, (c) that the Spirit and Christ are fully divine, and (d) that the Spirit is as distinct from Christ and the Father as they are from each other. This "modification" of Paul's understanding of the one God lies behind much that makes his treatment of salvation dynamic and effective.

Whatever else, the Spirit was not for Paul some mere "it" or "invisible force or power." The Spirit was none other than the way the eternal God and his Christ are forever personally present in and among his people. For salvation is both effected through the work of Christ and made effective in people's lives through the work of the Spirit. So Paul can urge others to join in his struggle through prayer on the basis of "our Lord Jesus Christ and the love of the Spirit" (Rom 15:30) — in part, because Christ is "in heaven interceding for us" (8:34), while the Spirit is "in our hearts" doing the same (8:26).

6. Paul's understanding of God as Trinity, including the role of the Spirit, is thus foundational to the heart of his theological passion — that is, to the experience and proclamation of *salvation in Christ*. Salvation is God's activity, from beginning to end: God the Father initiated it, in that it belongs to God's eternal purposes (1 Cor 2:6-9); it has its origin in God and God as its ultimate goal (1 Cor 8:6); and it was set in motion by God's having sent both the Son and the Spirit (Gal 4:4-7). Christ the Son accomplished salvation for the people of God through his death and resurrection, a complex of events that is the central feature of all of Paul's theology. The effective application in believers' lives of the love of God as offered by the Son, however, is uniquely the work of the Spirit.

So much is this so that when Paul reminds believers of their conversion experience or of their present status in Christ, he almost always does so in terms of the Spirit's activity and/or presence. There is no salvation in Christ that is not fully Trinitarian in this sense. Therefore, there is no salvation in Christ that is not made effective in the life of the believer by the experienced coming of the Spirit, whom God "poured out on us generously through Jesus Christ our Savior" (Titus 3:6, NIV).

7. The goal of God's eschatological salvation is to create a people of his name. These are the people who comprise the true succession of the old covenant people of God, and as a people they are the object of God's saving activity in Christ. But they are now newly constituted through the death and resurrection of Christ and the gift of the eschatological Spirit. Discontinuity with the old covenant people of God is in how one becomes a part of God's new covenant people — that is, *individually* through faith in Christ and the experience of the Spirit.

Formed by the Spirit, the newly constituted people of God are an eschatological people, who live the life of the future in the present as they await the consummation. They are God's family, evidenced by the Spirit's crying "Abba" from within their hearts (Gal 4:6); they are God's temple, the place of his habitation on earth by his Spirit (1 Cor 3:16; Eph 2:21-22); and they form Christ's body, made so by their common lavish experience of the one Spirit (1 Cor 12:13).

8. The Spirit's major role in Paul's view of things is in his being *the absolutely essential element of the whole of the Christian life,* from beginning to end. The Spirit empowers ethical living in all of its dimensions — whether individually, within the community, or to the world. Believers in Christ, who are "Spirit people" first and foremost, are variously described as living by the Spirit, walking in the Spirit, being led by the Spirit, bearing the fruit of the Spirit, and sowing to the Spirit. Likewise, ethics for Paul is founded in the Trinity, for the Spirit of God conforms the believer into the likeness of Christ to the glory of God. The Spirit, therefore, is the empowering presence of God for living the life of God in the present.

There is no Christian life that is not at the same time a *holy* life, made so by the Holy Spirit whom God gives to his people (1 Thess 4:8). At the same time, life in the Spirit also includes every other imaginable dimension of the believer's present end-time existence — including being empowered by the Spirit to abound in hope, to live in joy, to pray without ceasing, to exercise self-control, to experience a robust conscience, to have insight into

God's will and purposes, and to endure in every kind of present hardship and suffering. To be a believer means nothing less than being "filled with" and so to "live in/by the Spirit."

9. Finally, the Spirit is the key to all truly Christian *spirituality*. At the individual level, the life of the Spirit includes "praying in the Spirit" as well as with the mind (1 Cor 14:15; Eph 6:18). In so doing, the Spirit not only helps believers by interceding for them in their weaknesses, but also gives them great confidence in such times of prayer — since God knows the mind of the Spirit, and since the Spirit prays through the believer in keeping with God's own purposes (Rom 8:26-27).

At the same time, the Spirit's presence, including his *charismata*, helps to build up the believing community as its members gather together to worship God. In Paul's churches, therefore, worship is "charismatic" simply because the Spirit is the key player in all that transpires. The Spirit, who forms the body and creates the temple, is present with unity and diversity, so that all may participate and all may be built up.

As I perceive them, then, these are the central features in Paul's understanding of the Spirit. It does not take much imagination to recognize that these are also the vital factors in any valid Pauline theology. What remains to be shown is that the key to such an understanding of the Spirit's central role in all things Christian is to be found in the dynamically experienced way that believers — including Paul himself — entered into the Christian life.

2. The Conversion Texts

Although Paul had occasion at various times to speak of his own conversion, his concern at those times had to do with either his calling as an apostle to the Gentiles (e.g., Gal 1:13-16) or his former relationship to the law (e.g., Phil 3:4-11; cf. 1 Tim 1:8-16). In both cases the nature of the argument did not lend itself, it seems, to refer to his experience of the Spirit.

Quite the contrary, however, prevails when Paul reminds his converts of their conversion(s), which he does from time to time — whether to call them back to their senses (cf. 1 Cor 2:4-5; 6:11; 2 Cor 3:3; Gal 3:1-5), or to encourage them in their Christian lives (cf. 1 Thess 1:4-6, 9-10), or to reinforce a theological point of some kind (cf. 2 Thess 2:13-14; Col 1:6-8, 21-23; 2:13-15; Eph 1:13-14). The first two types of reminders are case-specific, and will be dealt with here in this section. The latter is more general and closely approximates Paul's various confessional, soteriological statements, and so will be treated in the next section.

Striking in the first two kinds of Pauline reminders, which call believers back to their senses or encourage them in their Christian lives, is the prominent role played by the Spirit. Indeed, the only instances where the Spirit is not mentioned are 1 Thess 1:9-10 (where he is presupposed from vv. 5-6) and Col 1:6-8, 21-23; 2:13-15 (where the issue is altogether christological). In all of the other passages, however, the Spirit is either (1) mentioned in a kind of presuppositional manner, without passion or argumentation, as in 1 Cor 6:11; 1 Thess 1:5-6; and 2 Thess 2:13-14, or (2) highlighted as being crucial to the argument itself, as in 1 Cor 2:4-5; 2 Cor 3:3; and Gal 3:1-5. Both kinds of passages reinforce the theological significance of the Spirit for Paul's understanding of the gospel, as noted above (for a more detailed exegesis of the following passages, and the argumentation supporting the perspective offered here, see my *God's Empowering Presence*).

Passages Where the Spirit Is Mentioned in a Presuppositional Manner

The significance of mentioning the Spirit in passages like 1 Cor 6:11 and 2 Thess 2:13-14, to offer but two examples, is (1) the otherwise unnecessary, and therefore altogether presuppositional, nature of the references, and (2) the latent Trinitarianism of such passages. Taking these passages in chronological rather than canonical order, a number of matters need to be observed.

In 2 Thess 2:13-14, by way of a repeated (or renewed) thanksgiving, Paul sets the Thessalonians over against those described in vv. 10-12, who have been taken in by "the Lawless One" (vv. 8-9). Such people have rejected "the truth" (vv. 10, 12) and through deceit have come to believe "the lie" (v. 11), and so have taken pleasure in unrighteousness (v. 12). By way of sharp contrast, Paul feels obliged in vv. 13-14 to thank God for the Thessalonian believers, who have been "elected" (by God), "loved by the Lord" (through his death on the cross), and "sanctified by the Spirit." The Thessalonians' part in this saving work of the three-personed God is "belief in the truth."

173

The reason for using "sanctification" as the metaphor for salvation in this instance, and for tying it to the effectual working of the Spirit, is case-specific. For not only has "holiness" been a concern throughout Paul's two letters to this community (e.g., 1 Thess 4:1-8; 5:23; 2 Thess 1:11-12). More particularly, as God's "sanctified" people who believe the truth, Paul's Thessalonian converts are being set in opposition to those who have been deceived by the "signs and wonders" that issue from Satan's (the deceiving spirit's) falsehoods, and who therefore take pleasure in wickedness.

What needs to be noted here is that putting the emphasis on the Spirit in his reminder of the Thessalonian believers' conversion is for Paul as natural as breathing. The only way to account for it adequately lies with the presupposed, experienced reception of the Spirit at their conversion — which, as 1 Thess 1:4-6 makes clear, was indeed a reality for them.

Likewise in 1 Cor 6:11, believers at Corinth are set in contrast to the wicked, who will not inherit the eschatological kingdom of God: "Such *were* some of you." Paul then reminds them explicitly of their conversion, which was effected by the Triune God. For it is God, who is the presupposed subject of these "divine passives," who has washed, sanctified, and justified them; while, at the same time, such salvation comes "in the name of our Lord Jesus" (referring to the authority of Christ's work on behalf of the believer) and is effected in their lives "by the Spirit of our God."

As with the Thessalonian passage, the references in 1 Cor 6:11 to both "sanctification" (as a metaphor for salvation) and the Spirit are related to the Corinthian situation. In this case the situation probably stemmed from the believers' own false sense of "spirituality." For while their sense of spirituality generated considerable enthusiasm for the manifestation of the Spirit in their worship, it was without a concomitant concern for the Spirit's manifestation in holy living.

Also, as with 2 Thess 2:13-14, the almost casual way in which the Spirit is brought into this passage presupposes the dynamically experienced nature of the Corinthian believers having received the Spirit at the time of their conversion, as 1 Cor 2:4-5 makes clear. Almost certainly, moreover, the "demonstration of the Spirit's power" that Paul speaks about in 1 Cor 2:4-5 refers not to accompanying signs and wonders (although these were also present, as 2 Cor 12:12 makes clear) but to their actual conversion, with its coincident gift of the Spirit — with that gift probably evidenced by various manifestations of the Spirit, especially speaking in tongues.

Passages Where the Spirit Is Highlighted
as Being Crucial to the Argument

This view of things is further (and especially) demonstrated by the most significant of the conversion passages in Paul's letters, that is, by Gal 3:1-5. For in this case the role of the Spirit as a dynamically experienced reality — both in conversion and in the ongoing Christian life — is absolutely crucial to the argument of the entire letter.

At issue for Paul in Galatians is the place of Gentile believers in the newly constituted "people of God" under the new covenant — in particular, whether their place and identity as that people demand Torah observance as well as faith in Christ. In effect, Paul's own calling and mission having to do with a law-free gospel for the Gentiles, and so his understanding of the gospel itself, were at stake. The question lay at the heart of Paul's proclamation: Is the gospel predicated on grace alone, or on grace plus Torah observance. Thus Paul comes out fighting.

The argument of Galatians begins with a series of three autobiographical narratives in 1:11-24; 2:1-10; and 2:11-14, each having to do with the relationship of Paul's apostleship and gospel to Jerusalem. At the end of the third narrative he starts to reiterate in 2:15-21 a "speech" given to Peter at Antioch, which in fact turns out to be a speech directed toward the Galatians. In that speech he argues: Not only is salvation predicated on faith in Christ and not on "works of Torah" (2:16), but if one "builds up again" what has been dismantled in Christ (v. 18) — as Peter, in effect, was doing at Antioch — then everything collapses. Grace is then nullified and Christ has died for nothing (v. 21).

Significantly, in setting out to argue this point with his Galatian converts in the first go-around of 3:1–4:7, Paul begins and ends his argument not with the work of Christ or with Scripture but with an appeal to the experienced reality of their own conversions, an experience that was marked by their having "received the Spirit." He begins this way precisely because he knows that he has his converts on this one: their experience of the Spirit absolutely belies any of the Judaizers' supposed biblical or theological arguments that lie behind their readiness to accept Torah observance as a requirement for Gentiles to be included in the newly constituted people of God.

"Did you *receive the Spirit* by Torah observance," he challenges them, "or by believing what you heard? Are you so foolish? Having *begun by the Spirit,* are you now trying to come to completion through the 'flesh'?" (Gal

3:2-3). Notice that he did not put it our way, with some such question as: "Were you saved?," "Did Christ come into your heart?," or the like. His question works precisely because of the *experienced* nature of their having received the Spirit.

And this is exactly the point of his final two questions in Gal 3:4-5: "Did you *experience* [not "suffer," since this is the common verb for "experience" and there is not a hint of "suffering" in this community; cf. my *God's Empowering Presence,* 387] so many things in vain?" (v. 4), and "He *who supplies you with the Spirit and performs miracles among you,* is this by faith or by doing the law?" (v. 5). For Paul the Spirit is the crucial element in *all* of the Christian life. Therefore, his argument stands or falls on their recalling their own experience of conversion at the *beginning* in terms of the Spirit, to which he appends an appeal to their ongoing experienced life in the Spirit since their conversion.

All of this is made even more clear by the way Paul's argument in Gal 3:1–4:7 concludes in 4:4-7. For after Paul has turned to Scripture to verify that Christ's death was *not* in vain, but in fact did away with the curse of having to "do the law" as opposed to "living by faith" — and the "righteous" can only live by faith, not by doing the law — he wraps up his argument in 3:1–4:7 by bringing the work of Christ and the Spirit into conjunction in his conclusion of 4:4-7: (1) God sent forth his Son both to redeem those who are under the curse of "doing law" and to provide us with "adoption as 'sons'"; (2) Abraham's true descendants are therefore God's true children, his heirs; and (3) the evidence for this is Paul's and their common experience of the Spirit of the Son, whom God also "sent forth," now "into our hearts, crying out *Abba* [the language of the Son]" to God the Father. One may simply note in passing that Paul's Trinitarian soteriology is in full display in this passage.

Finally, and especially crucial both for the argument of Galatians and for our understanding of Paul's theology as a whole, it needs to be pointed out that the experienced nature of their beginning and ongoing life in the Spirit serves as the presuppositional predicate for the final argument in the letter in 5:13–6:10, in which Paul argues for the sufficiency of the Spirit over against life in the flesh, once the time of the Torah is over. His primary ethical imperative, "Walk in/by the Spirit, and you will not fulfill the desires of the flesh" (5:16), assumes the *sufficiency* of the Spirit precisely in keeping with *the lavish experienced reality* to which Paul has already appealed in his earlier argument.

One may readily grant that the above texts do not, in their first instance, demonstrate that Paul's understanding of the Spirit grew out of *his own* experience of the Spirit at his conversion. Nonetheless, what can be pointed out is (1) the rather commonplace, presuppositional nature of these texts, and (2) their occurrence in letters to three different churches (and Ephesians could be added to this list as well). On the basis of this evidence, it could legitimately be argued that Paul's expectations and experience with regard to those who receive the Spirit when they put their trust in Christ are predicated first of all on his own experience of the Spirit at conversion. And that this is almost certainly the case can be demonstrated by another series of soteriological texts that are simultaneously both theological and confessional in nature, of which Gal 4:4-7 is a primary example.

3. The Confessional Texts

One of the more remarkable features of Paul's letters is the frequency of various soteriological affirmations. These affirmations occur in a variety of places — including, in one instance, a letter's salutation (Gal 1:4) — with no two of them even remotely similar in language or structure. Some appear to be so formalized that they are often argued to be pre-Pauline creeds that Paul takes up and fits into his argument. But while there can be little question that some of them have a very creedal ring, both their diversity (i.e., Can there have existed so many different creeds so early, and did Paul know them all?) and the fact that they come to us in Pauline sentences full of Pauline linguistic and theological features should give "pan-creedalists" reasons for pause.

Among these passages, including several from the previous section, are (listed in my view of their chronological order) the following: 1 Thess 1:9-10; 5:9-10; 1 Cor 15:3-5; 2 Cor 1:21-22; Gal 1:4; 3:13-14; 4:4-7; 5:24-25; Rom 3:21-26; 5:1-5; 7:4-6; 8:15-17; Col 2:13-15; Eph 1:11-14; 2:8-10; 1 Tim 1:15; Titus 2:11-14; 3:3-8; 2 Tim 1:6-7; 1:9-10. My interest in these passages is twofold: (1) to point out the frequency with which the Spirit is mentioned in these soteriological affirmations; and (2) to observe that in almost every case (Rom 3:21-26 being the notable exception) the sentences appear in a confessional format, in the sense either that they are expressed altogether in the first person plural or that Paul shifts from second- or third-person plural to first-person plural somewhere in the middle of the passage. Noting this phenomenon in Paul, C. E. B. Cranfield suggests "we might call it a 'confessional first person plural'" ("Changes of Person and Number," 284).

What seems to be happening in these passages is that they are, indeed, intended primarily for his readers, and so begin by duly asserting something about them (or about others in general). But when in the middle of his affirmation Paul comes to the part where his own life has been impacted by the gospel, he shifts to the first-person plural — thereby including himself along with his readers in a kind of confessional way. My interest in these passages lies in several (actually the majority) of them that exhibit both features: the mention of the Spirit and the appearance of the confessional "we."

We begin by returning to the *Abba* confession of Gal 4:4-7, with its companion occurrence of that confession in Rom 8:15-16. Our interest initially lies in the casual — for most readers, nearly imperceptible — way in which Paul moves in Gal 4:4-7 from "those under law," to "we," to "you," back to "our hearts," and finally back to "you":

> in order that he might redeem *those under law,* in order that *we* might receive adoption as children; and because *you* are children, God sent forth the Spirit of his Son into *our hearts,* crying out "Abba, Father." So then, *you* are no longer a slave but a child.

To say, however, that this movement appears to be "casual" does not mean that it is thoughtless. On the contrary, for the "you" in vv. 6 and 7 indicates that Paul's focus is still on his argument with the Galatians. Likewise, his saying "those under law," rather than "us under law" (as in 3:13), reflects his concern to bring the Jews under the same terms of redemption as his Gentile readers.

But Paul's use of the first-person plural in the next clause is neither "editorial" nor exclusive (of the Jews). Rather, the "we" is confessional and inclusive — that is, of both himself and the Galatians. Subtle as this may seem, it makes perfectly good sense in context, so that his sentences should be understood thus:

> in order that he might redeem those under law [i.e., Jews, as well as Gentiles, need to be delivered from the curse of having to "do Torah"], in order that we [i.e., both you Galatian Gentiles and Jews like myself]

might receive adoption as children; and given that you [i.e., Galatian believers] are children [through the work of Christ], God [gave concrete and experiential evidence of that reality by having] sent forth the Spirit of his Son into our hearts [i.e., both yours and mine], crying out "Abba Father." So then you [i.e., singular, as a way of individualizing his point for each of his readers] are no longer a slave but a child.

The identical thing happens in Rom 8:15-16, which is the companion text to Gal 4:4-7:

For in receiving the Spirit *you* were not brought under bondage and fear, but *you* received the Spirit who gave you adoption as children, through whom *we* cry "Abba Father." The Spirit himself bears witness with *our* spirits that *we* are God's children.

Right at the point where argumentation yields to soteriological affirmation, the "you" turns to "we." Of interest in this case, however, is that the "we" does not begin with the mention of "adoption as children," as in the Galatians parallel. That is almost certainly because the sentence has been set up as part of the argument, having to do first of all with his readers. The result is that the "we" begins ungrammatically right in the middle of the sentence.

In a similar way, earlier in the argument of Gal 3:13-14 Paul affirms that Christ redeemed "us" from the curse of the law "in order that the blessing of Abraham might be in Christ Jesus *for the Gentiles,* in order that *we* might receive the promise of the Spirit by faith." As before, it is at the point of mentioning the "receiving" of the Spirit that Paul shifts to the first-person plural, so as to include himself along with his readers.

That Paul intended the "we" in these cases to include himself along with his readers, and not to be understood as simply a "general" confessional "we," is made clear by the earlier occurrence of this phenomenon in 2 Cor 1:21-22. As is well known, Paul's use of "we/us" in 2 Corinthians presents commentators with considerable exegetical difficulties. Because so much of 2 Corinthians is written in the first plural, one is never quite sure whether this usage is "editorial" or intended to include Silas and Timothy. In any case, in the passage at hand Paul twice clarifies the "we" so as to remove any possible ambiguity for his readers. The first clarification appears in v. 19, where what Paul meant by having said "what was preached by us" is clarified to mean "by me and Silas and Timothy."

179

In vv. 21-22, however, the nature of the sentence and its clarification are decidedly different. The whole sentence is thoroughly confessional. And to make sure that the Corinthians understood it to include them and not just himself and Silas and Timothy, Paul inserts the clarifying phrase "along with you" after the first appearance of the first person plural. The result is a soteriological confession that reads: "Now the one who establishes *us*, along with *you*, unto Christ, and has anointed *us* is God, who indeed sealed *us* and gave *us* the down payment of the Holy Spirit in *our* hearts." In the case of the Corinthians, this harks back to their conversion, as recalled in 1 Cor 2:4-5. In the case of Paul, it must also be understood to refer back to his conversion, as the shift from the present tense ("establishes us") to aorist participles (anointed/sealed/gave) seems to indicate.

The confession in Rom 5:1-5 (which actually begins at 4:23), however, is of a quite different sort. The passage is transitional, serving both to conclude the argument up to this point, by way of application and appeal, and to anticipate what follows. Hence the whole is expressed in the confessional "we," and so is intended to include both Paul and his Roman readers. In affirming, therefore, that "the love of God has been poured out in *our* hearts through the Holy Spirit who has been given to *us*" (5:5), Paul is almost certainly reflecting on his experience of the Spirit at the time of his own conversion.

The significant common denominator in all of these confessional texts is that Paul includes himself along with his readers (mostly his own converts) at the key point of "receiving the Spirit": "God sent the Spirit of his Son into *our* hearts" (Gal 4:6), the "Holy Spirit has been given to *us*" (Rom 5:5), God has "given *us* the down payment of his Spirit" (2 Cor 1:22; cf. 5:5), and "*we* have received the Spirit" (Gal 3:14; cf. 1 Cor 2:12). So Pauline is this feature, in fact, that it continues as one of the clearly Pauline elements of the Pastoral Epistles. Thus Paul tells Timothy to "stir up the gift that is in *you*," since "in giving *us* his Spirit, God did not give us cowardice but love, power, and sound-mindedness" (2 Tim 1:6-7). And the clearly creedal, fully Pauline, sentence in Titus 3:4-7 likewise affirms that "God . . . saved *us* through the washing of regeneration and renewal of the Holy Spirit, whom he poured out on *us* richly through Jesus Christ *our* Savior."

My concern in all of this is to point out that not only does Paul regularly remind his converts of their reception of the Spirit at their entry point into the Christian faith, but that he also regularly and consistently includes himself along with them as a recipient of the Spirit when theological argument turns into Christian confession. I would suggest that this phenomenon is clear evidence that Paul's understanding of the Spirit stems from his own reception of the Spirit at his conversion.

4. Conclusions

Where, then, does this lead us with regard to Paul's conversion and his understanding of the Spirit? It must, of course, be acknowledged that there is no specific linguistic link between Paul's references to his own conversion and his understanding of life in the Spirit. Nonetheless, the fact that he so readily — sometimes even to the point of being ungrammatical in so doing — joins himself to his converts when he uses "received the Spirit" language, leads one to suspect that what he says of their conversions applies to his conversion as well. And, significantly, the Spirit plays an absolutely crucial role in most narratives where he is reminding his readers of their conversions. Moreover, the evidence seems compelling that the reason for reminding them of the Spirit's crucial role is precisely because of their having "received" the "outpoured" Spirit in a dynamically experienced way.

Only by Paul's having himself so experienced the Spirit at the beginning of his life in Christ can one easily explain how the Spirit came to play such a significant role in his theology. For it was surely only through the experience of the Spirit — coupled with his experience of Christ at his conversion and his former knowledge of God — that led him to express himself so often in Trinitarian ways. Likewise, it was that same experience of the Spirit, as the Spirit of God and of Christ, that best explains his thoroughly *personal* understanding of the Spirit. Hence, his soteriology is simply laced through with the twofold work of Christ and of the Spirit.

Furthermore, it is the experienced nature of the Spirit at his conversion that best accounts for one of Paul's apparent theological imprecisions, which has disturbed so many later believers. For, as we noted earlier, the most significant role that the Spirit plays in Paul's understanding of things Christian pertains to the ongoing life of the believer and the believing community. And in that ongoing life of the believer and the believing community, the Spirit's role is consistent, thoroughgoing, and all-embracing — including not only ethics ("the fruit of the Spirit") and spirituality (especially the life of prayer), but also worship (in the form of special giftings in the gathered community for the people's edification).

What is striking in Paul's letters is the frequent number of times he expresses these realities in terms of "present-tense" giftings of the Spirit. As Timothy is urged to "fan into flame" the gift of the Spirit, other believers are likewise reminded that God "gives his Holy Spirit" to them (1 Thess 4:8) or that God "richly supplies you with his Spirit and performs miracles among you" (Gal 3:5; cf. Phil 1:19). Still others are exhorted to "be filled with the Spirit," which is presented as the key not only to their worship but also to their relational life within the community of faith (Eph 5:18–6:9).

Our problem with theological precision takes the form of the question, How can people who have received the Spirit at conversion be urged to receive him again and again? But this is a problem of our theological making, not Paul's. His concern lies with the ongoing, dynamically empowering work of the Spirit in believers' lives. As they began, so they are to continue to live. But language fails him at this point — not because believers received the Spirit only partially at the beginning, but because they received the Spirit so dynamically.

Paul's concern lies with the freshness of the experienced reality of the Spirit. His language leads him to urge believers to experience again what they experienced at their conversion: the gift of the Spirit. So he says to the Ephesians, and through them to us all today: "Do not be drunk with wine, but be filled with the Spirit, so that you may admonish and teach one another in various kinds of Spirit-inspired singing." All of this, I argue, is best understood as stemming from Paul's own vital experience of the Spirit as the life-giving Spirit of the living God at his conversion.

Selected Bibliography

Bruce, F. F. "The Spirit in the Letter to the Galatians." In *Essays on Apostolic Themes: Studies in Honor of Howard M. Ervin,* ed. P. Elbert. Peabody, MA: Hendrickson, 1985, 36-48.

Cosgrove, C. H. *The Cross and the Spirit: A Study in the Argument and Theology of Galatians.* Macon, GA: Mercer University Press, 1988.

Cranfield, C. E. B. "Changes of Person and Number in Paul's Epistles." In *Paul and Paulinism: Essays in Honour of C. K. Barrett,* ed. M. D. Hooker and S. G. Wilson. London: SPCK, 1982, 280-89.

Dunn, J. D. G. *Baptism in the Holy Spirit.* London: SCM; Philadelphia: Westminster, 1970.

————. *Jesus and the Spirit.* London: SCM; Philadelphia: Westminster, 1975.

Ervin, H. M. *Conversion-Initiation and the Baptism in the Holy Spirit.* Peabody, MA: Hendrickson, 1984.

Fee, G. D. *God's Empowering Presence: The Holy Spirit in the Letters of Paul.* Peabody, MA: Hendrickson, 1994.

————. *Paul, the Spirit, and the People of God.* Peabody, MA: Hendrickson, 1996.

Gunkel, H. *The Influence of the Holy Spirit.* Philadelphia: Fortress, 1979. German original, 1888.

Stalder, K. *Das Werk des Geistes in der Heiligung bei Paulus.* Zurich: Evangelische Verlag, 1962.

Turner, M. M. B. "The Significance of Spirit Endowment for Paul." *Vox Evangelica* 9 (1975) 58-69.

Paul on Women and Gender:
A Comparison with Early Jewish Views

JUDITH M. GUNDRY-VOLF

WHAT impact did Paul's conversion have on his views regarding women and gender? The question presupposes that we can determine Paul's views on this subject both before and after his powerful experience on the road to Damascus. But on both of these matters there is much room for debate. Paul's post-conversion views on women and gender are disputed due to what many see as inconsistencies in his letters. And previous scholarly assumptions about his pre-Christian views are seriously called into question by newer research on women in Judaism and the Greco-Roman world.

It is impossible here to engage in a thorough investigation of either of these problems. I will begin, therefore, by simply sketching an overview of Paul's thought regarding women and gender, as based on the main texts in his letters on this subject. It will become evident that Paul's thought retains a considerable degree of tension. Then I will relate this conclusion to current discussions about how Paul's views compare with those of his non-Christian contemporaries, in particular, by asking: How do we account for the tension in Paul's view on women and gender? In this section I will raise briefly the relevant issues about Paul's background in Judaism as explanations for his thought. Third, the main part of this essay will compare the views on women of three Jewish authors who wrote during the period of Early Judaism with those of Paul as present in the key texts in his letters. Here I hope to illuminate Paul's thought by demonstrating that the tension it exhibits can also be found in other Jewish writers of his day. Finally, some implications of Paul's conversion for his views on women and gender will be highlighted.

1. An Overview of Paul's Thought Regarding Women and Gender

Paul's views on women and gender can be characterized as including both some egalitarian features and the all-pervasive patriarchalism of the ancient world. On the one hand, an egalitarian note is sounded in the assertion that in Christ "there is no male and female" (Gal 3:28). In addition, Paul gives Christian wives and husbands equal rights and responsibilities in sex (1 Cor 7:2-5); he recommends celibacy, which was a path of greater freedom and autonomy for women (1 Cor 7:7-8, 32-35, 40); and he accepts women's praying and prophesying in the assembly (1 Cor 11:4-5). Likewise, he recognizes the important leadership role of women in his circle — including Priscilla the teacher (Acts 18:26; cf. 2 Tim 4:19); Junia the apostle (Rom 16:7); Phoebe the minister *(diakonos)* and Paul's own "helper" *(prostatis,* Rom 16:1-2); Euodia and Syntyche in the Philippian church, "who struggled beside me in the work of the gospel, together with Clement and the rest of my co-workers" (Phil 4:2-3); Mary, Trypheona, Tryphosa, and Persis who "worked hard in the Lord" (an expression denoting the work of ministers of the gospel, Rom 16:6, 12); and other women who appear to have been leaders in various house-churches (Chloe at Corinth, 1 Cor 1:11; Nympha at Laodicea, Col. 4:15; and possibly Appia, Phlm 2).

On the other hand, Paul reveals his patriarchal background when he insists that women cover their heads while praying and prophesying (1 Cor 11:4-6, 13). Such a command suggests that he accepted the traditional view of women as being subordinate in their status and roles. Paul also sounds rather patriarchal when he says that "man is the head *(kephalē)* of woman" (1 Cor 11:3, with *kephalē* signifying "ruler," "source," or "preminent one"); that "man is the image and glory of God, but woman is the glory of man"; and that "man is not from woman but woman from man, and man was not created for woman but woman for man" (1 Cor 11:7-9).

In 1 Cor 14:34-35 we find a prohibition of women speaking in church and an instruction that they keep silent and ask their husbands at home if they want to learn anything. It must be noted, of course, that considerable text-critical arguments can be made against the authenticity of these verses. But even if we accept them as authentic, it would seem necessary to interpret them as compatible with the instructions in 11:2-16, which speak about women's prophesying and praying in the assembly. Thus they can hardly form a general prohibition but would have to be understood as a prohibition of speaking in a certain way or under certain conditions — though they still, of course, prohibit certain behavior by women in church. Likewise, 1 Tim 2:11-15 forbids women to teach or have authority over a man, affirms women's silence and submission with an appeal to Genesis 3, and declares that women will be "saved through childbearing." Here again, however, there is doubt about the Pauline authorship of this passage — this time not because of text-critical difficulties, but because of doubts that Paul wrote 1 Timothy.

In sum, Paul seems to affirm *both* equality of status and roles of women and men in Christ *and* women's subordinate or secondary place. He appears to think that sometimes the difference between male and female is to be expressed in patriarchal conventions and that sometimes these conventions should be transcended or laid aside. Robin Scroggs, therefore, clearly overstates the case for a "feminist Paul" when he says that the apostle can be construed as "the one clear voice in the New Testament asserting the freedom and equality of woman in the eschatological community" ("Paul and the Eschatological Woman," *Journal of the American Academy of Religion* 40 [1972] 283-303, quoting from 302). On the other hand, dismissals of Paul as a chauvinist or misogynist also appear to miss the mark. Rather, it seems that we cannot avoid the conclusion that there really is a tension in Paul's thought on women and gender — that is, that he is neither a consistent egalitarian nor a consistent patriarchalist. This tension has led, for example, Judith Plaskow to describe Paul as "deeply ambivalent about women's status" ("Anti-Judaism," 123), and Luise Schottroff to speak of "contending tendencies within Paul's thought" (*Let the Oppressed Go Free: Feminist Perspectives on the New Testament* [trans. A. S. Kidder [Louisville: Westminster/John Knox, 1993] 50).

2. Explanations of the Tension in Paul's Thought

How do we account for these different strands in Paul's thought on women and gender? Scholars have usually answered this question in one of two ways. The first is to say that the liberating tendencies in Paul's thought flowed from his gospel, whereas the patriarchal elements were products of "pagan" pressures, given the general patriarchalism of the Greco-Roman world. The second answer also attributes Paul's egalitarian strand to his gospel, but traces his patriarchalism to an unreconstructed Jewish past (as noted by Wegner, "Philo's Portrayal," 41-44). Both explanations attribute Paul's egalitarianism *only* to his Christian thought and his patriarchalism *only* to something essentially extraneous to his Christian thinking.

The pictures of first-century Jewish and Greco-Roman society with which these explanations operate, however, are skewed. For research on the social history of women has shown that both Hellenism and Judaism were a mixed bag when it came to women's status and roles. Though both cultural systems were patriarchies, women in both milieus enjoyed various rights and freedoms — an extension of their social roles was underway in Paul's day (see K. Thraede, "Frau," *Reallexikon für Antike und Christentum* 8, 211-27; J. P. V. D. Balsdon, *Roman Women: Their History and Habits* [London: Bodley Head, 1962]; S. Pomeroy, *Goddesses, Whores, Wives, and Slaves: Women in Classical Antiquity* [New York: Schocken, 1975]; Corley, *Private Women*, 24-79; Kraemer, *Her Share of the Blessings;* Brooten, *Women Leaders*). Such evidence points to the complexity and variety of views on women held by Paul's contemporaries.

In particular, with regard to the status and roles of women in Jewish society, Jewish feminists have criticized Christian feminists for failing to note the ways in which the personhood and rights of women were acknowledged and guarded in Judaism. Christian feminists, they say, have used Jewish sources selectively, and so have portrayed Judaism as completely negative — thereby setting up Christianity as the great liberator of women (so, e.g., L. Swidler, *Women in Judaism: The Status of Women in Formative Judaism* [Metuchen, NJ: Scarecrow, 1976]). This negative and inaccurate portrait of Judaism has even been seen as having been motivated by anti-Judaism (cf. Plaskow, "Anti-Judaism," 118-24).

It is clear that we cannot go on glibly repeating the commonplaces that Paul rose above his non-Christian contemporaries when he exhibited nonpatriarchal attitudes toward women or that he succumbed to the influence of those contemporaries when he exhibited patriarchal attitudes. Rather, what is called for is careful comparison of Paul's views with the views of those who did not share his belief in the gospel. How do Paul's views parallel and how do they diverge from those of his non-Christian contemporaries? By means of such comparisons we can come closer to seeing how Paul's experience on the road to Damascus might have impacted his thought on women and gender. Moreover, the critique of Christian feminist exegesis that comes from Jewish feminists makes it especially imperative to explore afresh the relation of Paul's thought on women and gender to that found in the Judaism of his day. The present investigation is intended as a modest contribution toward that end.

3. Women and Gender in Judaism: A Comparison with Paul

It is entirely appropriate to compare Paul's views on women and gender with other sources that reflect a Palestinian or Hellenistic Jewish milieu. For though Paul was a Jew, he was born in the Diaspora city of Tarsus and was well versed in Greek. And though he probably received his rabbinic training in Jerusalem, Hellenistic influences were by no means absent even there. Moreover, in the Jewish capital there flourished a variety of Jewish communities and pieties holding divergent views (cf. Martin Hengel, *The Pre-Christian Paul* [London: SCM; Philadelphia: Trinity Press International, 1991] 44).

While many Jewish sources include significant material for the study of women and gender — including the Mishnah (see Tomson, *Paul and the Jewish Law*, 97-149) and the *Testament of Job* (see Chesnutt, "Revelatory Experiences") — I have chosen to analyze three from the period of Early Judaism (roughly, from the first two centuries BCE to the second two centuries CE), namely, Sirach, Philo of Alexandria, and *Joseph and Aseneth*. These particular writings have been selected, not because they represent "Judaism" — either of a "Palestinian" or a "Diaspora" type — or because they accurately portray the actual lot of Jewish women, but because they provide extensive material on the subject and illustrate varieties of views within Judaism around Paul's time. The Pauline texts chosen for comparison include Gal 3:28; 1 Corinthians 7; and 1 Cor 11:2-16, which provide the most significant and extensive portrayals of the apostle's views.

Sirach and Paul

The book known as The Wisdom of Jesus the son of Sirach, or in the Latin tradition as Ecclesiasticus (i.e., the "Church's book"), was composed in

Hebrew by Joshua ben Sirach about 180 BCE in Palestine and translated into Greek by his grandson about 130 BCE in Egypt. It gives us a Palestinian Jewish view of women that was exported into a Hellenistic setting and presumably found an echo among Diaspora Jews in Egypt.

Sirach divides women into two categories: (1) the good, submissive, modest, and continent woman, and (2) the evil, insubordinate, shameless, and sexually promiscuous woman. The harlot or strange woman falls into the latter category, and Sirach warns that a man should beware lest he come to ruin through such a woman (Sir 9:3-4, 6-7). Wives can fall into either category. There is the "good wife," who is understanding and silent, continent and modest, full of grace, a good housekeeper, who "honors her own husband and appears wise to all" (26:26) and makes her husband happy (25:8; 26:1-4, 13-18). Marriage to such a woman is good for a man (36:24-26 [29-31]), and such a woman is a man's "choicest possession."

There is also, however, the "evil wife," who "has a tongue," is shameless and full of malice and makes her husband "sigh bitterly" (25:16-26; 26:24-25, 27). She "dishonors [her husband]" and "is known to all as one that is godless in [her] pride" (26:26). Indeed, for Sirach there is no greater evil than the wickedness of a woman and no greater wrath than the wrath of a woman (25:13, 15). He opines, "I would rather dwell with a lion and a dragon than keep house with a wicked woman" (25:16).

What then is a man to do? He must keep away from the seductive woman (9:3-9), and realize that taking hold of a wicked woman is to "grasp a scorpion" (26:7). He must not give power to a wicked woman (25:25), and "if she go not as [he] would have her," he must "cut her off from [his] flesh" (25:26). Sirach reminds his readers that "from a woman did sin originate, and because of her we all must die" (25:24). (The latter text is the earliest extant evidence for the view that Eve is the origin of sin and death.) So in Sirach's view, a woman has a proclivity to evil and, if given power, she can ruin a lot of things. For this reason it is crucial that women be subordinate to men.

Just as wives divide into two kinds, so also for Sirach there are two kinds of daughters: the prudent and modest daughter, who is a treasure to her husband (22:4), and the headstrong, bold, and shameless daughter, who brings shame to her father and husband (22:5; 42:11). The potential for daughters to cause trouble for their fathers is so great that Sirach can say, "a daughter is born to [her father's] loss" (22:3). He has in mind primarily the problems associated with a woman's sexuality — her virginity, marriageability, continence, and fertility. Thus,

> A daughter is to a father a treasure of sleeplessness,
>> and the care of her banishes slumber;
> In her youth, lest she pass the flower of her age,
>> and when she is married, lest she be hated;
> in her virginity, lest she be seduced,
>> and in the house of her husband, lest she prove unfaithful;
> in her father's house, lest she become pregnant,
>> and in her husband's house, lest she be barren.

(42:9-10)

A daughter, like a bad wife, is seen as prone to evil in the form of sexual promiscuity. Her father must "keep a strict watch" over her lest she bring disgrace on him.

> In the place where she lodges let there be no lattice,
>> or spot overlooking the entrance round about.
> Let her not show her beauty to any male,
>> and among wives let her not converse.
> For from the garment issues the moth,
>> and from a woman a woman's wickedness.

(42:11-13)

And if a headstrong daughter is given liberty, she is sure to use it for sexual license, Sirach declares:

> As a thirsty traveller that opens his mouth,
>> and drinks of any water that is near,
> so she sits down at every post,
>> and opens her quiver to every arrow.

(26:12)

Clearly, Sirach has an ideology of male control over women based on women's perceived susceptibility to evil, especially to sexual immorality (see also, however, the critique of the sexually promiscuous male in 23:16-21; 9:3-9). In particular, Sirach wants to secure the man's control over the woman's sexual function on which his honor as a father or husband, as well as his ability to raise up legitimate heirs, depends (cf. 23:22-23 regarding this latter concern). The good wife or prudent daughter is always a woman who is under male control, not an autonomous woman or a woman who challenges the authority of a man.

For Sirach a woman's subordination to man is apparently also grounded in the fundamental superiority of the man. Because of his superior status, Sirach implies, it is a disgrace for a man to be controlled by a woman: "Give not yourself unto a woman [i.e., into her power] so as to let her trample down your manhood" (9:2; cf. 33:19a, b). To be lured into a subordinate position through a woman's beauty or riches is to bring shame on oneself: "Fall not because of the beauty of a woman, and be not ensnared for the sake of what she possesses, for hard slavery and a disgrace it is, (if) a wife support her husband" (25:21-22). To show weakness in the face of a woman's seductive power, as King Solomon did by taking many wives, is shameful for a man: "You gave your loins unto women, and gave them to rule over your body. Yea, you brought a blemish upon your honor" (47:19-20, cf. vv. 12-18). The point is not simply that Solomon *defiled* himself with *foreign* women but that he *shamed* himself by falling under women's power. Here kingly glory contrasts with the shame of being dominated by women.

How do Paul's views compare with Sirach's? Paul's discussion of marriage and sex in 1 Corinthians 7 and his treatment of male and female headdress and gender identity and roles in 1 Cor 11:2-16 suggest that Paul shared some basic patriarchal assumptions with Sirach. Yet there are important points of divergence. Paul did not view women as morally weaker than men, or idealize marriage and its patriarchal concomitant, the subordination of women to men. And although shame played a role in determining gender roles along traditional patriarchal lines, he sometimes broke loose from this criterion in significant ways.

First, woman's moral nature. In 1 Corinthians 7 and 11 there is no suspicion of women as being especially prone to evil and to sexual immorality, as in Sirach. The situation in the Corinthian church, of course, partly explains this fact, for Paul seems to be facing the exact opposite inclination on the part of some women — that is, some of the Corinthians, apparently some of the women especially, wanted to live as celibates (cf. chap. 7). They wanted to be "holy in body and in spirit" (7:34). Paul turns the Corinthians' attention toward the danger of falling into immorality *(porneia)* if they are not able to live a continent life. Now if Paul had thought that women especially were in danger because they are morally weaker, he would have indicated so. Yet he does not. Instead he treats men and women as having the same weakness and the same responsibility and rights:

> But on account of sexual immoralities, let each husband have [sexually] his wife, and let each wife have [sexually] her own husband. Let the husband fulfill his duty to his wife, and likewise the wife to her husband. The wife does not have authority over her own body, but the husband does, and likewise the husband does not have authority over his own body, but the wife does. (1 Cor 7:2-4)

The parallelism of the instructions to the woman and the man implies the equality of their moral natures as well as their equal responsibility and personhood. Paul's warning not to withdraw permanently from the marriage bed in order to devote themselves to prayer "lest Satan tempt you on account of your lack of self-control" (7:5) also lacks any differentiation between women and men. So also, he makes no distinction in his recommendation of marriage if continence proves impossible (7:8, 27), and of celibacy if one has this spiritual gift (7:7-8, 37-38, 40). Women are thus neither more likely candidates for marriage nor less likely candidates for celibacy on account of some difference in their moral nature.

Further, Paul does not view woman as man's tempter. Rather, Satan is the tempter of them both (1 Cor 7:5). The only statement in 1 Corinthians 7 that might put women in a negative moral light is 7:1: "it is better for a man not to touch a woman." It suggests that women are a hindrance to male virtue. This statement, however, should be taken as a Corinthian slogan, and not as coming from Paul. He cites it in order to qualify it in the following discussion (see 7:2, "but . . .").

It follows that Paul does not develop an ideology of male control over women because of a woman's supposed moral weakness and lack of sexual self-control, as Sirach did. Instead of asserting a woman's need to be controlled by a man, Paul accepts "autonomous women" who are consecrated to the Lord in body and in spirit, rather than to a man (7:34). By contrast, the autonomous woman in Sirach is always negatively defined. She is either a harlot or a woman who is "cut off from [her husband's] flesh" because she refuses to submit to him. Also in contrast to Sirach, Paul restricts the man's power by prohibiting both husbands and wives from initiating divorce (7:10-16, recalling Jesus' teaching), and possibly also by stipulating that they must reach agreement about abstaining from sex temporarily in order to devote themselves to prayer (7:5).

Second, on marriage Paul differs from Sirach. Paul's comments on marriage in 1 Corinthians 7 are consistent with the views on gender just described. He does not recommend marriage as the ideal in which woman is subordinate to man. Rather, as often observed, Paul's attitude toward marriage in this chapter is less than enthusiastic. He regards it as more of a hindrance and a source of "tribulation in the flesh" than of happiness, for he is viewing married life from the perspective of "the impending crisis" (7:26-29), and from this perspective it is better to be single. Paul's Christian eschatological outlook therefore leads him to sit loose to traditional gender roles and embrace untraditional ones that eschew marriage and procreation.

Third, shame, or loss of social acceptability, which was so central a value in the ancient Mediterranean world, has in Paul's thought a significant, but not always determinative, function in drawing the lines for appropriate male and female behavior — shame, that is, defined in patriarchal terms. Paul agrees with the general view that behavior that crossed gender boundaries brought shame, both shame to oneself and shame to the person whose honor depended on one's own. In 1 Cor 11:2-16 shame is the reason why, according to Paul, a woman should not uncover her head while praying and prophesying: it is shameful to her and to her "head," the man (who is above her in the social ladder), by going against traditional expectations for women's covered heads. Likewise a man should not cover his head while praying and prophesying, lest he incur shame and cause shame to his divine "head," Christ, by crossing gender boundaries through "unmanly" headdress. In 1 Cor 14:34-35 shame is also the ground for prohibiting the woman from speaking in the assembly, but, as already noted, this statement may very well be an interpolation.

Paul's insistence on avoiding shame by observing gender boundaries in headdress (as is characteristic of many cultures) reinforces patriarchal notions of gender. This is clear from the theological arguments Paul gives to support his practical instructions. "The head *(kephalē)* of every man is Christ, and the head *(kephalē)* of the woman is the man" (11:3); "Man is the image and glory of God, but woman is the glory of man, for man is not from woman but woman from man" (11:7-8). Both of these texts presume the preeminence or priority of man in relation to woman. In the cosmological order man is preeminent — which, in my view, is the connotation of the much disputed term *kephalē*, or "head." And according to the creation story, man has chronological and therefore ontological priority. The man's preeminence or priority is the ground of the woman's owing him honor instead of shame.

Paul applies the principle of avoiding shame when it comes to head-dress that transgresses gender boundaries, but, significantly, he does not apply it across the board. He accepts women's crossing traditional gender boundaries by taking the same roles as men through prophesying and praying in the assembly as the Spirit leads them. This behavior is not excluded as shameful. Patriarchy is here undermined. He also gives the wife the "authority over" her husband's body — that is, for sex (7:4) — which is precisely what Sirach objected to in the case of King Solomon as bringing shame on the man. Patriarchy is again undermined. Paul disregards the priority and preeminence of the man in both of these examples of crossing gender boundaries. Here other considerations weigh more heavily than the avoidance of shame. Thus patriarchal notions of gender are not sacred for Paul. His inconsistency in applying the principle of avoiding shame by respecting gender hierarchy illustrates this fact. In contrast to Sirach, for Paul shame based on the idea of the man's fundamental priority does not govern the *entire* relationship of man and woman in the Lord.

We have seen that Paul participates in the patriarchal worldview of Sirach. But he breaks out of it as well — in some cases for specifically Christian reasons (though parallels in Judaism can also be pointed out, as Tomson, *Paul and the Jewish Law,* 103-24, has shown). He is much less bound to the patriarchal framework of Sirach than the author of 1 Tim 2:12-15, who calls for women to be silent, to submit, and not to exercise authority over a man. These instructions are grounded not only in the man's priority according to the creation story, but also in the woman's being deceived and becoming a transgressor, according to the fall narrative. There is no hint of an impact on gender roles of the apocalyptic shift through Christ's death and resurrection. The "woman will be saved through [or in the process of] bearing children, if she continues in faith and love and holiness, with modesty."

Sirach's obvious misogynism has earned him the label of one of the most conservative voices on women in Judaism. The comparisons of Paul and Sirach made here do not serve to portray Paul the Christian as a hero of liberation in comparison to Sirach the Jew. The fact that Paul transcends the patriarchal framework of Sirach in important ways simply shows that Paul, thinking about gender in the light of Christ, significantly differed from one of the most conservative traditions within Judaism.

Philo of Alexandria and Paul

Philo was a Jewish philosopher and a contemporary of Paul who lived in the city of Alexandria in Egypt and interpreted the Jewish Scriptures using Platonic categories of thought. His views on women and gender are characterized by a distinctive blend of Jewish and Hellenistic thought patterns (see further Wegner, *Chattel or Person?*; Sly, *Philo's Perception,* 207). The result, as we will see below, is not only the reinforcement of patriarchy but also, remarkably, the possibility for women to attain the same status and roles as men.

Philo's social thought is deeply patriarchal. He thinks a woman is inferior to a man by nature (*On the Special Laws* 2.124). He attributes to her both intellectual inferiority — she is more easily deceived than a man (*Questions and Answers on Genesis* 1.33) — and moral inferiority, as seen in his approving description of the reason why Essenes do not marry: "a wife is a selfish creature, excessively jealous and adept at beguiling the morals of her husband and seducing him by her continued impostures" (*Hypothetica* 11.14-17).

Consistent with Philo's view of a woman's "natural" inferiority are his beliefs about her "proper" place and role. A woman belongs in the lesser, domestic sphere, while the greater, public sphere is proper to a man (*On the Special Laws* 3.169-70). Because of a woman's "natural weakness" (*On the Special Laws* 4.223) she is "best suited to the indoor life which never strays from the house," "a life of seclusion" (*On the Special Laws* 3.169-71). A woman's life is "naturally peaceful and domestic" (*On the Special Laws* 4.225). "To a man are entrusted the public affairs of state; while to a woman the affairs of the home are proper" (*Questions and Answers on Genesis* 1.26). A wife, of course, should be subordinate to her husband (*Hypothetica* 7.3).

For Philo the boundaries of gender identity and roles are fixed. A woman who transgresses those boundaries loses her sexual identity, as well as her respectability. If, for example, she engages in the public conflicts that are a man's domain, she will "unsex herself by a boldness beyond what nature permits" (*On the Special Laws* 3.172-75). And to appear in public, which is not proper for a woman, is to "show herself like a vagrant in the streets before the eyes of other men" (*On the Special Laws* 3.171). She can, however, cross gender boundaries in a way that is impossible to discredit, as did Julia Augusta by adorning the Temple, but in so doing she will transcend her sexual identity — or, in Philo's words, "excell all her sex" and

195

through training "supplement nature and practice" and exhibit "virility" in her reasoning power" (*On the Embassy to Gaius* 319-20). That is, she can sometimes overcome her inferiority by acting like a man. The practical barriers to participation in the higher, male sphere, however, are great. For example, Philo sanctions women's going to the Temple to make oblations and say prayers only "when most people have gone home" (*On the Special Laws* 3.171; on the patriarchalism in Philo's social thought, see further Sly, *Philo's Perception*, 179-209).

In Philo's philosophical thought, we find the same division between male and female spheres and the same higher valuation of the male over the female as in Philo's social thought. Influenced by Platonism, Philo characterizes all that is positive or superior — that is, mind, activity, self-control, etc. — as "male," and all that is negative or inferior — that is, passion, sense perception, body, irrationality, passivity, etc. — as "female" (cf., e.g., *Allegorical Interpretation of the Laws* 2.38; 2.49-50; 3.49-50; 3.222-24; *On the Special Laws* 1.200; *On the Creation of the World* 165-67; *Questions and Answers on Genesis* 1.43; 4.15-18; *On Flight and Finding* 51; see further Baer, *Philo's Use*, 38-44; Wegner, *Chattel or Person?* 48-50; Sly, *Philo's Perception*, 96-97).

The ultimate goal in Philo's philosophical system is the attainment of divine wisdom. To reach this goal it is necessary for the soul to strip off the body and passion — that is, leave the "female" sphere and become "male" (*On the Cherubim* 50; cf. *On Rewards and Punishments* 159; see further Baer, *Philo's Use*, 45-49). A woman, however, suffers great disadvantage at this point in Philo's system, just as we would expect, since the basic polarity is built around the more "sensual" feminine and the more "spiritual" masculine. For in Philo's philosophical scheme, she belongs to the sphere of sense and passion — just as in his social scheme she is relegated to the domestic sphere. Indeed, she is quasi-bound to the sphere of sense and passion by her female body.

The resulting disadvantage of a woman becomes clear when Philo discusses sex. For him sex is a potential problem for both men and women because it links them to the realm of desire. Philo would like to think of the patriarchs as *not* having had sex at all with their wives, and argues in *On the Cherubim* 40-41 that their wives were, in reality, not real women but virtues. Nevertheless, when a man has sex he can keep from "emasculating" himself through desire and do it just for procreation; he simply sows his male seed in the "cornfield" of the woman's body at the right time when it can reproduce (*On the Special Laws* 3.32-34; cf. *Questions and Answers on Genesis* 4.154). But a woman cannot keep herself so far removed from the world of the senses, for her monthly flow of blood symbolizes passion and sense (cf. *On the Special Laws* 2.54; *On Flight and Finding* 188-93). Her womb, in fact, is "nature's laboratory" where the living creature is molded, and ties her to the sensate world (*On the Special Laws* 3.33). Thus a woman appears to be slated by her female body not to participate in the higher realm of the mind and of knowledge, which "comes into being through estrangement from sense and body" (*On the Cherubim* 41).

Nevertheless, there is a way also for a woman to attain divine insight. It emerges precisely from the division between the spheres of the mind and the body that initially excluded her from the realm of knowledge and tied her to the realm of sense perception. A woman, just like a man, can exit the "female" sphere of the body and desire. This is done by abdicating desire and sexual activity, which puts the soul on the path of heavenly ascent.

For a woman, however, it also includes ceasing her reproductive functions, which tie her to the sensate world. She must return to a state of "virginity," or inability to conceive and give birth. The ideal of "virginity" in the sense of barrenness appears in Philo's discussions of the soul's attainment of divine wisdom. The soul must "become barren and cease to produce . . . children," which are "pleasures" and "desires," and must be "transformed into a pure virgin" (*On Rewards and Punishments* 159-60; see Baer, *Philo's Use,* 51-53). "When God begins to consort with the soul, he makes what before was a woman into a virgin again, for he takes away the degenerate and emasculate passions which unmanned it" (*On the Cherubim* 50). Sarah is Philo's allegorical representation of the revirginized soul that is able to commune with God: God "will not talk [with Sarah] till she has ceased from all that is after the manner of women (Gen xviii.11), and is once more as a pure virgin" (*On the Cherubim* 50).

There are also real flesh-and-blood women in Philo's world who attain divine insight through re-virginization, or continence and barrenness. They are the women of the Therapeutic community (the "Therapeutae"), a group of Jewish ascetics who had withdrawn to the desert where they lived in solitary cells and came together only for divine worship. They devoted themselves to contemplation of the law, and they saw visions and spoke in ecstatic speech (*On the Contemplative Life* 12, 26, 84).

The reason why the women were able to attain such heights is clear. Philo says that most of them were "*aged* virgins," that is, abstinent women past their childbearing years. They were not only continent but barren: "In their ardent yearning for wisdom they have spurned the pleasures of the body and desire no mortal offspring"; rather, they seek "those immortal children which only the soul that is dear to God can bring to birth unaided because the Father has sown in her spiritual rays enabling her to behold the verities of wisdom" (*On the Contemplative Life* 68). In other words, the female Therapeutae had escaped the realm of passion by not only renouncing desire but escaping their female bodies that tied them to this realm and exchanging physical conception and childbirth for its spiritual equivalent. In this way they attained divine insight just as the men did.

This equality of women with men through asceticism and revirginization is made tangible in the Therapeutics' "sacred vigil," where men and women came together — just as the Israelites did at the Red Sea to sing of the miracle of their redemption — to "form a single choir" (*On the Contemplative Life* 85-87). Daniel Boyarin (*Radical Jew*, 188) has argued that "this ritual of the Therepeutae is a return to the originary Adam," which in Philo's view is an *"incorporeal"* androgyne, "neither male nor female" (*On the Creation* 134). The Therapeutics' ecstatic "joining of the male and the female in a mystical ritual recreates in social practice the image of the purely spiritual masculo-feminine first human of which Philo speaks in his commentary [on Genesis]." It is through the disappearance of gender distinctions through return to a primal disembodied state, then, that equality is attained in Philo's thought, if Boyarin's analysis is correct. Such equality was lived out in the sect of the Therapeutae.

Philo, then, reinforces patriarchal values by applying Platonic categories in his thinking on women and gender. He also, however, because of his Neoplatonism, opens up for women the possibility of equality with men in access to the divine sphere — but at the cost of their becoming defeminized and "disembodied" (cf. Baer, *Philo's Use*, 100-101).

There are both striking similarities and profound differences between Philo and Paul with respect to women and gender. Both entertain an ideal of humanity beyond gender inequality, at least implicitly. And both, significantly, express that ideal in very similar terminology. Philo speaks of the ideal human being, created in the image of God, as "neither male nor female." Paul's foundational statement about the new humanity in Christ in Gal 3:28 contains the words: "there is no longer male and female, for all of you are one in Christ Jesus."

Despite these similarities in formulation, the way Philo and Paul ground their respective statements and what they do with them are profoundly different. Philo grounds his ideal of androgyny in the denial of the body — that is, bodily differences are stripped away, and so in the realm of the pure spirit there is neither male nor female. But this notion presupposes a Platonic and radically non-Jewish denigration of the body that Paul does not share. Paul, on the other hand, grounds the claim that there is "no male and female" in baptismal unification with Christ, which entails not the stripping away of the body, but coming to be "in Christ" as real men and women on the same basis — Christ's death and faith in him — and thus as equals.

Paul's lack of sympathy for Philonic denigration of the body, in fact, results in there being no need to practice sexual asceticism to commune with God or to attain divine inspiration, as Paul's treatment of the question of celibacy in 1 Corinthians 7 shows. While it is true that Paul considers celibacy a better choice than marriage, he does so for practical reasons related to the eschatological character of the present age — the "impending distress" and the special burdens that it causes for the married — and not because denial of the body is a precondition for receiving the Spirit. He positively commands marriage for those who cannot live a continent life. At the same time, he raises the Corinthians' expectations for spiritual gifts of inspiration: "Now I would like all of you to speak in tongues, but even more to prophesy" (1 Cor 14:5); "Strive for the spiritual gifts, and especially that you may prophesy" (14:1); "When you come together, each one has a hymn, a lesson, a revelation, a tongue, or an interpretation" (14:26). Thus the indulging of desire does not prevent one from partipicating in spiritual realities — though some Corinthians may have assumed so. In contrast to Philo, then, Paul disassociates the sphere of divine wisdom from a denial of the body and of passion.

Since for Paul the body is not a hindrance to life in the Spirit, a woman, who possibly has a stronger body-identification than a man, does not suffer any disadvantage in her aspirations to participate in the Spirit. To be a pneumatic she does not need to "defeminize" herself by denying her female body through sexual asceticism. Nor do her reproductive functions need to cease. When Paul affirms a difference between the sexes — a difference rooted in the body — as, for example, in 1 Cor 11:2-16, it does not lead to a view of woman as barred from, or more distant to, the world of divine insight. And he does not expect the Corinthian women to dis-

199

continue praying and prophesying in the assembly, but simply to "cover" their heads in order to symbolize their female identity. In Paul's thought, women can become pneumatics, attaining divine insight, while remaining women. He does not idealize "virgin" prophetesses in the sense of the women Therapeutae, who were beyond femaleness. For Paul prophets are clearly male and female. He does not deny or denigrate the gender of either.

Nevertheless, precisely because a woman remains a woman and does not escape her femaleness — rooted in the body — a woman in Paul's thought seems to be vulnerable to a subordinate, even inferior, status in relation to man. Paul requires a woman to cover her head in manifestation of her female identity, which is a cultural symbol of her secondary status and role in relation to man. Paul, in fact, says that a woman can shame a man by not covering her head, which also implies that she is his social inferior.

So in his supporting arguments for the requirements (1) to maintain the symbols of sexual difference and (2) to avoid shame through the abandonment of these cultural signposts, Paul uses a hierarchical framework in his "Christian cosmology" and theology of creation: "the head of man is Christ, and the head of the woman is the man" (1 Cor 11:3); and "man is the image and glory of God, but woman is the glory of man" (11:7-9). Thus, although a woman's difference, as rooted in her female body, does not make her inferior to a man as far as access to the Spirit and divine revelation are concerned, there remains a gender hierarchy and inequality in some other respects — which Philo's virgins escaped (or, at least, minimized) by "exiting" the body.

There appears, therefore, a tension in Paul's thought between, on the one hand, equality in Christ, as lived out in the pneumatic worship of the community before the world, and, on the other hand, inequality as evident in his explicit approval of patriarchal relations. For Paul, in contrast to Philo, there is no escape from this tension. The reason there is no escape is not that Paul is willingly or unknowingly falling back to his alleged Jewish patriarchal persuasions. Rather, it is because of his genuinely Christian, and at the same time Jewish, belief that the body, marriage, and sex are "goods" to be affirmed. Yet given the pervasive patriarchal culture of the time, such an affirmation of the body could only be lived out under the conditions of inequality. And insofar as there is no escape from the body, which must be either male or female, there is no escape from this culturally conditioned inequality.

There is also, however, another, more Christian, reason why Paul affirms inequality while at the same time affirming equality, as he does in Gal 3:28: the Church has a mission to accomplish, and so it cannot withdraw from the world into the kind of community that the Therapeutae formed. Living in the world, and for the sake of a world that is patriarchal, and affirming that the body, marriage, and sex are good meant — to some degree, at least — living out the inequality inherent in that world. Hence, within the framework of Paul's thought and within the context of his world, both egalitarianism and patriarchy could be — indeed, had to be — affirmed on genuinely Christian grounds.

Joseph and Aseneth *and Paul*

Joseph and Aseneth is best described as a Greco-Roman romance, or novel, of Jewish origin, which probably dates from between the first century BCE and the early second century CE. It tells the story of the conversion of an Egyptian woman named Aseneth to Judaism and of her marriage to Joseph, which is mentioned in Gen 41:45.

The story may have been intended as an apologia for women proselytes to Judaism, who were not few (cf. Chesnutt, "Revelatory Experiences," 112-13). Further, it can be read as portraying how, through conversion to Judaism, Aseneth is freed from a social milieu oppressive to women and gains an impressive new status and role, while still remaining within a patriarchal context. This work, therefore, portrays Judaism in favorable terms for women — though of the two textual traditions in which it is preserved, the shorter version gives a more positive view of Aseneth and lacks some of the more patriarchal features of the longer version (cf. Kraemer, "Book of Aseneth," and Standhartinger, *Das Frauenbild*, on the differences and the dispute regarding which version is earlier).

The book opens by describing Aseneth as a ravishing eighteen-year-old virgin fought over by all the most eligible bachelors in Egypt because of her famed beauty, which no man has ever espied (1:3-9). For her part, she hates men and secludes herself in a high tower (2:1) where "her virginity was being fostered" (2:7) and where she worships and fears all the Egyptian gods and sacrifices to them daily (2:3). In other words, Aseneth is a very pious young woman with the highest sexual morals who is determined to resist objectification by men. She will not be prize male bounty. When her father tries to marry her off to Joseph, she protests that she will have only the Pharaoh's firstborn son for a husband, not some son of a Canaanite shepherd sold as a slave and with a reputation for sleeping with his mistress. Aseneth stages a rebellion against the system that would deprive her of the identity she has created for herself, quite apart from male interests. And she succeeds in her plan by converting to Judaism.

In *Joseph and Aseneth* the Jewish religion is pictured as one that offers women the following benefits: escape from being treated as mere objects of male lust; access to ineffable divine mysteries and revelations; transformation to immortality in a ritual reversal of Eve's eating the forbidden fruit; a public salvific role; and a new ability to speak to God and be heard by God, so as even to utter miracle-working prayers. Aseneth receives all these benefits because of her conversion. Aseneth's sexuality, however, remains intact. And the gains she makes are set within a patriarchal framework in which women have a subordinate, secondary status.

As the story unfolds, Aseneth is completely swept away by Joseph once she actually sees him in his physical beauty and royal glory. She now wants her father to give her to Joseph "for a maidservant and slave," claiming that she "will serve him for ever and ever" (6:8). She comes to greet Joseph with a kiss, but he, unlike all the other men, resists. He will not take her simply because she is beautiful and desirable. He will only take her when she worships the one true God. His lips will not touch the mouth that blesses dead and dumb idols (8:1-7). He sees Aseneth not as a sexual conquest but as a person with religious commitments that are to be taken seriously. We have to wait a whole week for the kiss while Aseneth repents by prayer and fasting in sackcloth and ashes.

After seven days Aseneth gets an angelic visitation (14:1–15:10). A man from heaven comes and assures her that her words of repentance have been heard and that she is from that day transformed to life incorruptible — and she will also get to marry Joseph. Furthermore, her new name is "City of Refuge" because, as the angel forecasts, "in you many nations will take refuge with the Lord God, the Most High, and under your wings many peoples trusting in the Lord God will be sheltered, and behind your walls will be guarded those who attach themselves to the Most High God in the name of Repentance" (15:7). And so Aseneth is not only herself made new, but she becomes a salvific figure: "in her" many others will experience the salvation of God.

202

At the conclusion of the book Aseneth fulfills this role toward her own would-be assassins in a dramatic display of mercy (chap. 28). The sons of Bilpah and Zilpah, who have joined in a plot to kill her, raise their swords against her. But Aseneth prays to God and their swords turn to ashes. They repent and plead for mercy, and she hears their request and hides them. Then she appeases the wrath of Simeon and his brothers against these traitors and insists that they should be pardoned and not shown evil for evil. Aseneth has, indeed, become a "City of Refuge" where the repentant find shelter and where the vicious circle of evil and vengeance is broken. Like Joseph, the savior of Egypt in time of famine, Aseneth also becomes a savior (cf. Kraemer, "Book of Aseneth," 881). And in all of this, as well as in the other parallels between Aseneth and either Joseph or Levi throughout the book, Aseneth is exalted as a woman (see Chesnutt, "Revelatory Experiences," 112, 115).

Aseneth's ignorance as an idolater, which is thematized in the beginning of the book, is replaced by a supernatural knowledge of divine mysteries, which are revealed to her by an angel (chap. 16). For example, when a wonderful honeycomb miraculously turns up in her storeroom, she knows that it originates from the mouth of the angel. The angel then proclaims her "blessed," "because the ineffable mysteries of the Most High have been revealed to [her]" (16:14). The angel is the one who reveals these mysteries to her, and the revelation is portrayed dramatically: he "called her to himself, and stretched out his right hand, and grasped her head and shook her head with his right hand. And Aseneth was afraid of the man's hand, because sparks shot forth from his hand as from bubbling (melted) iron. And Aseneth looked, gazing with her eyes at the man's hand" (16:12-13). Later on Aseneth utters a miracle-working prayer that contrasts with her prayers as a repentant idolater, which she initially could not even say out loud and which she was not even sure God would hear. She is also privy to the revelations of "unspeakable [mysteries] of the Most High God" to Levi the prophet, who saw "letters written in heaven by the finger of God" and then passed on these mysteries to Aseneth in secret (22:13). Aseneth's new status as an enlightened mystic is thus sustained throughout the book.

The angel instructs Aseneth to eat from the honeycomb angelic food that is "[full of the] spirit of life" and that bestows immortality. He breaks off a piece, takes a bite, puts the rest in Aseneth's mouth, and tells her that she now partakes of immortality (16:7, 14-16). The scene apparently symbolizes an undoing of primal history, for it depicts a reversal of the story about Eve's deception by the serpent, her giving to Adam of the forbidden fruit, his listening to the voice of his wife, and their both being banished from the Garden and the tree of life (cf. Kraemer, "Book of Aseneth," 880).

Aseneth, therefore, is the new Eve. She is a recipient of divine knowledge and a sharer in immortality. Genesis 3 no longer defines her status and role as a woman. Instead, her participation in a new, incorruptible life, as a result of repentance and as characterized by divine knowledge — here ritualized in the eating of the honeycomb — signals her new status and role. Ross Kraemer gives this portrait of woman an ironic twist by suggesting that in the longer text the "subliminal mesage is that paradise is restored when women are properly obedient to their husbands" ("Book of Aseneth," 881). But this interpretation depends on identifying the angel whom Aseneth obeys, with Joseph, which seems rather questionable.

When the angel beckons, "Come!", thousands of bees arise from the honeycomb and encircle Aseneth from head to foot. They make on her lips another honeycomb and eat from it. Swarming bees around a person can symbolize inspiration or eloquence, as in the case of Pindar, Plato, Ambrose, and others (cf. C. Burchard, "Joseph and Aseneth," in *The Old Testament Pseudepigrapha*, vol. 2, ed. J. H. Charlesworth [Garden City, NY: Doubleday, 1985] 230, note f2. [citing M. Philonenko and I. Opelt, though Burchard himself demurs]). If so here too, then Aseneth's reception of divine revelation is again depicted, though this time more symbolically, and she is portrayed as being divinely inspired. And when the angel tells the bees to go off, the ones that wanted to harm her fall to the ground and die, while the others fly away into heaven (16:17y-23) — a detail that may suggest a plurality of good and evil inspiring agents, Aseneth being protected from the evil ones.

As the plot develops it becomes clear that through Aseneth's conversion to Judaism and marriage to Joseph she has escaped the objectification by men that plagued her as a virgin. Yet throughout, she never has to deny her sexuality. She marries the one man who did not treat her as a sex object. She abandons the seclusion of her tower and enters into relationships with other men that are intimate, yet not eroticized. She is especially close to Joseph's brother Levi. At one point the story relates how Levi sat beside her and how she grasped his hand and "loved Levi exceedingly"; similarly, how he loved Aseneth "very much" (22:12-13; cf. 28:15). Their relationship seems to be characterized by the intimacy of fellow mystics, since it centers around Levi's sharing of divine mysteries with Aseneth.

Furthermore, the motif of Aseneth's escape from the sexual advances of men dominates the whole second part of the book (chaps. 22–29), which tells the story of a failed plot by Pharaoh's son to kidnap her and make her his own. Pharaoh's son had been "cut to the heart" by Aseneth's beauty and was filled with jealousy by her marriage to Jospeh. Levi, however, gets a supernatural revelation of the plot and orchestrates a counterattack. In the end, Pharaoh's son dies and Aseneth is forever freed from that threat.

Aseneth's conversion to Judaism, therefore, sets her free from the unwanted sexual advances of men. Likewise, it replaces her ignorance with divine knowledge, gives her a public role in the salvation of others, and transforms her from mortality to immortality as a new Eve.

For Paul, as for the author of *Joseph and Aseneth,* conversion and initiation had significant implications for the status and role of women. We need only look at Gal 3:27-28, which mirrors the baptismal tradition associated with Christian initiation, to see that Paul thought this was the case: "For as many of you as were baptized into Christ have put on Christ. . . . there is no male and female, for you are all one in Christ Jesus." But neither for Paul nor for *Joseph and Aseneth* does initiation obliterate the difference between males and females — as life in the community of believers, as portrayed by both authors, indicates.

Just as Aseneth remains within the bounds of a traditional female identity by wearing her veil and marrying, so Paul expects the Corinthian women to "cover" their heads to signify their gender identity. He gives them the option, however, of marrying or remaining celibate — which is a possibility that does not emerge for Aseneth — and so departs significantly from assumptions about traditional female roles.

Two interrelated motifs appear in the description of Aseneth's and the Corinthian women's initation into a new life, motifs that help to account for their new status and roles: (1) the presence of the divine Spirit, and (2) the revelation of divine mysteries or inspiration. The Corinthians' initation is a baptism "by one Spirit" (1 Cor 12:13), from whom they receive gifts of inspiration. These gifts are identified as prophecy, which Paul describes as the knowledge of mysteries (1 Cor 13:2); tongues, which he characterizes as human and angelic (1 Cor 13:1); knowledge; revelation; interpretation; etc. (1 Cor 13:2; 14:26). These gifts of inspiration are apparently mediated by angels (cf. 1 Cor 11:10). Similarly, Aseneth at her initiation eats of the honeycomb "full of the spirit of life" and receives knowledge of "ineffable mysteries" from an angel. Bees, which may symbolize inspiration, come out of the honeycomb to encircle her and land on her lips. Levi the prophet passes on his revelations to her in secret.

Thus both Paul and *Joseph and Aseneth* portray women initiates as pneumatics or enlightened mystics, in contrast to their former ignorance when they lacked the divine spirit. But whereas the Corinthian women are active prophets and pneumatics in their community (cf. 1 Cor 11:4-5, 10, 13), Aseneth herself does not become a prophet. Instead she develops a close relationship with Levi the prophet, who mediates his revelations to her privately. She has an elite status as a mystic, but she is clearly not the equal of the mystic Levi — a man, who stands between her and the Revealer.

Aseneth's experience of angelic inspiration may supply the background for Paul's enigmatic statement in 1 Cor 11:10, "the woman ought to have control over her head because of the angels." Aseneth experiences a violent shaking of her head when the angel puts his spark-shooting hand on her head, which presumably signifies the mediation of the ineffable mysteries to her. The psychological effect on Aseneth is emphasized: she is afraid and gazes at the man's hand. The scene thus portrays inspiration as accompanied by violent physical effects — in particular, to the head, the part of the body representing the person on whom the divine revelation comes — and as psychologically overwhelming. Against this background it becomes clear why Paul, in the context of women prophesying and praying under inspiration, can speak about the need for a woman to control her head. For the experience of inspiration could be so dramatic as to make one lose control over one's body and speech.

In 1 Cor 14:30-32 Paul expresses precisely such a concern — prophets who lose control under inspiration create such pandemonium that their hearers cannot understand what they are saying, and so are not instructed or encouraged by their prophecies. To deal with this situation, Paul says that the "spirits of prophets [i.e., the inspiring agents] are subject to prophets [i.e., to those being inspired]." The instruction in 11:10 apparently has a similar intent: a woman prophet ought to have control over her head because of the angels — that is, she must keep control under potentially violent angelic inspiration, lest her inspiration become merely a private experience rather than a means of directing the community. Whether Paul also thinks that such a woman is open to some harm through malevolent inspiring agents, as Aseneth was through malevolent "bees," is uncertain.

Corinthian women, it seems certain, had public roles as prophets and leaders in communal prayer. Though this is different from Aseneth's salvific role as a "City of Refuge," it is comparable in its significance and effects, for the Corinthian women's divinely inspired words had power to nurture the community spiritually. Paul describes the effect of glossolalia and prophecy in 1 Cor 14:22-25 in dramatic terms that compare with the powerful effect of Aseneth's miracle-working prayer at the scene of her rescue of the sons of Bilpah and Zilpah from death. An unbeliever who comes into the Corinthians' assembly when all are prophesying, says Paul, will be convicted. The secrets of the unbeliever's heart will be revealed, and that one will fall down on his or her face and worship God, saying, "God is among you." In other words, a Christian woman's prophecy can lead to the salvation of her hearers as well as the edification of other believers.

Just as men are the object of Aseneth's mercy and protection in the exercise of her new public role, so in the fellowship of Christians are men dependent on women in their new roles as pneumatics. Paul makes this point in 1 Cor 11:11: "Neither is woman without man nor is man without woman in the Lord." Being "in the Lord" creates a new interdependence of men and women. As the context suggests, it is an interdependence based on spiritual gifts. The inspired prayer and prophecy of women are indispensable to men, and vice versa.

For this mutual interdependence in the Lord for spiritual nurture Paul finds an analogy in the mutual interdependence of men and women for their physical existence: "For just as the woman is from the man, so also the man is through the woman" (11:12). Thus in both Paul and *Joseph and Aseneth,* women play key roles in the public arena associated with the salvation and spiritual good of others, including men. These roles are the result of their initiation, as well as the powers and expectations that are bestowed in conjunction with that initiation.

Like the author of *Joseph and Aseneth,* Paul defines a woman's new status and roles against the backdrop of primal history. *Joseph and Aseneth* retains the gender difference based on creation as male and female — even while transcending it by portraying Aseneth as a new Eve, elevating her to the level of a mystic who has angelic inspiration, and delegating to her a salvific role comparable to Joseph's. The book, however, appears to retain a gender hierarchy among mystics, for Aseneth's continued access to divine mysteries is still only through the prophet Levi. Paul may appear to negate gender difference based on creation in Gal 3:28: "there is no male and female." Yet interpreted in its context, this statement only makes maleness and femaleness adiaphorous — they are irrelevant for membership in the eschatological community — and does not declare them abolished.

Further, Paul does not set aside all of the implications arising from the difference between male and female, which is what some of the Corinthians seem to have been doing. In fact, Paul insists on expressing gender difference through distinct male and female headdress (1 Cor 11:2-16), and he does so by appealing to creation in 1 Cor 11:7-9: "man is the image and glory of God, and woman is the glory of man"; "man is not from woman but woman from man"; and "man was not created for woman but woman for man." On the other hand, he does not insist on different roles for women and men *in the community's worship* on the basis of the difference between male and female, but implicitly approves both women's and men's praying and prophesying in the assembly. Thus both Paul and *Joseph and Aseneth* can be seen to be moving beyond an understanding of gender identity and roles based simply on created differences. We can attribute this development, in both cases, to the way in which the s/Spirit that brings immortality shapes a woman's new identity and empowers her for new roles.

In addition, Paul goes on to support a Christian woman's new identity and roles by developing fresh perspectives on women from creation itself — which betrays his concern to hold on to creation as a theological determinant of gender identity and roles in Christ. He argues from the created order that "the man is through the woman," as well as from the notion of God as creator that "all things are from God" (11:12), in order to support the statement that "man is not without woman in the Lord" (11:11). Taken as a reference to the "spiritual" dependence of men on women *pneumatics,* this verse essentially reverses the *exclusive* male/female gender hierarchy on the basis of Genesis 2 by pointing to a parallel female/male hierarchy in the body of Christ, which has its mundane analogy in creation (i.e., the priority of a woman to a man in procreation; for a more detailed argument on the interpretation of 1 Cor 11:2-16 given in this essay, see my "Gender and Creation in 1 Corinthians 11:2-16: A Study in Paul's Theological Method," in *Evangelium — Schriftauslegung — Kirche* [Essays in Honor of P. Stuhlmacher; ed. O. Hofius et al.; Göttingen: Vandenhoeck & Ruprecht, 1997] 152-71). Paul's novelty over against *Joseph and Aseneth* is in seeing a Christian woman's *new* identity in relation to men as *consistent with creation* read in the light of the new creation.

The foregoing discussion has reviewed three partly overlapping, partly distinctive constructions of women and gender within Judaism, all of which have a certain degree of Hellenistic influence. Sirach operates with a thoroughly patriarchal, at points misogynist, perspective. Philo shares the patriarchalism of Sirach, but merges it with Platonic categories and so produces the possibility of gender equality at the price of disembodiment and denial of sexuality and sexual difference. *Joseph and Aseneth* also works within an overall patriarchal framework but, in contrast to Philo, conserves a Jewish regard for the body and gender difference. Within this framework, however, Aseneth — and, by implication, other women who convert — attains impressive social gains and freedom from severe forms of oppression through patriarchy as a result of her transformation to new life through the power of the divine spirit. Paul's view of women and gender has much in common with *Joseph and Aseneth*. But what is striking about the women in Paul's first letter to the Corinthians — that is, about those who break out of a patriarchal mold and become by the inspiration of God's Spirit prophets and community leaders — is that not only are they indispensable in their roles, but they are also just ordinary, even nameless, women, and not (necessarily) exceptional virgins or individuals like Aseneth.

4. The Implications of Paul's Conversion for His View of Women and Gender

Did Paul change his mind on women and gender as a result of his experience on the road to Damascus? From our brief sampling of Jewish authors, we have seen that a variety of views were current in various strands of Early Judaism in Paul's day. Furthermore, it is difficult to know exactly what Paul would have believed before his conversion, since we have only his Christian writings, in which no direct statements on his pre-conversion view of women appear. Some inferences, however, may be drawn, though drawn somewhat guardedly.

That there is some commonality as well as difference between Paul's Christian views and those of his non-Christian Jewish contemporaries seems apparent. The commonality and difference apply both to the more patriarchal and to the more egalitarian features of his thought. So Paul does not appear to be entirely unique in a first-century Jewish setting, especially in the Diaspora. Nevertheless, Paul develops specifically Christian grounds for his views, and that is what we must draw attention to in conclusion.

Paul's ideal of one humanity without gender discrimination (Gal 3:28) is grounded in the reality of incorporation into Christ by faith, but this is not understood to entail a rejection of the body that bears the marks of gender difference. A believer's new identity in Christ does not erase maleness or femaleness, which Paul's Jewish heritage taught him to value. Rather, it is as either women or men — not as beings beyond sex and gender — that Christians live out their new lives. And the lives of believers in Christ are characterized by the gifts of the Spirit of Christ, who does not discriminate according to gender.

In Paul's day, of course, Christians lived out their lives under the conditions of patriarchy. And we find Paul himself *advocating* certain patriarchal forms of expressing the distinction between male and female. Yet he also has specifically Christian reasons for doing so. In his view, Christians had to live "in the world," and they had a mission to that world which was dominated by a patriarchal culture. Christian presence and mission within such a world, therefore, necessarily took on certain of its patriarchal characteristics, including a degree of inequality between men and women. We probably ought not, however, to speak of "accommodation" to patriarchy, as if Paul could have completely abstracted from his socio-cultural context and distinguished between what the gospel implies about gender identity and roles, and what the cultural situation demands.

It would be unjustified, therefore, to portray Paul at his conversion as having experienced a radical transformation from patriarchalism to egalitarianism. Nevertheless, it is also clear that the gospel was central in his thinking about women and gender. It is precisely because of Paul's understanding of what it means to be "in Christ" and a part of "the body of Christ" that he can burst out of a patriarchal framework — at points quite dramatically — without resorting to a denial of the body. This novelty was also possible within a Hellenistic Jewish framework, as we observed in *Joseph and Aseneth;* that is, it does not necessarily depend on specifically Christian beliefs.

Whatever his beliefs before conversion, however, it is clear that Paul's *Christian* beliefs played a key role in his theologizing about gender after Damascus. His letters, in fact, suggest that those beliefs were formed communally with women and men who shared his faith in Christ. More precisely, his letters show that his Christian beliefs about women and gender were formed in interaction with these women and men in common reflection on the central events in the Christian life: baptism and corporate worship, which was rich in *pneumatika,* or spiritual gifts, especially inspired speech.

Though the task of this essay was not to reflect on the implications of Paul's views on women and gender for Christians today, it is appropriate to note here that his views are both culturally determined and grounded in the common gospel faith that Christians of all cultures share and in the work of God's Spirit in God's people. This points to the need for contemporary Christian reflection on a culturally appropriate, as well as gospel- and Spirit-oriented, theology of gender.

Selected Bibliography

Archer, L. J. *Her Price is Beyond Rubies: The Jewish Woman in Graeco-Roman Palestine*. Sheffield: JSOT Press, 1990.

Baer, R. *Philo's Use of the Categories Male and Female*. Leiden: Brill, 1970.

Boyarin, D. *A Radical Jew: Paul and the Politics of Identity*. Berkeley: University of California Press, 1994.

Brooten, B. J. *Women Leaders in the Ancient Synagogue: Inscriptional Evidence and Background Issues*. Chico, CA: Scholars Press, 1982.

Chesnutt, R. D. "Revelatory Experiences Attributed to Biblical Women in Early Jewish Literature." In *"Women Like This": New Perspectives on Jewish Women in the Greco-Roman World*, ed. A.-J. Levine. Atlanta: Scholars Press, 1991, 107-26.

Corley, K. *Private Women, Public Meals: Social Conflict in the Synoptic Tradition*. Peabody, MA: Hendrickson, 1993.

Ilan, T. *Jewish Women in Greco-Roman Palestine: An Inquiry into Image and Status*. Tübingen: Mohr-Siebeck, 1995.

Kraemer, R. S. *Her Share of the Blessings: Women's Religions Among Pagans, Jews, and Christians in the Greco-Roman World*. New York: Oxford University Press, 1992.

————. "The Book of Aseneth." In *Searching the Scriptures. Volume 2: A Feminist Commentary*, ed. E. Schüssler Fiorenza. New York: Crossroad, 1994, 859-88.

Plaskow, J. "Anti-Judaism in Feminist Christian Interpretation." In *Searching the Scriptures. Volume 1: A Feminist Commentary*, ed. E. Schüssler Fiorenza. New York: Crossroad, 1993, 117-29.

Sly, D. *Philo's Perception of Women*. Atlanta: Scholars Press, 1990.

Standhartinger, A. *Das Frauenbild im Judentum der hellenistischen Zeit: Ein Beitrag anhand von 'Joseph & Aseneth'*. Leiden: Brill, 1995.

Tomson, P. J. *Paul and the Jewish Law: Halakha in the Letters of the Apostle to the Gentiles.* Assen/Maastricht: Van Gorcum; Minneapolis: Fortress, 1990.

Trenchard, W. C. *Ben Sira's View of Women: A Literary Analysis.* Chico, CA: Scholars, 1982.

Wegner, J. R. *Chattel or Person? The Status of Women in the Mishnah.* New York: Oxford University Press, 1988.

————. "Philo's Portrayal of Woman — Hebraic or Hellenic?" In *"Women Like This": New Perspectives on Jewish Women in the Greco-Roman World,* ed. A.-J. Levine. Atlanta: Scholars Press, 1991, 41-66.

Paul's Conversion and His Ethic of Freedom in Galatians

G. WALTER HANSEN

How does one determine the impact of Paul's conversion on his ethics? One clue can be found in tracing the thread of his references in Galatians to God's gracious *call*. The first reference to God's call points to the conversion of the Galatian Christians: "I am amazed that you are so quickly deserting the one who *called* you by the grace of Christ" (1:6). The second discloses Paul's own experience: "He *called* me though his grace" (1:15). The third introduces Paul's ethical appeal: "You were *called* to freedom, brothers and sisters" (5:13).

These three references to the call of God cast considerable light on both the nature of Paul's conversion and the basis of his ethics. For the way in which Paul parallels his own call by grace (1:15) with the Galatian believers' experience of God's call by grace (1:6) indicates what he meant by the term "call" in both cases. Certainly in the case of the Galatian Christians, God's call was the effective cause of their conversion. And this use of "call" in 1:6 is consonant with Paul's use of the term elsewhere in his letters to refer to God's initiative in the salvation process (cf. Rom 8:30; 1 Cor 1:9; 1 Thess 4:7). Likewise, Paul's rebuke of the Galatians for their desertion from the call of God leads to his account of his own loyalty to God's call (1:15).

In Galatians, of course, Paul explicitly says that when God called him, he was summoned to a new career as an apostle to the Gentiles (1:16). But Paul's experience of God's call cannot adequately be described as merely

213

an appointment to the apostolic office. His autobiography is crafted to demonstrate that, in contrast to the Galatian errorists, he remained true to the "truth of the gospel" (2:5, 14) because he was radically transformed by being personally identified with the events of the gospel: "I am crucified with Christ!" (2:19-20).

The change of perspective that was caused by God's gracious call led Paul to oppose anyone who proposed that righteousness comes through adherence to the law. "I do not nullify the grace of God," he declares (2:21a). "For if righteousness comes through the law," he goes on to assert, "then Christ died in vain" (2:21b). Thus for Paul the antithesis between righteousness based on the law and righteousness based on the death of Christ stemmed from the transforming effect of God's call on his life.

The entire Galatian rebuke section of 1:6–4:11 serves as the background for Paul's personal appeal in 4:12 to "become like me." His portrayal of his own practice of freedom in Christ in 1:13–2:21, as well as his explanation of his theological perspective on freedom in Christ in 3:1–4:11, forms the basis for his presentation of himself as a paradigm of loyalty to God's gracious call. Furthermore, his personal appeal to follow the pattern of his life and thought leads to his ethical appeals in 5:13–6:10, where obedience to God's gracious call to freedom is spelled out in terms of ethical principles drawn from his own experience of God's call by grace. So his conversion establishes the foundation for his ethics.

There are, of course, many other threads to trace out in the complex fabric of Paul's ethics. We could, for example, study the connections between Paul's ethics and his Jewish heritage. His quotation in 5:14 of Lev 19:18 ("Love your neighbor as yourself"), which stands at the beginning of the ethical section of Galatians, points to the impact of a Jewish background on his ethics. Likewise, relations between a pervading Hellenistic milieu and the formulation of his ethics could also be examined. For his lists of vices and virtues in 5:19-24 (cf. also Rom 1:29-31; 13:13; 1 Cor 5:9-11; 6:9-10; 2 Cor 12:20-21; Eph 4:31-32; 5:3-5; Col 3:5-8; 1 Tim 1:9-10; 2 Tim 3:2-5; Titus 3:3), as well as his moral aphorisms in 6:1-10 (and elsewhere throughout his letters), have often been seen as material that Paul borrowed from Hellenistic moral philosophy to contextualize his ethical principles for a Gentile audience.

Another fascinating thread to follow out would be Paul's use of the teachings and example of Jesus. His reference to the "law of Christ" in 6:2, his list of moral fruit in 5:22-23, and his use of the love commandment to summarize the whole law in 5:14 seem to echo the words of Jesus. In addition, we could explore the way that Paul's ethics are rooted in his theological convictions. For while he used the indicative mood to state the facts of God's redemption — "For freedom Christ has set us free" (5:1); "You were called to freedom" (5:13); "We live by the Spirit" (5:25) — the way that each of these indicatives leads to an imperative suggests that Paul always sought to provide theological warrants for moral actions.

These are all essential elements to consider in any comprehensive study of Pauline ethics. Paul was quite eclectic in his use of ethical materials, and he mounted a number of diverse arguments to defend his ethical positions. We certainly can point to Jewish and Hellenistic sources, to parallels with the words and actions of Jesus, and to warrants derived from redemption in Christ. But we will have missed the dynamic force in Paul's ethics if we do not see how all of these factors have been refracted through the prism of his own conversion experience.

In what follows, therefore, I propose to explore the connection between Paul's conversion and his ethics — using his letter to Gentile believers in the Roman province of Galatia as something of a case study. In particular, I intend to investigate four major themes in Galatians that have to do with his ethic of freedom: (1) freedom from slavery; (2) freedom through the cross; (3) freedom by the Spirit; and (4) freedom to love.

1. Freedom from Slavery

The ethical section of Paul's letter to the Galatians begins in 5:13 with a declaration that the Galatian believers were "called to freedom." That declaration echoes the command to defend freedom from slavery in 5:1: "For freedom Christ has set us free. Stand firm, therefore, and do not submit again to a yoke of slavery." Our understanding of what Paul meant by freedom from slavery will be enhanced by a review of what precedes this call to freedom. For in the material in Galatians that precedes this call, freedom from slavery is (1) exemplified by Paul's autobiographical accounts (1:13–2:21), (2) defended by his biblical arguments (3:1–4:11), (3) modeled by his personal appeal (4:12-20), (4) illustrated by his biblical allegory (4:21-31), and (5) commanded by his apostolic authority (5:1-12).

Autobiographical Accounts (1:13–2:21)

Paul's autobiographical accounts in Galatians begin with the story of his conversion in 1:13-16. We are given "before and after" snapshots. Twice Paul refers to his pre-conversion life as his life "in Judaism" (1:13-14). Although he strongly affirmed that he continued to be a Jew after his conversion (cf. Rom 11:1, "I am an Israelite myself"), Paul nevertheless used the phrase "in Judaism" only to describe his life before his encounter with Christ. The term "Judaism" itself was coined in the Maccabean era to distinguish the law-observant Jewish way of life from alternative lifestyles in the Hellenistic world. 2 Maccabees 14:37-38, for example, describes Razis, one of the elders of Jerusalem, as follows: "In former times, when there was no mingling with the Gentiles, he had been accused of Judaism, and he had zealously risked his life for Judaism."

In Galatians Paul describes his life "in Judaism" as having been characterized by an extremely zealous devotion to the Jewish traditions (1:14). His zeal was a mark of the Jews of his time who fought to maintain the purity of the Jewish way of life from pervasive Hellenistic influences. Such zeal had been inspired by the deathbed speech of Mattathias, the father of the Maccabean leaders:

> Now my children, show zeal for the law, and give your lives for the covenant of our ancestors. . . . You shall rally around you all who observe the law, and avenge the wrong done to your people. Pay back the Gentiles in full, and obey the commandments of the law. (1 Maccabees 2:50, 67-68)

It is, in fact, not difficult to see why Paul's zeal for his Jewish traditions made him "try to destroy the church" (1:13). For the message of the church that Jesus, the crucified and risen Messiah, offers salvation to all people negated the message of the Jewish traditions that salvation was only to be found in the law-observant Jewish nation.

But when God revealed his Son to Paul so that he would preach him among the Gentiles (1:16), Paul was set free from "Judaism." He was no longer a zealot demanding adherence to the Jewish way of life. Instead, he became an apostle preaching salvation in Jesus Christ.

We know that Paul viewed his conversion as freedom from a zealous observance of the law by what he says in his Galatian account about the early church's conference at Jerusalem in 2:1-10. For in that account he tells of his refusal to submit to those "who slipped in to spy on the freedom we have in Christ Jesus, so that they might enslave us" (2:4-5). Furthermore, he insists that his resistance to pressures to have Titus, who was a Greek, to be circumcised was so as to protect the truth of the gospel for the Galatian Christians (2:5). Any capitulation to the requirement to keep the law as a basis for inclusion among God's people, therefore, would have denied the truth of the gospel that all believers — regardless of racial, cultural, or social status — are already included by God's grace in Christ. So Paul defended the freedom of Titus, standing in opposition to pressures that he should be circumcised.

Paul's account of his confrontation with Peter at Antioch in 2:11-14 likewise revolves around the basic issue of freedom from slavery to the requirements of the law. The withdrawal of Peter and the rest of the Jewish Christians from table fellowship with the Gentile Christians implied that Gentile Christians had to keep the requirements of the law in order to be accepted within God's covenant people. In this case, the requirements had to do with Jewish food laws, which prohibited table fellowship with Gentiles.

Paul accused Peter of hypocrisy. For Peter had already demonstrated by his initial willingness to eat with Gentile Christians that his convictions permitted him to be free from Jewish food regulations so that he could "live like a Gentile and not like a Jew" (2:14a). But his separation from table-fellowship with Gentiles forced Gentiles Christians "to live like Jews" (2:14b) if they wanted to remain in fellowship with Jewish Christians. So Paul confronted Peter for "not acting consistently with the truth of the gospel" (2:13). Because when the requirements of the law divide the fellowship of believers in Christ along ethnic lines, then keeping the law negates the truth of the gospel.

Paul moves in 2:15-21 from the account of his confrontation with Peter to a very personal statement of his own freedom from slavery to the law. Here he says that if he rebuilt what had been destroyed, he would, indeed, then be proved to be a lawbreaker (2:18). In other words, if the law was reinstated for the supervision of the Christian life, he would be condemned by the law as a transgressor of the law for breaking purity regulations in his table-fellowship with Gentile Christians. But, Paul declares, he died to the law by being crucified with Christ (1:19-20). So the law can no longer be used to direct or condemn his behavior. He has been set free from slavery to the law by his union with Christ.

Biblical Arguments (3:1–4:11)

Paul's biblical arguments in Galatians serve to drive a wedge between the works of the law and faith, (3:2, 5), between the law itself and faith (3:12), and between the law and the promise (3:15-18). The law pronounces a curse (3:10), points out transgressions (3:19), cannot impart life or righteousness (3:21), imprisons all under sin (3:22-23), and serves as a disciplinarian (3:24). Paul's exposition of the purpose of the law discloses two functions of the law: (1) as a universal moral standard to reveal the sinfulness of all humankind (3:22); and (2) as a social boundary marker to separate Jews from Gentiles (3:23).

Imprisonment and slavery under the law was to last only "until faith would be revealed" (3:23), "until Christ" (3:24), and "until the date set by the father" (4:1-2). Freedom from this slavery came when "God sent his Son . . . to redeem those who were under the law" (4:4-5). Although the law had been given by God to supervise the behavior of his people, now that God has sent his Son and the Spirit of his Son, believers are to live no longer as slaves under the supervision of the law but as free children of God (4:4-7).

It is important to note, as Richard Longenecker points out, that "Paul not only opposes in Galatians a soteriological legalism but also the necessity for a nomistic lifestyle" (*Galatians,* 176). In other words, Paul rejected not only the idea that the law can be used to give life (i.e., "legalism"), but also the understanding that the law is still meant to supervise and direct the life of believers in Christ (i.e., "nomism"). "Having begun by the Spirit," Paul asks, "are you now going to be made perfect by the flesh?" (3:3). His question was intended to show that the Spirit is needed not only for the beginning of the Christian life but also for the believer's ongoing progress in that new life.

Paul's characterization of the law as a "disciplinarian" portrays the constant supervision of the law over all of life. And his assertion that "we are no longer under a disciplinarian" (3:25) points to freedom from the control of the law over the whole of life. On a practical level, he instructs the Galatians not to be enslaved by the Jewish calendar — that is, not to be enslaved to the observance of special days and months and seasons and years (4:10). So the law was not to control the Galatian believers' diaries or agendas. All of Paul's biblical arguments, in fact, were directed against a "nomistic lifestyle."

Personal Appeal (4:12-20)

On the basis of his autobiographical accounts and his biblical arguments, Paul makes his personal appeal in Galatians: "Become like me, for I became like you" (4:12). Here is the irony: as a Jew, Paul had become so free from his slavery to the Jewish way of life that he was able to become like Gentiles in order to preach Christ to them; but now his Gentile converts were turning from their faith in Christ and becoming enslaved by the Jewish way of life. So Paul pled with them to be free from slavery to the law, as he was, so that they might be conformed to Christ, as he was (4:12, 19).

Biblical Illustration (4:21-31)

Since the Galatian believers wanted "to be under law" (4:21), Paul asks them if they know what the law says. We do not have space here to explore the details of Paul's allegorical treatment of the Hagar-Sarah story in 4:21-31 (cf. my *Abraham in Galatians*, 141-54). It is clear, however, that he uses the story to set up the freedom/slavery and spirit/flesh antitheses that provide the basic framework for his ethics in the next section of the Galatian letter. For those who are born of the flesh and teaching observance of the covenant made at Mount Sinai are in slavery, whereas those who are born of the Spirit are children of promise and free.

Apostolic Command (5:1-12)

The illustration of the free son, Isaac, and the son born into slavery, Ishmael, immediately precedes and prepares the way for the command to protect freedom in Christ from a yoke of slavery (5:1). Paul explains that the "yoke of slavery" that the Galatians would be submitting themselves to if they accepted circumcision would be the obligation "to obey the entire law" (5:3). It is unlikely that Paul meant that they would be required to live a life of sinless perfection by keeping every commandment. What he meant, evidently, was that accepting circumcision was but the first step in accepting the total Jewish way of life.

Paul knew very well from his earlier life "in Judaism" all the demands of the Jewish way of life. But since his conversion his identity was found

219

in union with Christ, not in zealously adhering to the Jewish way of life. The Galatian believers were in danger of moving from their identification with Christ to identification with the Jewish way of life. If they did so, Paul asserts, Christ would be of no benefit to them (5:2). They would, in fact, be cut off from Christ and fall away from grace (5:4). For Paul, a great reversal in life had come when he turned from seeking to obey the entire law to living by faith in Christ. His Galatian converts, however, were on the verge of moving in the opposite direction, with their obedience to the truth of the gospel being endangered by their attraction to the law (5:7).

All that Paul has said to this point gives force to his strong imperative to stand firm in their freedom from the obligation to keep the whole law. He begins his ethical section by reminding them of their call to freedom: "You were called to freedom, brothers and sisters" (5:13a). But the question arises: Are the ethical instructions given in 5:13b–6:10 directed toward a problem different from the problem addressed in the previous sections of his Galatian letter?

Many interpreters have thought so. It is common, in fact, to see a major shift in Paul's direction right in the midst of 5:13 — that is, up through the middle of this verse he has been warning against the danger of a law-centered life; afterwards, however, he warns against the dangers of a lawless life. For immediately after his reminder in 5:13a of their call to freedom, Paul directs the believers of Galatia in 5:13b not to abuse their freedom: "Do not use your freedom as an opportunity for self-indulgence, but through love become slaves to one another." According to this common interpretation, the imperatives of 5:13b–6:10 were aimed at some Galatian believers who were either characterized as being antinomian or were tempted to live lives of moral license and libertinism.

But there are good reasons to interpret all of 5:13–6:10 as a continuation of Paul's arguments against slavery to the law. One major reason has to do with context, for 5:13–6:10 is both preceded (5:1-12) and followed (6:11-14) by sharp words against those who were teaching submission to the law. It would seem reasonable, therefore, to see the ethical instructions of 5:13–6:10 as directed against that same threat.

A second reason has to do with the repeated subject and implied addressees of this section. For 5:13–6:10 constantly refers to the law (5:14, 18, 23; 6:2), and the passage is still directed toward those who want to live under the yoke of the law. As John Barclay asserts, "It is precisely because of the Galatians' attraction to the law that Paul has to demonstrate the sufficiency and practical value of his proposal for ethics — 'walking in the Spirit' " (*Obeying the Truth*, 218).

Paul described freedom from the law as freedom from a disciplinarian (3:24-25). But such freedom did not mean that there was no moral discipline or moral direction. Moral discipline, for Paul, is applied through identification with the cross of Christ: "Those who belong to Christ Jesus have crucified the flesh with its passions and desires" (5:24). And moral direction is provided by the Holy Spirit: "If you are led by the Spirit, you are not subject to the law" (5:18).

Paul claims that in his conversion to Christ he died to the law so that he might "live for God" (2:19). For him, freedom from slavery to the law did not mean freedom for self-indulgence. Rather, it meant freedom to live for God. And so in 5:13–6:10 he goes further in drawing from his own conversion experience to describe the ethical pattern of that freedom to live for God in terms of freedom through the cross.

2. Freedom through the Cross

There is no question that a central feature of Paul's conversion experience was his change of perspective regarding the cross of Christ. Before his conversion, undoubtedly one of the most objectionable features of the gospel message had been its proclamation of a crucified Messiah. Belief in a Messiah who died on a Roman cross would certainly have infuriated a Jew who expected the Messiah to rule the world from David's throne. In Paul's pre-conversion days he may have tried to refute the message of the church by quoting Deut 21:22-23, which pronounces God's curse on anyone who has been hanged on a tree or a cross. After his conversion, however, Paul's view of the crucified Messiah was so radically changed that he quoted that same passage to proclaim that the cross was the way of redemption: "Christ redeemed us from the curse of the law, having become a curse for us — for it is written, 'Cursed is everyone who hangs on a tree' " (3:13).

In a very real sense, Christ died through the law since he died under the curse of the law. So Paul says: "Through the law I died to the law, that I might live for God. I am crucified with Christ" (2:19). A believer's death "through the law" and "to the law" is, therefore, accomplished by identification with the death of Christ. The perfect tense of the verb "I am

crucified" (2:19) points to a permanent condition in relation to the law —
that is, to the believer having been fully punished by the law and become
absolutely dead to its claims. The law can neither condemn nor make any
further claim on one who has been crucified with Christ. Thus in his use
of the first person singular "I am crucified" Paul not only points to his own
conversion experience, but also suggests that his experience serves as the
paradigm for all believers: that freedom from slavery to the law is accomplished by death through the cross.

Paul turns to his own conversion again at the end of the Galatian
letter, that is, in the subscription of 6:11-18. And in that subscription he
again speaks of his conversion experience in terms of identification with
the cross of Christ: "But may it never be that I should boast except in the
cross of our Lord Jesus Christ, through which the world has been crucified
to me and I to the world" (6:14). Here Paul describes his conversion in
apocalyptic terms. It was the end of the world for him!

Paul's apocalyptic metaphor of the crucifixion of the world does not
mean, of course, the end of the world in a literal, cosmic sense. It signifies,
rather, an end to the old world order — that is, as he explains in 6:15, an
end to understanding the world as structured by the opposition of "the
circumcised" and "the uncircumcised." For after his personal identification
with the cross of Christ, Paul no longer identified himself on the basis of
ethnic or social distinctions such as circumcision and uncircumcision, Jew
or Gentile. Rather, he contrasted himself with those in the old world order
who used the law to draw such divisions (6:12-14). The perfect tense of the
verb "has been crucified" (6:14) points to a permanent change, with the
crucifixion of the world to Paul and of Paul to the world unable to be
reversed. Now all that matters is the "new creation" (6:15) where there is
no longer the opposition of "Jew or Gentile, slave or free, male and female,
for you are all one in Christ Jesus" (3:28).

Before his conversion, Paul's zealous devotion to the traditions "in
Judaism" drove him to attempt to destroy the church, because the church
was proclaiming salvation in Christ. Such a proclamation was, at least
implicitly, a denial of any significance to the distinction between those who
were circumcised and those who were not (1:12-13). The crisis in the
Galatian churches was caused by teachers of the law who had the same zeal
for the Jewish traditions as Paul did before his conversion. They were
emphasizing the distinction between "the circumcised" and "the uncircumcised," believing that such a distinction would preserve the integrity of God's

222

people. But their campaign to force the Galatian churches to live under the law was, in fact, destroying those churches.

We can see something of the tragic condition of the Galatian churches in Paul's warning: "If you bite and devour one another, take care lest you be consumed by one another" (5:15). Just as Paul's pre-conversion life was a life of fierce competition to advance beyond his contemporaries by being more zealous than they were in his devotion to the Jewish traditions (1:13-14), so the Gentile believers' attraction to the law in the churches of Galatia was causing disruptive and destructive competition. Thus Paul pleads, "Let us not become conceited, competing against one another, envying one another" (5:26).

The irony is that such passionate competition to surpass one another in "works of the law" actually expressed itself in "works of the flesh." Paul makes this link between "works of the law" and "works of the flesh" when he impugns the motive of the law teachers: "It is those who want to make a good showing in the flesh who are compelling you to be circumcised" (6:12). Here the good showing in the flesh was circumcision, the mark of Jewish identity. And when there is such a preoccupation with ethnic identity (i.e., "the flesh"), the sinful nature (i.e., "the flesh") acts in all kinds of ways to destroy the unity of the church.

Paul's list of the works of the flesh in 5:19-21 is heavily weighted in the direction of social breakdown, particularly with its eight references to social divisions: "enmities, strife, jealousy, anger, quarrels, dissensions, factions, envy." Attempting to live under the supervision of the law had not eradicated a person's sinful passions or desires. It had, in fact, only stimulated them. For when "the flesh" is expressed in a preoccupation with keeping the law, the law is broken by a multiplication of the "works of the flesh."

Paul points to the teachers of the law themselves for evidence when he observes: "They do not keep the law themselves, but they want you to be circumcised so that they may boast about your flesh" (6:13). Their campaign was to bring Gentile Christians into submission to the law. But in boasting about their attempts to have Gentile Christians circumcised, they were breaking the law by their boasting in the flesh. Their promotion of law observance was, therefore, providing an "opportunity for the flesh" (5:13), which resulted in "works of the flesh" (5:19-21).

The only cure for "the flesh," Paul held, was the cure that he himself had experienced in his conversion — that is, full identification with the cross of Christ (2:19; 6:14). So drawing from his own conversion experience, he points to the way of freedom through the cross: "Those who belong to Christ Jesus have crucified the flesh with its passions and desires" (5:24). Paul knows from experience that only crucifixion with Christ will bring an end to the patterns and passions of the old world order, which have divided the church along ethnic and social lines. Only personal participation by faith in the cross of Christ breaks the power of the sinful propensity to boast in the flesh.

Paul's ethic of freedom demands that freedom from slavery to the law must not result in a self-indulgence of the sinful nature (5:13). For freedom from slavery to the law only comes through the cross of Christ. And identification with Christ's cross means nailing one's sinful nature to that cross and leaving it there to die.

Paul's teaching here echoes the teaching of Jesus about "taking up the cross" and following him. But Paul is not simply repeating the words of his master. These ethical principles were forged in the red-hot heat of Paul's own conversion and were hammered out in the application of that experience to the crisis in the Galatian churches. His own conversion experience, therefore, supplies the substructure for his ethics (cf. Styler, "Basis of Obligation," 183).

3. Freedom by the Spirit

To understand the link between Paul's conversion experience of union with Christ (1:16; 2:20) and his ethic of freedom by the Spirit (5:16-25), it is essential to see that the affirmation "Christ lives in me" (2:20) means the same thing as the affirmation "We live by the Spirit" (5:25). Paul describes his own conversion as that event when God "was pleased to reveal his Son in me" (1:16), with the inwardness of God's revelation of his Son being stressed by the phrase "in me." Galatian believers, according to Paul, had essentially the same inward experience when "God sent the Spirit of his Son into our hearts" (4:6).

The result of Paul's conversion and of the conversion of the Galatian believers was essentially the same as well. For Paul, the result of the inward revelation of God's Son was to "live by faith in the Son of God" (2:20). For the Galatian believers, the result of receiving the Spirit of his Son should be to follow the guidance of the Spirit (5:16, 18, 25). So freedom by the Spirit is the same thing as freedom by union with Christ.

If we separate the Spirit from the Son, we might make the mistake of thinking that the Spirit was given merely to empower obedience to the law. But Paul did not tell the Galatian believers that the Spirit had been given to them so that they would have the power to submit to the yoke of the law, to receive circumcision, to keep the food laws, to obey the Sabbath laws, or to live "under the obligation to keep the whole law." No! By interpreting the empowerment of the Spirit apart from reference to the Son, we are led straight back into legalism, "seeking to be justified by the law" (5:4). Paul warned the Galatians that if they turned in that direction they would be "cut off from Christ" (5:4). Rather, the Spirit was given for participation in the life of Christ. So when we receive the Spirit of the Son into our hearts, we then say with the Son, "Abba! Father!" (4:6). And by the Spirit we are given the moral power of Christ to live the life of Christ.

Paul's assertion, "If you are led by the Spirit, you are not under the law" (5:18), clearly establishes the fundamental contrast between his ethic of freedom by the Spirit and obedience to the law. For life under the law is a life of moral impotence. As a *paidagōgos* or disciplinarian (3:24-25) the law could only present objective moral standards, but could not produce subjective moral transformation. Where, however, the directive power of the law fails, the Spirit succeeds. Thus after his command to "walk by the Spirit," Paul expresses his supreme confidence in the moral power of the Spirit with this promise: "You will absolutely not gratify the desires of the flesh" (5:16) — with "absolutely" being added to bring out the force of the double negative in the Greek, and so understanding Paul to mean: Those who follow the guidance of the Spirit will absolutely not carry out the evil intentions of their sinful nature.

Paul explains the basis for his confidence in the moral power of the Spirit in 5:17. Here he realistically portrays the reality of the incessant warfare that exists between the Spirit and the flesh: "The flesh desires what is contrary to the Spirit, and the Spirit what is contrary to the flesh, for these are at war with one another." Inner spiritual warfare, therefore, is the nature of the normal Christian life. But Paul says that the outcome of this war between the Spirit and flesh is that "you do not do what you want."

Many interpreters take the phrase "you do not do what you want" as an admission of defeat — or, at best, a stalemate — and so interpret the statement to mean either (1) that the flesh negates "what you want" (i.e., Spirit-given desires) or (2) that the flesh and Spirit neutralize each other. But such an admission of defeat undermines Paul's confident promise of victory in the immediately previous verse. For if the Spirit is defeated or neutralized by the flesh, what is the advantage of living under the direction of the Spirit over living under the supervision of the law? In that case, life by the Spirit would be a life of moral impotence as well.

Those who interpret 5:17 as an admission of defeat usually equate this verse with the moral struggle described in Rom 7:14-25. But the struggle depicted in that passage differs in significant ways from what we see in Gal 5:17. For one thing, there is no mention of the Spirit in Rom 7:14-25. What Paul is describing there is life under the law without the power of the Spirit.

In Gal 5:17, however, Paul is presenting a basis for his confidence in the Spirit's moral power over the flesh. Although believers are always involved in a spiritual battle that determines every moral choice and action, they are not left morally frustrated and defeated. Moral freedom by the Spirit does not mean that believers can use their freedom as "an opportunity for self-indulgence" (5:13). No! For if you walk by the Spirit, you do not do what your self-indulgent desires want (5:16-17). Instead, you do what the Spirit leads you to do. And since you are under the control of the Spirit, it is unnecessary for you to be under the supervision of the law (5:18).

So freedom by the Spirit is freedom from the supervisory control of the law precisely because it is freedom from the destructive influence of the flesh. But freedom by the Spirit is not only freedom *from* the law and the flesh, it is also freedom *to* love (5:22-23). For the fruit of the Spirit is love.

4. Freedom to Love

When Paul received the revelation of God's Son (1:16), he received a revelation of love that transformed his life. We learn this from his affirmation in 2:20: "It is no longer I who live, but Christ lives in me; and the life I now live in the flesh, I live by faith in the Son of God, who loved me and gave himself for me." Before his conversion, of course, Paul knew about God's love. He heard the Scriptures describe God's love for his people. And he read the commands to love God and one's neighbor. But his conversion experience gave love a new shape — that is, now the shape of the cross of Christ.

After his conversion, Paul defined love by always pointing to the self-sacrificing love of the Son of God: "He gave himself for our sins" (1:4); "he loved me and gave himself up for me" (2:20); "Christ redeemed us from the curse of the law, having become a curse for us" (3:13); "God sent his Son, born of a woman, born under the law, in order that he might redeem those who were under the law" (4:4-5). That revelation of the redemptive love of Christ gave the overall shape to all of Paul's ethics. And since faith in Christ expresses itself through love (5:6), the central task of Paul's ethics became to spell out how to express Christ-like love.

Two Paradoxes of Love: Being Slaves of Others and Fulfilling the Law

Paul creates two paradoxes in his exhortations to express love. The first has to do with the concept of slavery. For having commanded the Galatians to stand firm in their freedom and not to submit to a yoke of slavery (5:1), and then reminding them that they were called to freedom (5:13a), Paul exhorts his converts in 5:13b to be slaves of one another through love. To put it simply, he says to them: Since you were called to freedom, be slaves of one another. The only way to understand this apparent contradiction is to observe that freedom in Christ resists one kind of slavery and expresses itself through another kind of slavery. Slavery under law is contrasted to slavery under others through love. We are, therefore, not to be slaves under law, but we are to be slaves of one another to demonstrate love.

Then Paul adds another paradox concerning keeping and not keeping the whole law. For in 5:14 he tells his readers: "The whole law is fulfilled in one word, 'You shall love your neighbor as yourself'" (5:14). But how can Paul object to being "under obligation to do the whole law" (5:3) and then advocate fulfilling the whole law (5:14)? We cannot even begin to survey the discussion generated by this apparent contradiction. Of all the alternative explanations, however, two seem to be problematic and two are particularly attractive.

One way of dealing with the paradox, which I consider to be a problematic explanation, is to posit a fundamental distinction between justification and sanctification — that is, between "getting in" and "staying in." According to this line of interpretation, Paul meant to refute the use of the law for the purpose of justification (i.e., getting into covenant relationship with God) but advocated the use of the law for the purpose of sanctification (i.e., staying in that relationship). In the first part of his Galatian letter — that is, up to 5:12 — he argues strenuously against any attempt to be justified, or declared righteous by God, on the basis of keeping the law. So in 2:15 he writes: "We know that a person is justified not by works of the law but through faith in Jesus Christ." But having made that point, Paul then, it is argued, turns to the ethical conduct of the Christian life in 5:13–6:10, and in that section he bases his ethics on the precepts of the Mosaic law. So in 5:14, at the beginning of his ethical instructions, he appeals to the law by quoting from Lev 19:18: "You shall love your neighbor as yourself."

Since the love commandment of Lev 19:18 is so central to Paul's ethical counsels, it is understandable why many interpreters of Paul have concluded that the origin of Paul's ethics is the Mosaic law. But if we interpret Paul's ethical instructions as stemming basically from the Mosaic law, we seem to imply that Paul's conversion did not make a substantial difference in the content of his ethics. Although he may have changed some of his theological convictions because of his encounter with Christ, he was still a practicing Pharisee in the realm of ethical obligations. Of course, those who espouse this perspective grant that Paul's motivations and empowerment for keeping these ethical obligations were the result of his new-found faith in Christ. But, according to this perspective, he still derived his moral demands from his Jewish background.

Such an understanding, however, misses the major ethical change that occurred for Paul when he moved from his former life "in Judaism" to his new residence "in Christ." There are, of course, parallels between the ethical demands in those two places of residence, and certainly Paul's ethics reflect his Jewish heritage at many points. Nevertheless, for Paul the old world order controlled by law had come to an end (6:14). He was no longer under the supervision of the law (3:25). His arguments against the law were aimed not merely at the use of the law at the beginning of the Christian life, but also the supervision of the law in the continuation of the Christian life (3:3). For Paul, in fact, the Christian life is under the direction of the Spirit, not under the discipline and control of the law (5:18).

A second solution to the paradox of not keeping the whole law and yet fulfilling the whole law, which I also consider to be a problematic explanation, builds on the postulated distinction between ceremonial laws and moral laws — that is, between the social and the moral functions of the law. According to this interpretation, Paul, when speaking against the law, was speaking against circumcision, purity regulations, and Sabbath rules. These demands of the law were all ceremonial in nature. They served as social boundary markers for the Jewish people to separate them from the Gentiles. But since there is now no distinction between Jews and Gentiles (3:28), these ceremonial requirements have become obsolete. Nevertheless, according to this perspective, the moral requirements of the law are still in force as the basis of Paul's ethics. He may be negative about the works of the law that point to ethnic identity. But he is positive about the necessity to keep the moral demands of the law. After all, he quotes the moral demands of the law.

But this understanding dilutes the full force of Paul's proclamation of freedom from the obligation to keep the whole law (5:3). The whole point of his assertion that acceptance of circumcision carries with it an obligation to keep the whole law is that a person cannot be selective — that is, that one cannot unravel the law and discard some strands and keep other strands. The law is a whole unit. The whole Mosaic law cannot impart life or produce righteousness (3:21). It can only point out transgressions and imprison all under sin (3:10, 19, 22). So it is impossible to make progress toward moral perfection by trying to observe the law (3:2-3). Nor is it possible to gain moral victory over the desires of the sinful nature by submitting to the control of the law (5:13-18).

The first of the more attractive explanations of the above paradox regarding keeping and not keeping the whole law posits a difference between using the law to divide and using the law to unite. According to this approach, Paul objected in 5:3 to the use of the law to divide — in opposition to those who were pressing for the Galatian believers to be circumcised, thereby using the law to divide between Jews and Gentiles. In this case "the whole law" refers to the whole distinctive Jewish way of life (both ceremonial and moral) within the ethnic boundaries that separated Judaism from Hellenism (cf. Dunn, *Galatians*, 290). Before his conversion, therefore, the shape of Paul's ethics "in Judaism" was determined by his zeal for the Jewish traditions, and he was concerned to preserve the entire Jewish way of life so that there would be a sharp line of demarcation between "the circumcised" and "the uncircumcised." After his conversion, however, Paul held that "in Christ Jesus neither circumcision or uncircumcision counts for anything; the only thing that matters is faith working through love" (5:6). The shape of his ethics was then determined by his call to express the love of Christ. And he was opposed to any use of the law that divides between Jew and Gentile, slave and free, male and female (3:28), for all believers are united by the redemptive love of Christ. Yet since his Galatian converts desired to be under the law (4:21), Paul accommodated himself to their desire by giving them a command that summarizes the whole law: "Love your neighbor as yourself" (5:14). Here Paul was using "the whole law" to unite rather than to divide.

A second, even more helpful solution to the above Pauline paradox, however, argues for a difference in Paul's language between *doing* the law (5:3) and *fulfilling* the law (5:14). Advocates of this understanding point out that Paul resists using the law to *prescribe* what Christians should do, but that he refers to the law to *describe* the results of a life lived in obedience to Christ in the power of the Spirit (cf. Betz, *Galatians*, 275; S. Westerholm, "On Fulfilling the Whole Law (Gal. 5:14)," *Svensk Exegetisk Årsbok* 51-52 [1986-87] 229-37; idem, *Israel's Law*, 201; Barclay, *Obeying the Truth*, 139-42; Longenecker, *Galatians*, 241-43). Those who are "under the Law" are required "to do the whole law." Those who are led by the Spirit are not under law (5:18). Therefore they are not required to do the whole law. And yet when they are led by the Spirit to serve through love, fulfilling the whole law is the result of expressing the self-giving love of Christ.

Love in Relation to the Law of Moses and the Law of Christ

Paul clarifies the meaning of fulfilling the law by changing the object of fulfillment from "the whole law" (5:14) to "the law of Christ" (6:2). The immediate context for his reference to the law of Christ establishes a striking contrast between the law of Moses and the law of Christ. The law of Christ is fulfilled by restoring sinners and bearing their burdens (6:1-2), whereas the purpose of the Mosaic law is "to point out transgressions" (3:19). Paul's letter to the Galatians is replete with illustrations of ways that the law of Moses was being used to separate "sinners" from the church. The purpose of the law of Christ, however, is to serve sinners in the church.

Yet despite this important contrast between the law of Moses and the law of Christ in Galatians, there is a striking parallel between Paul's quotation of the love commandment from the law of Moses (5:14) and his reference to the law of Christ (6:2). Both "laws" are prefaced by commands to render mutual service: "Serve one another in love" (5:13) and "Bear one another's burdens" (6:2). And in both places the term "fulfill" is used to describe the results of this mutual service.

Some have suggested that such a close connection points to the essential identity of the law of Moses and the law of Christ — that is, that while Christ may have redefined to some extent the meaning of the law, the law that he promulgated was essentially the same as the Mosaic law. So fulfillment of the law of Christ involves fulfillment of the commandments of the Mosaic law. But this simple equation does not work in Galatians, for Paul clearly indicates that at least some commandments of the Mosaic law — such as the dietary laws (2:14), the Sabbath and festival regulations (4:10), and circumcision (5:2-4) — are not applicable to Gentile Christians. And he goes on to argue strongly against taking on any obligation to keep the whole law of Moses (5:3).

Others interpret the connection between fulfilling the love commandment from the law of Moses and fulfilling the law of Christ as evidence that only the command to love — apart from any other external principles or directives — is the law of Christ. But such an understanding is refuted by the evidence that Paul (as well as Jesus) defined and applied the love command in terms of external principles and specific directives. For, as we will see (below), Paul enunciates certain specific instructions for the church in 6:1-10.

Still others say that the love commandment, as defined and illustrated by the teachings and example of Jesus, is "the law of Christ." This interpretation is true as far as it goes, but it does not go far enough. It seems to imply that Paul simply replaced one set of precepts, the Mosaic law, with a new set of regulations derived from the words and works of Jesus. In other words, that the Messianic law now takes the place of the Mosaic law. But such a perspective misses the centrality of the cross of Christ and the resurrection presence of Christ by his Spirit in the life and ethical teaching of Paul.

Certainly Jesus taught the love command of Lev 19:18 by his words and actions. But Paul did not focus on the words or acts of Jesus. We do not find any explicit reference in Galatians to anything that Jesus ever said or did during the course of his ministry. Paul's focus, rather, is on the cross of Christ and Christ's redemptive work on that cross: that Christ loved us and gave himself for our sins (1:4; 2:20) by becoming a curse for us (3:13) in order to set us free from the burden of the yoke of slavery (5:1). Paul wants to draw the "foolish" Galatians back to his dramatic portrayal of

Christ crucified (3:1). Therefore it must be insisted that for Paul, Christ crucified is the law of Christ. It is his cross that sets the standard for self-giving, self-sacrificing love. It is his cross that is the supreme measure of love. Any definition of the law of Christ that loses sight of the cross loses the center of Paul's ethics.

Those who are led by the Spirit will express the same self-giving love of Christ (5:22-23). Like him, they will restore sinners by bearing their burdens (6:1-2). Such love will express the love of Christ and so fulfill the law of Christ. And such Christ-like love fulfills the whole intent of the law of Moses, which is summarized in the love command of Lev 19:18: "Love your neighbor as yourself."

Love as Exemplified in the Life of Paul

Paul not only sets forth Christ crucified as the normative pattern ("law") for the Christian life, he also presents his own conversion and life as a reenactment of that normative pattern. His exclamation "I have been crucified with Christ!" is not only personal, it is paradigmatic. He commands the Galatian believers: "Become as I am."

Like Christ, Paul identified with sinners. When he ate with "Gentile sinners" (2:15) at Antioch, he was labeled a sinner (2:17). He was, in fact, so identified with Christ that when he arrived in Galatia the first time he was welcomed as if he were Jesus Christ himself (4:14). Paul does not chide his converts for their initial welcome; he only wishes they had not changed their minds about him.

Paul ends his Galatian letter by claiming total identification with Christ: "I bear on my body the stigmata of Jesus" (6:17). Whatever "the marks of Jesus" were and how they were caused, they clearly portray Paul as crucified — with the fulfillment of the law of Christ established by Christ crucified. When Paul said that "God was pleased to reveal his Son in me that I might preach him among the Gentiles" (1:16), he meant not only that Christ was revealed through his proclamation but also that he was revealed in his person (cf. Hays, "Christology and Ethics," 281).

When Paul commands his readers to "bear each other's burdens," he speaks from experience because he has borne the burden of the welfare of the Galatian believers within him like a pregnant woman. "My little children," he writes, "with whom I am again in labor until Christ is formed in you" (4:19). The birth pangs that Paul experienced in his labor for the Galatians signal the incredibly intimate union of Paul with his converts, who were his "children" in Christ and for whom he was their example of love. When "Christ is formed" in them, the normative pattern established by the cross of Christ will be seen in the Galatian community as Christians serve one another in love and bear each other's burdens. So the Christ-form will be seen in a cruciform community.

Love as Expressing the Character of Christ and Empowered by the Spirit

Freedom to love is expressed not only in deeds but also in character — or, more aptly, in deeds that flow from the character of the doer. That is why Paul in 5:22-23 highlights qualities of character that are produced by the Spirit: "love, joy, peace, patience, kindness, goodness, faithfulness, gentleness, and self-control." Paul's metaphor of "the fruit of the Spirit," which heads this list, resonates with overtones from the ancient biblical prophecies of the fruitfulness of Israel through the outpouring of the Holy Spirit (cf. Isa 32:15-16; Joel 2:18-32) and the promises of Jesus regarding the fruitfulness of his disciples because of his abiding presence (John 15:1-17). The prophet Isaiah lamented that, while God expected the fruit of righteousness from Israel, the vineyard he had planted, all he got were wild grapes of bloodshed (Isa 5:1-7). Now, however, Paul proclaims that God's expectations for his people are being fulfilled in a full harvest of moral qualities produced by the Spirit — moral qualities against which no law can be found (5:23). The law, in fact, has no power to produce moral fruit (3:21). It is only the Spirit who can produce an abundance of such fruit of righteousness.

Immediately after his description of the fruit of the Spirit, Paul identifies in 5:24 those who bear this fruit as being "those of Christ Jesus." The connection of Christ Jesus with the fruit of the Spirit suggests that this list of moral qualities provides a "character sketch of Christ" (Dunn, *Galatians*, 310). All who can say with Paul, "It is no longer I who live, but Christ who lives in me," will express the moral character of Christ — an argument, again, that highlights how Paul can apply the fruit of his own conversion experience to his ethics.

In 6:1-10 Paul shows how the freedom to love works itself out in specific actions on behalf of the community. Some have seen his exhortations in this section as a random collection of moral maxims drawn from Hellenistic philosophy. For example, Paul counsels those who would "restore" anyone caught in a transgression to "look to yourselves that you may not also be tempted" (Gal 6:1). Hans Dieter Betz argues that the term "restore" is "a highly significant concept from Hellenistic philosophy, where it describes the work of the philosopher — 'psychotherapist' — and educator" (Betz, *Galatians,* 297). The command "look to yourself" sounds very much like the famous words of Socrates: "Know yourself." So Betz asserts that this maxim "comes from the Socratic tradition and no doubt goes back to Socrates himself" (ibid., 298).

According to Betz, Paul applied the general standards of popular Hellenistic philosophy to the needs of his churches. Supporting teachers (6:6) and doing good (6:9) were common moral obligations in Hellenistic philosophy. Indeed, Betz asserts that Paul did not develop a distinctively Christian ethic:

> The Christian is addressed as an educated and responsible person. He is expected to do no more than what would be expected of any other educated person in the Hellenistic culture of the time. In a rather conspicuous way Paul conforms to the ethical thought of his contemporaries. (ibid., 292)

Betz does point to Paul's belief that the Holy Spirit provides the power to do what is good. But what is good, as Betz understands Paul's ethical teaching, is defined by Hellenistic thought and culture.

Such an interpretation of Paul's ethics leads to the rather disappointing conclusion that the redemptive work of God's Son and the empowering work of God's Spirit merely accomplish adherence to the values of a Hellenistic intellectual outlook and cultural environment. From this perspective, Paul's conversion did not have any significant impact on his ethics. His moral expectations for his churches were those of a good Hellenistic philosopher.

Admittedly, Paul's use of the Greek language inevitably resulted in the use of words that were common in the Greco-Roman world. And no doubt his use of common Greek terms enabled him to build rapport with his audiences. But the meaning of Paul's terms and imperatives cannot be adequately explained simply by tracing their use in Greek philosophical literature. In fact, as John Barclay's examination of the Hellenistic literature cited by Betz demonstrates, there is "remarkably little to support Betz's sweeping statement about the Hellenistic character of Paul's ethics" (*Obeying the Truth,* 173). Rather, Paul's moral maxims need to be interpreted in a context where his concern is to show how the character of Christ (5:22-23) is expressed by "keeping in step with the Spirit" (5:25).

Paul's ethical instructions in 6:1-10, it needs to be noted, spell out in concrete fashion how the moral qualities listed in 5:22-23 are to be expressed in practical ways for the welfare of the Christian communities in the province of Galatia — that is, how such moral qualities as "gentleness" (6:1), "love" (6:2), "self-control" (6:4), "patience" (6:9-10), and "goodness" (6:6, 10) are to be expressed in practical ways to build relationships within those communities. Sowing to the Spirit (6:8), therefore, means bearing "the fruit of the Spirit" within the relationships of the church. And those who choose to sow to the Spirit will from the Spirit reap eternal life.

In Paul's ethical understanding, it is the Spirit's empowering that enables believers to express the life of Christ. So he exhorted his converts: "If we live by the Spirit, let us also walk by the Spirit." It is also the major tenet and goal of his ethics that the character of Christ is to be the inward formation and outward expression of a Christian's life. Because he knew the reality in his own experience of the words "Christ lives in me," his desire for believers was that "Christ be formed in you" (4:19). Thus his ethics were the expression of his own conversion experience.

Conclusion

We have traced only a single thread of the impact of Paul's conversion in the complex fabric of his ethics. But that strand holds the whole fabric together. Pull out that strand and the whole fabric falls apart.

It would be profitable — but beyond our limits — to trace this thread in Paul's other letters. It would also be beneficial to explore, if possible, the circumstances and catalysts that motivated Paul to develop the implications of his conversion in his ethics. His ethical instructions in his letter to the Galatian churches were developed to answer the crisis in those churches. How did crises in other churches spark other ethical insights? Such explorations and questions must wait for another time.

What is important to grasp here, however, is the enduring relevance of Paul's ethics. What we have endeavored to demonstrate in this essay is this: that, essentially, Paul's ethic of freedom has to do with (1) expressing the content of love that is displayed in the cross of Christ, and (2) appropriating the moral power to love that is provided by the Holy Spirit.

In Dostoevsky's *Brothers Karamazov,* Father Zossima says that the lack of love is the punishment as well as the substance of sin. To the question "What is hell?," Father Zossima replies: "I maintain that it is the suffering of being unable to love." He then goes on to appeal: "Love a man even in his sin, for that is the semblance of Divine love and is the highest love on earth."

Dostoevsky has captured the essence of Paul's ethic of freedom to love. The shape of love is the shape of the cross of the Son of God, who loved us and gave himself for us. The strength to love is the strength of the Spirit of the Son, who leads us and forms within us the character of the Son so that we can freely express the love of the Son.

Paul's ethics were born in that time when God revealed his Son in him. For him, that was an apocalyptic time when the world ended and there was a new creation. May we also experience such an apocalypse so that we may be free to love!

Selected Bibliography

Barclay, J. M. G. *Obeying the Truth: A Study of Paul's Ethics in Galatians.* Edinburgh: Clark, 1988.

Betz, H. D. *Galatians: A Commentary on Paul's Letter to the Churches in Galatia.* Philadelphia: Fortress, 1979.

Dunn, J. D. G. *The Epistle to the Galatians.* Peabody, MA: Hendrickson, 1995.

Fee, G. D. *God's Empowering Presence: The Holy Spirit in the Letters of Paul.* Peabody, MA: Hendrickson, 1994.

Furnish, V. P. *Theology and Ethics in Paul.* Nashville: Abingdon, 1968.

Hansen, G. W. *Abraham in Galatians: Epistolary and Rhetorical Contexts.* Sheffield: Sheffield Academic Press, 1989.

————. *Galatians.* Downers Grove, IL: InterVarsity, 1994.

————. "A Paradigm of the Apocalypse: The Gospel in the Light of Epistolary Analysis." In *Gospel in Paul: Studies on Corinthians, Galatians and Romans for Richard N. Longenecker,* ed. L. A. Jervis and P. Richardson. Sheffield: Sheffield Academic Press, 1994, 194-209.

Hays, R. B. "Christology and Ethics in Galatians: The Law of Christ." *Catholic Biblical Quarterly* 49 (1987) 268-90.

Lategan, B. C. "Is Paul Developing a Specifically Christian Ethic in Galatia?" In *Greeks, Romans, and Christians: Essays in Honor of Abraham J. Malherbe*, ed. D. L. Balch, E. Ferguson, and W. A. Meeks. Minneapolis: Fortress, 1990, 318-28.

Longenecker, R. N. *New Testament Social Ethics for Today*. Grand Rapids: Eerdmans, 1984.

————. *Galatians*. Dallas: Word, 1990.

O'Donovan, O. *Resurrection and Moral Order: An Outline for Evangelical Ethics*. Grand Rapids: Eerdmans, 1986.

Rosner, B. S., ed. *Understanding Paul's Ethics: Twentieth-Century Approaches*. Grand Rapids: Eerdmans, 1995.

Styler, G. M. "The Basis of Obligation in Paul's Christology and Ethics." In *Christ and Spirit in the New Testament. In Honour of C. F. D. Moule*, ed. B. Lindars and S. S. Smalley. Cambridge: Cambridge University Press, 1973, 175-88.

Westerholm, S. *Israel's Law and the Church's Faith: Paul and His Recent Interpreters*. Grand Rapids: Eerdmans, 1988.

Index of Subjects

Index of Modern Authors

Index of Scripture and Other Ancient References

243